Ladies of the Ticker

Ladies of the Ticker

*Women and Wall Street
from the Gilded Age
to the Great Depression*

GEORGE ROBB

**UNIVERSITY OF
ILLINOIS PRESS**
Urbana, Chicago, and Springfield

Library of Congress Cataloging-in-Publication Data
Names: Robb, George, author.
Title: Ladies of the ticker : women and Wall Street from the
    Gilded Age to the Great Depression / George Robb.
Description: Urbana : University of Illinois Press, [2017] |
    Includes bibliographical references and index. |
Identifiers: LCCN 2016057350 (print) | LCCN 2017014261 (ebook)
    | ISBN 9780252099748 (E-book) | ISBN 9780252041174 (cloth :
    alk. paper) | ISBN 9780252082719 (pbk. : alk. paper)
Subjects: LCSH: Women in finance—United States—History. |
    Women capitalists and financiers—United States—History. |
    Finance—United States—History.
Classification: LCC HG181 (ebook) | LCC HG181 .R575 2017 (print)
    | DDC 332.64/27308209041—dc23
LC record available at https://lccn.loc.gov/2016057350

For Netty
BFF, 30 Years and Counting...

Contents

Acknowledgments

The research and writing of a book can be a long, lonely, and expensive endeavor, so I am grateful to the many institutions and individuals that provided me with assistance. The president and provost of William Paterson University granted me a sabbatical leave in 2007–8, during which I began the project. Subsequent travel grants and release time from teaching enabled me to complete the book. My research assistant, William Peniston, helped in ways too numerous to detail.

I owe an enormous debt to many librarians and archivists, especially those at the New York Historical Society; the New York Public Library, Research Division; and the Boston Public Library. I am also grateful for assistance from Janet Linde at the New York Stock Exchange Archives; Kristin Aguilera at the Museum of American Finance, New York; Shaun Kirkpatrick at the ACE Insurance Archives, Philadelphia; Paul Israel at the Thomas Edison Papers, Rutgers University; Amanda E. Strauss at the Schlesinger Library, Harvard University; and Gail Malmgreen of the Newark Archives Project.

I could never have completed this book without the enormous generosity of my colleagues and friends. Janette Rutterford, Timothy Alborn, David Koistinin, Bonnie Anderson, and Elaine Schwartz discussed different aspects of my research with me, providing valuable suggestions and leads. Amy Froide, Antoinette Burton, Patricia Cleary, and Lucia McMahon read and commented on certain chapters. The book has especially benefited from the astute suggestions of Nancy Henry and Ginger Frost, who kindly read the entire manuscript.

I would additionally like to thank the anonymous readers for the University of Illinois Press for providing intelligent, insightful, and constructive suggestions. The final book has certainly benefited from their advice. I must also thank my copyeditor, Angela Arcese, for her fine work and meticulous attention to the smallest details. Lastly, I am indebted to my editor at the press, Dawn Durante, for carefully shepherding the book through review and production. She made what is often a tedious and painful process a pleasure.

Ladies of the Ticker

Introduction

Opportunities and Obstacles

During the past twenty years, a veritable bonanza of new scholarship, literary and historical, has argued that women played a vital economic role in the rise of capitalism in Europe and the Americas. In particular, scholars of the British Isles and the United States have demonstrated how women helped promote the Commercial and Industrial Revolutions of the eighteenth and nineteenth centuries through their activities as property owners, domestic managers, consumers, laborers, and retailers.[1] Far less has been written, however, about women's engagement with finance, such as banking and the stock market. There is good evidence nonetheless that Victorian women were active investors and shareholders, that contemporaries were well aware of this activity, and that there was much comment about the phenomenon, most of it negative.

The new economy was dominated by joint-stock companies, which were financed by the investments of the faceless thousands—women as well as men. The period between the Railway boom of the 1870s and the Great Depression of the 1930s was one of almost continuous financial expansion in the United States. Although women were barred from politics, the professions, and many forms of enterprise, they could participate in the period's robust investment economy by buying and selling shares on the stock exchange. In their pioneering study of the origins of the Victorian middle class, *Family Fortunes*, Leonore Davidoff and Catherine Hall argue that shareholding was seen as especially suitable for women, who were less likely to inherit the family business than their brothers, but who were the primary "beneficiaries of 'passive' property yielding income only: trusts, annuities, subscriptions and insurance."[2]

Until recently, long-standing assumptions about Victorian women's passivity, political subordination, and domestic isolation have colored historians' discussions of women's economic roles. Supposedly, the ideology and practice of "separate spheres" banished women from the marketplace and deprived them of financial autonomy. Standard economic histories had little or nothing to say about American women's contributions to capital formation. More recently, historians have acknowledged women's greater financial autonomy but have been unable to provide many details about how women invested their money. As business historians Nancy Robertson and Susan Yohn recently summarized our knowledge of American women investors during the Gilded Age: "What women did or did not do, we do not know."[3]

This book seeks to broaden our understanding of "what women did" as financial players during the nation's most intense period of economic development. It provides new and detailed information regarding women's investment choices, their levels of expertise, their sources of information, and the nature of their interactions with financial agents. This study also provides ample evidence about how women investors and financiers were depicted by a wide assortment of observers and commentators, as well as how the women themselves strove to present their financial activities to a skeptical and often unsympathetic public. In examining the nature and extent of women's investments during this period, the book will also explore how historical developments in finance capitalism and changes in married women's property rights created new and enhanced opportunities for female investors and financiers.

Women Investors Before the Gilded Age

While this study centers on American women investors and financiers from the Gilded Age to the Great Depression, it does not assume, as did many of these women's contemporaries, that the feminine invasion of Wall Street was an entirely new phenomenon. Indeed, as important work by Anne Laurence, Amy Froide, and Rosemary O'Day demonstrates, English and American women had been an important source of capital for business communities during the Early Modern and Colonial eras, their dowries and jointures invested in mortgages and trade. Women in merchant families inherited equally with their brothers and were trained to manage money, real estate, and rents, as they needed to safeguard their property.[4]

With the growth of national capital markets in the eighteenth century, new and expanded investment opportunities opened up for British and American women. In the fifty years following the Glorious Revolution of 1688, Great Britain and its American colonies experienced a profound shift, the Financial Revolution, which transformed the economy and opened many doors for resourceful investors. The Bank of England was created in 1694 to finance the national debt, and the government bonds, annuities, and lottery tickets issued by the bank, and traded in the coffee houses of Change Alley, soon became an important source of investment for the wealthier classes, as did the shares of large joint-stock corporations like the East India Company, the Africa Company, and the South Sea Company.[5]

As historians have pointed out, financial securities quickly became an important part of women's dowries and jointures. Aristocratic families tried to keep lands intact to pass on to the eldest son, but stocks, bonds, and annuities could provide income for daughters. Shareholdings were more easily divisible and transferable than land, and shares, unlike land, were not taxed. As financial securities became an important part of women's marriage portions, the language of investment came to color popular understandings of courtship. Women "invested" in marriage, or were themselves securities that prospective suitors bid upon.[6]

Single women with capital also saw government bonds and company shares as a good way to invest their money and obtain for themselves a secure income. As early as 1707, women constituted 20% of those who held government annuities. In 1709, women made up 17% of the Bank of England's shareholders and 11% of East India Company shareholders. By 1723, women were 20% of the South Sea Company's shareholders. As women acquired a significant portion of the nation's financial securities, they became increasingly knowledgeable about the stock market.[7]

Recent work by Rosemary O'Day and Amy Froide demonstrates that some upper-class English women became quite adept at the management of financial instruments. O'Day argues that during the eighteenth century, aristocratic women took advantage of new financial developments to enhance their traditional role in consolidating their family's position and providing a secure future for younger relations. O'Day documents the investment activities of Cassandra Willoughby Brydges, Duchess of Chandos, who purchased large amounts of Bank of England and South Sea Company stock to provide marriage portions for her twelve nieces. The duchess, who came from a gentry family with important merchant and banking connections, advised numerous female relations how to manage their money, and in 1720 she called in debts from these women to cover the duke's losses in the South Sea Bubble.[8] Amy Froide tells a similar story about Gertrude, Lady Cheyne, who invested money for herself, her husband, and a circle of female relations in the early 1700s. Lady Cheyne purchased securities herself at business offices in the City of London rather than conducting her affairs through a male agent. Although married, Lady Cheyne and the Duchess of Chandos both invested family funds themselves. Apparently their husbands agreed to this unusual arrangement as they respected their wives' financial acumen.[9]

Other business historians, in particular Anne Laurence and Ann Carlos, have studied the financial activities of less exalted women during the eighteenth century, concluding that while women investors were less numerous than men, they were no less energetic. Laurence points out how women were quick to take advantage of the expansion of credit and banking as means of engaging with the stock market. Ann Carlos and Larry Neal document the extraordinary career of Johanna Cock, a merchant's widow, who was one of the nation's most active dealers in Bank of England stock between 1716 and 1720. Although Cock's speculations ended in bankruptcy, Carlos and Neal found no evidence that "women as a group were unable to manage these assets." Indeed, in their analysis of stock trades involving shares of the Bank of England and Royal Africa Company for 1720, women overall did slightly better in the market than men.[10]

Eighteenth-century commentators told a different tale. As women's participation in the share market grew, so too did public condemnation, especially in the aftermath of the South Sea Bubble in 1720. Women's stock "gambling" was now denounced as aggressive and inappropriate and was linked to the instability of the market. Women were satirized as hapless speculators and the dupes of dishonest brokers. Typical of this approach was Thomas Foxton's *Jesina, or Delusive Gold: A Pastoral Lamenting the Misfortunes of a Young Lady of Quality, Ruined by South-Sea Stock* (1721). In an important pioneering article about gendered representations of the market, Catherine Ingrassia demonstrates how satiric accounts of the South Sea Bubble depicted women gambling their household allowances in a frenzied pursuit of luxury and excitement. "Criticism of women's financial interests, like contemporaneous criticism of their fascination with popular fiction, confronted the spell these new imaginatively based pursuits cast over women's emotions and desires."[11] Assumptions about women's fundamental financial incapacity came to be crystallized in advice books such as Thomas Mortimer's *Every Man His Own Broker* (1761), which characterized the buying and selling of shares as "an activity suitable for patriotic and prudent gentlemen, but ill-advised and dangerous for women." According to Mortimer, women were too ignorant and unstable to manage their own investments and should seek the guidance of a male relation.[12] As we shall see, such prescriptive literature came to dominate the historical understanding of women investors.

Eighteenth-century America underwent many of the same commercial and financial transformations as the mother country, and American women, like their British counterparts, were quick to profit from them. It has been estimated that 10% to 25% of women in colonial North America engaged in some form of entrepreneurship. In some towns nearly half the shopkeepers were women. Some female traders, like Elizabeth Murray and Mary Alexander, achieved important commercial positions as wholesalers. Facetiously referred to as "she-merchants," these women had no counterparts in Great Britain. American women's capital also played a vital role in establishing family businesses, as was the case with Sarah Todd's $300 dowry, which enabled her husband John Jacob Astor to found his fur-trading business during the 1790s. As Ellen Hartigan-O'Connor emphasizes, eighteenth-century urban society was inherently commercial and thus necessitated that housewives engage in all sorts of economic activities like borrowing and lending money.[13]

During the colonial era and early republic, women owned significant amounts of stocks and bonds and held a large proportion of the nation's bank deposits, as Robert Wright has documented. Nineteen of the thirty-one subscribers to Pennsylvania's bonds for financing the French and Indian War were women. During the Revolution, women invested heavily in bonds issued by the Continental Congress. In 1810, 14.5% of the original shareholders of the Commercial and Farmers Bank of Baltimore were women, as were 12% of the initial subscribers to the Bank of Chester County, Pennsylvania. In 1812, women constituted almost 25% of the shareholders of the Philadelphia Bank. Wright argues that "the considerable extent of female shareholding shows that the early financial markets were impersonal and inclusive." Financiers welcomed women's capital no less enthusiastically than men's.[14]

Abigail Adams was a heavy investor in government securities, as Woody Holton points out in a recent biography. Early in her marriage she realized that the family money could be invested more profitably in U.S. government bonds than in land. In spite of her husband's initial skepticism, she used her "pin money" to purchase bonds, frequently employing her uncle to act as her agent. During the 1780s, Abigail bought up large blocks of depreciated federal bonds in which the public had lost faith. She, however, believed that "one must wait for interest, and run risks, but at all events it will fetch what is given for it." The bonds were eventually redeemed, and Abigail made a fortune. John Adams was less interested in money matters than his wife, and she capably managed the family finances during her husband's lengthy absences on government business.[15]

Early American society prized financial literacy for women, who were expected to be efficient and capable managers of household budgets. In

1755, William Dawson ran an evening school for girls in Philadelphia that taught "accounts, by way of single entry, in a plain methodical manner." Early textbooks for girls frequently explained financial matters, such as how to calculate interest. In a 1762 letter to her niece Dolly, the Boston merchant Elizabeth Murray impressed upon her the importance of a woman's financial knowledge. Many families, Murray argued, were "ruined by women not understanding accounts."[16]

Women and Property Law

Women's financial accomplishments in both England and America were achieved in the face of the legal restrictions of English Common Law. Under the common-law doctrine of coverture, a married woman lost her separate legal identity. She was covered, or hidden, by her husband's identity, and became in the eyes of the law a *feme covert*. As such, any money or personal property a woman owned before her marriage became her husband's property upon marriage. Any money she inherited or earned after marriage was also her husband's to dispose of as he wished. Land was not subject to coverture, but a wife could not rent or sell her land without her husband's consent. It was also his to manage during the course of their marriage. Neither could a *feme covert* enter into contracts, make a will, or sue and be sued in courts of law. She was under her husband's guardianship, as if she were a child or a lunatic.[17]

A single woman, or *feme sole*, was not bound by coverture. She could own property on the same terms as a man, sign business contracts, and defend her property in court if necessary. Widows might find their financial autonomy constrained by the terms of their husbands' wills.[18] It was obviously far easier for single women, widows and spinsters, to engage in business, or to invest their money. In the eighteenth century, women shareholders were overwhelmingly widows and spinsters. As most people married, most women therefore found themselves restricted by the rules of coverture at some point during their lives. Some women must have resented the restrictions, and the first attack on coverture, *The Hardships of the English Laws in Relation to Wives*, was written by an anonymous woman in 1735. Many other popular handbooks, such as *The Lady's Law* (1732), explained the legal disabilities of married women, while also showing ways around them.[19]

Propertied families often insisted on marriage settlements for their daughters that would formalize "pin money"—an allowance paid by the husband to his wife for her personal use. If a wife wanted to spend her pin money on stock in the South Sea Company, rather than clothes or jewelry, that was her right. A marriage settlement might also specify that a woman's dowry be invested in a "jointure"—land purchased to produce income—which was the husband's to spend during his lifetime but would support his wife during her widowhood. Jointures became more common with the growth of financial securities, as a block of shares or bonds, rather than land, could more easily be set aside for the eventual support of the widow.[20]

In certain circumstances, married women could carry on business as independent players, in spite of the common law. In England, several towns, most notably London, allowed a married woman to engage in trade as a *feme sole*. Some British colonies, like Pennsylvania and South Carolina, passed laws granting married women similar exemptions to coverture. Husbands could also agree to let their wives carry on business on their own, which gave some married women greater economic independence but also protected husbands' property from wives' creditors. Other married women simply ignored the law, carrying on their own businesses with the full cooperation of the local business community, which accepted their bills of exchange and entered into contracts with them. Over the course of the eighteenth century, English courts even became more flexible in enforcing business contracts made by married women.[21]

The most effective remedies for coverture were through the laws of equity, a separate legal system that had developed since the Middle Ages to address the inadequacies of the common law. Equity allowed wealthy families to circumvent coverture by creating "trusts," whereby a daughter's property was not turned over to her husband upon marriage, but administered for her by a third party, her trustees, who would pay her the profits from the trust. Financial securities, especially government bonds, came to be a favorite choice for trusts, as they provided a set, guaranteed income (3% interest during the eighteenth century) and were easier to look after than land. Trusts enabled fathers to secure family property for their daughters' separate use and to preserve it for her children, but they denied women any control or management of the property.[22]

Prenuptial agreements were another equitable innovation, which gave married women direct control over separate property. They were favored by widows or businesswomen, who already had management of their own property and did not care to lose control to either trustees or their new husbands. Elizabeth Murray, a wealthy widow and "she-merchant" in colonial Boston, required her second and third husbands to sign prenuptial agreements guaranteeing her control over her property as if she were a single woman.[23]

Even when equity supposedly protected a wife's separate property, husbands could find ways around the law. The female author of *The Hardships of English*

Laws in Relation to Wives argued that a husband often held such psychological and physical sway over his wife that he could easily bend her to his will. She quotes an English judge's skeptical remark about trusts, that "he had hardly known an instance, where the wife had not been kissed or kicked out of such previous settlements."[24]

It remains unclear how many American women were protected by trusts and prenuptial agreements. Historians have usually assumed that these arrangements were the privilege of the very wealthy. Norma Basch, for one, argues that few women had the assets to pursue these options.[25] Based on her study of colonial Pennsylvania, Marylynn Salmon argues that "courts accepted separate estates for married women but discouraged their use." Rosemary O'Day, however, maintains that prenuptial contracts were "not uncommon" in colonial America. She sees evidence that "women maintained a lively interest in their own property rights as documented in wills, leases and settlements." Equity was certainly employed by savvy colonial businesswomen like Elizabeth Murray.[26]

Reform of married women's property law had been advocated by the female author of *The Hardships of the English Laws in Relation to Wives* as early as 1735, but substantial change did not take place until a century later. Erosion of coverture began in the United States a generation earlier than in England, though reforms were piecemeal, geographically uneven (each state had separate laws), and inspired by a wide variety of motives, not all of them progressive.

During the 1830s and 1840s, a few states passed married women's property acts that made modest adjustments to coverture. The earliest acts—in Arkansas (1835) and Mississippi (1839)—were especially concerned with protecting a wife's slaves from seizure for her husband's debts. The actual control and use of the slaves remained with the husband. Similar acts elsewhere expressed fathers' desires to protect their gifts from the depredations of sons-in-law. As Linda Kerber explains, "in protecting gift property from seizure for debts contracted by husbands, married women's property acts were debtor relief acts that directly benefited men."[27]

The growth of personal property in the form of stocks and bonds made the alteration of coverture more pressing. Real estate was better protected under common law than were other forms of property. Upon marriage, a woman's lands remained hers. Her husband could manage them, but he could not sell them without her consent, nor could they be seized to cover his debts. Personal property had no similar protections. When a woman married, her slaves, livestock, money, stocks, and bonds became her husband's. These rules of common law developed in an agricultural society, where most wealth was in the form of land. As Britain and the United States became more urbanized and commercialized, and as more people held financial assets, the law had to catch up.[28]

Legislative attitudes toward married women's property rights were influenced by a growing awareness of financial change. As more men provided for their daughters with stocks, bonds, and insurance, they wanted to shelter those assets from husbands and husbands' creditors. In 1840 the New York Legislature passed a married women's insurance act that enabled a wife to insure her husband's life and to receive the benefits free from the claims of his creditors.[29] A few years later, some politicians argued that the women of New York needed further protection from husbands who risked the family property in the "hazards and vicissitudes of trade and speculation." Major financial crises in 1837 and 1848, and their attendant bankruptcies, underscored the need to allow wives to protect their assets from their husbands' prodigal ways.[30]

In 1848, New York State passed a watershed married woman's property act. The law stipulated:

> The real and personal property of any female, who may hereafter marry, and which she shall own at the time of marriage, and the rents, issues and profits thereof, shall not be subject to the disposal of her husband, nor be liable for his debts, and shall continue her sole and separate property, as if she were a single female.[31]

The act also protected whatever property a married woman might inherit or be given after her marriage. It did not, however, give married women contractual powers. Wives could own property separate from their husbands, but they could not sell it or use it as a basis for operating a business. An 1849 law corrected this oversight.[32]

As New York was the nation's commercial and financial hub, its reform of coverture served as a model for similar acts in other states, especially in the Northeast. As more American wives could retain their own personal property, financial securities became an even more attractive form of wealth for women. Stocks and bonds could be bought and sold more readily and cheaply than real estate, and managed more easily than a business. To accommodate female investors, in 1851 the New York Legislature stipulated that a married woman who owned shares could vote in person or by proxy for corporate officers.[33]

While the Seneca Falls, Convention celebrated New York's 1848 act as a great victory for women's rights, twentieth-century women's historians have been less enthusiastic. They noted that states still gave husbands absolute control over their wives' wages. In many cases husbands also maintained management powers over wives' property, and wives usually could not sign contracts or make wills without their husbands' consent.[34] Massachusetts (1855) and New York (1860) were the first states that gave married women control over their own wages or money they earned through trade or business, as well as enabling them to make contracts on their own and to sue and be sued as a *feme sole*. On the eve of the Civil War, eighteen states (out of thirty-five) gave women "separate use" of their property, while another ten merely prevented a husband's creditors from seizing a wife's property. Three states (Virginia, South Carolina, and Delaware) gave wives no legal protection, and only four states (Massachusetts, New York, Connecticut, and Maine) gave wives contractual rights and rights to their own wages.[35]

In the decades following the Civil War, additional states granted married women property rights, a few for the first time, most others by expanding their existing but somewhat limited legislation. During Reconstruction, nine southern states adopted new constitutions that gave property rights to married women. By 1880, 90% of states gave wives control over separate property, but only 63% gave them rights to their own wages.[36]

None of the laws were retroactive. In states where the language of the act was vague, courts usually interpreted its provisions narrowly, for example giving women control over their wages only if they were abandoned by their husbands. Per Norma Basch, "the concept of a wife's separate estate continued to be based on easily identified gifts and legacies either brought to marriage or acquired afterward."[37] This principle favored wealthy or middle-class women, who were more likely to own real estate or stocks and bonds than working women or farmer's wives, who frequently ran businesses like boardinghouses, laundries, or egg and butter stalls. When wives' enterprises were operated in their families' residences or related to traditional domestic duties, courts usually construed them as belonging to husbands. In some states the statutes required wives to secure a special license or obtain a court decree before they could engage in trade. Buying and selling shares, however, did not constitute "trade" and was in no way inhibited by the new laws.[38]

Courts might nonetheless invalidate a woman's business contracts merely because she was a woman and unlikely to understand basic financial principles. Robert Chused gives one such example from 1872, when an Oregon judge nullified a woman's sale of land, even though the 1859 state constitution had granted women control over their separate property. The judge invoked separate-spheres ideology, arguing that "the sphere of married women's duties, as they have been heretofore generally recognized and acquiesced in, precludes the means of acquiring by them that knowledge of law and commercial transactions necessary to enable them, as a rule, to safely and understandingly enter into covenants concerning real estate."[39]

Despite the uneven and heterogeneous nature of married women's property law, women's-rights advocates celebrated each new act as an important victory for American women. For them, the acts legitimated women's presence in the marketplace. Carole Shammas argues that Victorian women's optimism was not misplaced, and that recent critics of the legislation are too pessimistic, since the acts allowed for a massive transfer of property into women's hands. Using wills, she demonstrates that by 1900, women inherited around a quarter of probated wealth, a dramatic advance over earlier periods. Indeed, between the 1860s and the 1890s, there was a greater increase in female wealth than "in the previous two hundred years of American history."[40]

Separate Spheres?

As women escaped the legal restrictions of coverture and gained control over a larger share of national wealth, were they able to participate more fully in the burgeoning economy of industrial America? Historians remain divided on this question. Until recently, most historians argued that industrial development in Europe and North America diminished women's entrepreneurial activities and that by the mid-nineteenth century there were far fewer women traders and shopkeepers than there had been in the eighteenth century. Supposedly, the separation of work from the home, embodied in the factory system and the corporate structure, meant that wives and daughters were less likely to be employed in the family business. The development of more formal and impersonal credit structures further marginalized women's businesses and starved them of capital necessary for growth and expansion. An apparent hardening of patriarchal attitudes, symbolized by the ideal of separate spheres, justified women's exclusion from the marketplace and idealized their domestic bondage.[41]

The American historian Gerda Lerner was among the first scholars to posit a deteriorating economic status for women during the nineteenth century. Lerner made her case in an influential article from 1969, "The Lady and the Mill Girl: Changes in the Status of Women in the Age of Jackson." Shortly afterward, Neil McKendrick made a similar case for industrializing England. During the next two decades, other scholars, such as Heidi Hartmann, Nancy Cott, Sonya Rose, and Louise Tilly, contributed to the notion that industrial capitalism devalued women's labor and limited their active participation in the market economy. Local, in-depth studies by Mary Ryan for the United States and Leonore Davidoff and Catherine Hall for England maintained that a gendered division of labor and an ideology of domesticity played a key role in forming the middle-class family.[42]

The concept of separate spheres has exerted tremendous influence in social and gender history but since the late 1980s has been questioned as an accurate representation of even middle-class women's lives. Linda Kerber, Amanda Vickery, and Margaret Hunt all argue that the assumption that middle-class women dropped out of business activities in the early nineteenth century rests primarily on prescriptive literature of the period. There was certainly an enhanced emphasis on woman's domestic role, but Vickery doubts whether the domestic ideal, "in and of itself, severely limited a woman's freedom of maneuver." She points out that "women, like men, were eminently capable of professing one thing and performing quite another."[43]

Other scholars, like Jeanne Peterson and Stephen Walker, note that the stereotype of Victorian women as "angels in the house" has been greatly exaggerated by women's historians. The proponents of separate spheres never expected housewives to be financially incompetent or merely possessed of ornamental skills like music, drawing, and embroidery. Middle-class women had to manage budgets, hire and supervise servants, and interact with tradesmen. Throughout the nineteenth century, household advice books emphasized the importance of managerial and bookkeeping skills.[44]

Historians on both sides of the Atlantic are now questioning whether there actually was a significant decline of women's entrepreneurial activity coincident with industrialization. They argue that women continued to play important roles as traders and business owners in spite of ideological objections by advocates of separate spheres. Much of this work makes use of city directories and newspapers to identify and quantify women's presence as shopkeepers and workers in American and British towns. For example, Claudia Goldin's research, comparing American business directories with census data, found only a slight decline in women's paid employment from the late eighteenth to the mid-nineteenth century and a steady presence of women shopkeepers in urban areas.[45]

Similar pathbreaking work by Wendy Gamber, Hannah Barker, Nicola Phillips, and others finds that British and American women remained fully engaged with business during the height of industrialization, playing vital roles as shopkeepers, artisans, and traders. Women's businesses were usually smaller than men's, and they tended to cluster in certain "feminine" sectors of the economy such as fashion, food, and hospitality. While women's businesses often had difficulty securing credit, many of them remained remarkably healthy and long-lived, and as a whole, they constituted a significant part of the urban economy.[46]

Most revisionist scholarship on Victorian women's economic activities has focused on their roles as workers and entrepreneurs, rather than as investors and financiers. While some pioneering work has been done on British women's investment activities, notably by Janette Rutterford, Josephine Maltby, Nancy Henry, and myself, very little research on nineteenth-century American women investors has occurred.[47] In my own earlier work on women investors, I emphasized women's economic disadvantages and vulnerability to exploitation.[48] Susan Yohn made this same point in a 2006 article, "Crippled Capitalists," arguing: "While women achieved gains, they did so despite huge challenges that limited their ability to exercise the power Americans commonly associate with financial success."[49] While this book certainly details the prejudices and disadvantages faced by women investors and financiers, it presents a more complicated cast of characters. Beside those women excluded from investment opportunities or cheated by businessmen were many others who managed their stock portfolios with great aplomb. These women were not crippled capitalists, but until now they have been hidden from history.

This study is not only sensitive to differences between male and female financial experience, but also to social and economic differences between different classes of female investors and financiers. Social class, unsurprisingly, was an important determinant of women's access to financial markets and an important indicator of their success as capitalists.

*   *   *

Before the Civil War, American women's investment opportunities were mostly local and somewhat limited: savings banks, farm mortgages, municipal bonds, canal companies, and insurance policies. This was to change dramatically as a result of postwar industrial and financial expansion. A tremendous boom in railroad building, and the formation of new national corporations to develop telegraphs, steel, oil, copper, and other industrial commodities, transformed investment possibilities for women with capital to spare. For propertied women, investments in stocks and bonds became another way to support themselves without compromising their status through waged work or trade. The New York Stock Exchange emerged as the nation's most important clearinghouse for all manner of financial securities, and "Wall Street" entered the American vocabulary as a byword for high finance. As growing numbers of women participated in the stock market, their investment actions attracted greater public scrutiny, much of it quite censorious.

Chapter 1 examines debates and sentiments regarding the appropriateness of women as investors utilizing a wide variety of genres: journalism, financial writing, advice books, fiction, and cinema. Although ideas about what role, if any, women should play in the world of finance varied considerably depending upon who was expressing them, most commentators remained skeptical about women's ability to invest money. Popular depictions of women investors usually characterized them as ignorant, capricious, and emotionally unstable. Women were especially enjoined to avoid the volatile stock market and to entrust their capital to the management of male financial advisors.

Chapter 2 compares the actual behavior and investment choices of American women with the largely negative judgments of contemporaries, as laid out in the first chapter. Drawing upon understudied archival sources—shareholder ledgers, stock portfolios, business correspondence—I argue that women investors were far more resourceful and capable than they were depicted in prescriptive sources. American women constructed stable and diverse securities portfolios that embodied the best financial thinking of the time.

Chapter 3 examines women as both victims and perpetrators of white-collar crime. Most commentators believed that women were more vulnerable than men to financial fraud, though this assumption does not always stand up to historical scrutiny. Women's supposed financial victimization was endorsed by conservatives, who cited it as evidence that the business world was too dangerous for women, and by progressives, who used it to justify a program of financial reform and regulation to better protect women. Ironically, the same freebooting financial system that offered women investors little protection also allowed some unscrupulous women to operate on its margins. Female financial criminals were rare, but they attracted widespread attention and condemnation out of all proportion to their numbers.

While the dominant public discourse during the nineteenth century favored women's economic subordination and proclaimed their incapacity for investment, there was a counterdiscourse, feminist and progressive, that sought to liberate women economically. Chapter 4 details feminist critiques of the traditional upbringing that sheltered some women from economic knowledge and deprived them of property rights and financial responsibility. Women's-rights advocates realized that financial independence was key to personal freedom and could lead to full political citizenship. Although suffragists often encouraged women to enter the male sphere of business, they remained deeply suspicious of American finance capitalism, which they typically saw as ruthless, predatory, and corrupt. Victoria Woodhull's career as both a stockbroker and as a critic of Wall Street embodied that contradiction. Woodhull and other Victorian feminists realized that the domestic sphere was often threatened by market forces over which women had little control, but to shun the market was hardly an option, as this would cut women off from an important source of wealth.

A handful of women financiers achieved national prominence. They were subject to especially intense scrutiny as to whether women could succeed in finance without becoming "unsexed." Chapter 5 examines the career of Hetty Green, a Wall Street tycoon who became a lightning rod for debates about women and money. A fearless speculator, she made millions in the stock market buying at times of financial panic. Some women cited Green as an example of women's capacity for moneymaking, if given the chance, but many male commentators demonized her as "the witch of Wall Street," a ruthless miser whose success was achieved at the expense of feminine modesty and grace.

Finally, a brief epilogue and conclusion recapitulate the book's most significant findings and trace some of its principal themes over the course of the twentieth century and up to the present, revealing that many Victorian stereotypes and prejudices concerning women investors and financiers persist. Although women now constitute half the nation's shareholders, financial institutions still treat them in a patronizing manner. Stockbroking also remains an extremely male-dominated profession, where female interlopers are still unwelcome, subject to harassment, and assumed to be unqualified simply by virtue of their sex.

1 The Vortex of Speculation

Picturing Women Investors

"I am so ignorant of money matters . . ."
—Lily Bart in *The House of Mirth* (1905)

Women who ventured into Wall Street in the late nineteenth century did so at a time when there was both great animosity toward the stock market and considerable skepticism regarding women's capacity for investment. This chapter will explore these sentiments as they were expressed by a wide variety of genres—journalism, financial writing, advice books, humor, fiction, and cinema—from the Gilded Age through the 1920s. While popular hostility to Wall Street was never monolithic or uncontested, it nonetheless remained a potent force in American culture in the late nineteenth and early twentieth centuries, the heyday of the Progressive Movement and muckraking journalism, with their attacks on trusts, monopolies, and financial fraud.[1] Criticisms of the stock market (that it was selfish, reckless, and unproductive) also remained remarkably consistent over time. Indeed, such criticism is alive and well today, as witnessed in the Occupy Wall Street protests around the country. Ideas regarding what role, if any, women should play in the world of finance have been more volatile over time, but, like opinions about the stock market itself, they have varied considerably depending upon who was expressing them and where they were being expressed.

Many Americans of the Gilded Age embraced free-market capitalism and industrial finance, and the period has often been defined by the freebooting activities of the robber barons. The very term "gilded age" was coined by Mark Twain and Charles Dudley Warner in 1873 to describe the lavish tastes of a nouveau riche American plutocracy of bankers, brokers, and entrepreneurs.[2] There were, however, powerful voices that denounced the "cash nexus" and a culture of "getting and spending." Henry David Thoreau was a notable and forceful critic of acquisitive materialism, as were his British contemporaries

Thomas Carlyle, Matthew Arnold, and John Ruskin, whose works were widely read and admired in America.[3] Much of the critique of finance capitalism came from the pens of writers like Thoreau and Carlyle, as well as like-minded journalists, academics, clergymen, and civil servants who were collectively part of a professional middle class that was frequently at odds with a commercial middle class of merchants, bankers, and industrialists. The historian Harold Perkin was among the first to elaborate how nineteenth-century bourgeois society was riven by a struggle between the ideals of businesspeople, who favored a society based on individualism, competition, and entrepreneurship, and the ideals of professionals, who condemned such a society as selfish and soulless and instead promoted the virtues of education, expertise, and service to the community.[4] Needless to say, much of the writing about finance that will be discussed in this chapter represented the worldview of the professional middle class, who, in their debates with businessmen, usually had the last word.

Another important influence over writings about both finance and women was religion. Puritan and evangelical strains of American Christianity had long insisted that one could not serve both God and mammon. The Social Gospel Movement at the turn of the century drew from this tradition and insisted that Christians had a duty to help the less fortunate.[5] The stock market was especially suspect, since making money on the rise or fall of shares appeared to be gambling. Honest people, according to the Social Gospel Movement, should work for their money. That women might speculate in shares was especially offensive to the religious point of view, as this was an affront to the greater modesty and spirituality expected from women. Women were to set a moral example for men; at the very least, their duty was to keep the home pure from the contaminating influences of the marketplace.[6]

Main Street Looks at Wall Street

Among the most negative views of the stock market and women investors were those found in the popular social commentary and journalism of the period. The most scathing accounts of Wall Street were often written in the aftermath of the financial crises that punctuated American history at fairly regular intervals: 1873, 1884, 1893, 1896, 1907, 1929. Books like *Bulls and Bears of New York* (1875) and *Plain Truths about Stock Speculation* (1887) were intended to be shocking exposés of the stock exchange and its victims, many of whom were assumed to be women.[7] Both books used biblical images of temptation and idolatry to convey their belief that the stock market was a place of sin. "Like the cup of abominations in the Apocalypse, it seems to drunken and madden all who touch it," wrote Matthew Hale Smith in *Bulls and Bears*.[8] The desire for sudden riches could be overpowering, and the votaries of Wall Street came to worship money itself. "Their chief god is Mammon," wrote Moses Smith in *Plain Truths*. "In the time of Aaron they would have bowed down in worship of the 'Golden Calf.'"[9] Both books also argued that playing the stock market was no better than gambling: "The haste to be rich, by a lucky stroke of fortune, by hazarding a few thousands in Wall Street, is the same spirit that leads thousands to the gambling table."[10] These early commentaries on Wall Street clearly depict the stock exchange as a wicked and ruinous institution.

That women would participate in stock gambling was especially shocking. In her 1863 survey *The Employments of Women*, Virginia Penny, who was usually eager to promote new fields of employment for women, noted with approval that there were no women stockbrokers in the United States. Penny argued that "women could not very well conduct the business without having to mix promiscuously with men on the street, and stop and talk to them in the most public places; and the delicacy of woman would forbid that."[11] During the 1870s and 1880s, the very presence of women on Wall Street seemed remarkable. Clarence Day remembered the New York financial district of the 1880s as "a tangle of little streets full of men and boys but no women. If some lonely bonnet chanced to be bobbing along in the crowd, we all stared at it."[12] Such women as appeared on Wall Street were not seen as moral exemplars. According to Matthew Hale Smith, they were the sort of women who "drive fast teams on the road" and "give their gentlemen friends a turn around the Park."[13]

Speculation on the stock market was just another form of excitement for "fast" women. The moral disapproval of the commentators is palpable. Words like "excited," "infatuated," and "intoxicated" are repeatedly used to describe the mental state of women who bought stocks. In Gilded Age America, female speculators were depicted as capricious and emotional, and thus utterly unsuited to manage their own money: "In speculation, as a rule, they are too impulsive and quick to jump at wrong conclusions. If they see prices going up a point or two they buy, thinking a big rise is coming sure. But four times out of six they find they have bought at the top and got left. Hence, they seem to suffer worse than the men who are more calculating, cautious and wary."[14] In these accounts, women are losers in the game of speculation but are offered little sympathy for their losses. Their reported aggressive and "unladylike" behavior has rendered them undeserving of pity.

By the turn of the century, most mainstream journalism had accepted the stock market as a fact of American life. A number of popular magazines like

Atlantic Monthly and the *Century* had begun to adopt a more pro-business, pro-investment stance. As Steve Fraser has demonstrated, these publications boosted the stock market as "a vital piece of economic machinery, lubricating the wheels of capital mobility. The century's progress depended on making sure that pools of investment capital didn't lie idle, stagnating in useless hoards."[15] In the 1890s, *Harper's Weekly* began running its column "The World of Finance," which explained the activities of Wall Street to ordinary readers, including many women.

Obviously, gender is not the only lens through which we should view women investors. Class is equally important. Bourgeois women were enjoined to be modest and maternal, but as members of a burgeoning capitalist class they were also steeped in mercantile ambitions. Separate-spheres ideology pushed women in one direction, but the middle-class worldview encouraged them to speculate, invest, and seek personal profit.

The stock exchange was finding champions in the popular media, but many commentators still remained hostile to women in Wall Street. Women's and family magazines were especially conservative regarding woman's proper sphere in society. An editorial from the *Ladies' Home Journal* in 1900 condemned woman's participation in business by asserting that "God had made her a woman and never intended her for the rougher life planned out for a man."[16] Women's magazines urged their readers to avoid the stock market and instead invest their money in more conservative alternatives like real estate, savings banks, or government bonds.[17] In an 1899 article, "Women in Wall Street," from *Frank Leslie's Popular Monthly*, the author, Mrs. Finley Anderson, was scathing in her denunciation of women who tried to make money in Wall Street. Such women were "born gamblers" unable to resist "the vortex of speculation" or the "bauble gold" that "flashes before their eyes." Anderson claimed that women have been driven to drink and suicide by their losses in the market, as they lacked men's ability to "jostle one another in the centers of trade" without losing their equanimity. She urged women to leave "the fascinating game of the Street to men who can buffet against its adversities."[18] Frank Leslie pushed this conservative line in his magazines, as a 1901 illustration from *Leslie's Weekly*, purportedly drawn from life, showed a group of women giving way to panic during a downturn in the market.

Although World War I greatly expanded women's participation in the securities market, in large part through the purchase of government bonds, there remained, nonetheless, considerable queasiness on the part of mainstream journals and magazines regarding women in Wall Street. America's leading journals of opinion, such as *The North American Review* and *The Forum*, consistently argued against women's involvement with the

Figure 1. Women reacting to a stock market drop. From *Leslie's Weekly* (May 25, 1901): 502. (Courtesy of the Library of Congress)

stock market. An article from *The Forum* in 1918, "Women Gamblers in Wall Street," by "One of Them," held that women were far more credulous than men, and thus more susceptible to outlandish investment schemes. Women were prey to the worst advice, often buying shares based on gossip or "tips" from ignorant friends. Even "women's intuition" came in for criticism, as some women had apparently "gotten a hunch" about a stock they saw advertised on a billboard or read about in a novel. In the final analysis, the article fell back on essentialism. Women simply weren't made for finance. "It's bad enough for a man . . . but to subject the highly-keyed nervous system of the average woman to stock gambling is little short of a crime."[19]

During the stock market craze of the 1920s, women were buying and selling shares almost as frequently as men, and opposition to them doing so further diminished. Even women's magazines now recommended share purchases in addition to the more conservative bonds they previously had endorsed. Most famously, the financier John Raskob gave an interview to the *Ladies' Home Journal* in which he proclaimed, "Everybody ought to be rich!"[20] Speculation was openly defended and advocated in mainstream magazines like the *Saturday Evening Post*.[21] Only a few lone voices held out against Wall Street's allure.[22] Some old prejudices, however, still remained. A 1929 article from *The North American Review*, "Ladies of the Ticker," by Eunice Fuller Barnard, chronicled women's advances as investors but was written in a rather patronizing tone. Barnard repeated the long-standing criticism that women were more troublesome as brokerage customers than men, and she characterized their obsessive concern with their stock portfolios as a "pseudo-maternal attitude." Although she claimed to be celebrating women's financial achievements, Barnard couldn't resist depicting female investors as an incongruous, even grotesque assemblage of "aggressive, guttural dowagers, gum-chewing blondes, [and] shrinking spinsters who look as if they belonged in a missionary society meeting."[23]

The Financial Press and Investment Guides

While most mainstream journalism and social commentaries about the stock market before the 1920s discouraged women from seeking their fortunes in Wall Street, new forms of financial writing had emerged in the nineteenth century that championed the nation's expanding financial system and were more supportive of women investors. The new genre of financial journalism sought to normalize and legitimate the workings of high finance for ordinary Americans through education and publicity. In the words of Mary Poovey, this journalism aimed to "translate the arcane jargon of the financial world into a language that any middle-class reader could appreciate."[24] From the 1860s, periodicals like *Hunt's Merchants' Magazine*, the *American Railroad Journal*, and the *Daily Financial News*, as well as money columns in many daily papers, familiarized readers with the workings of the stock exchange and supplied current information about share prices and interest rates.[25] In 1883 the brokers Charles Dow and Edward Jones began publishing their *Customers' Afternoon News Letter*, which evolved into the *Wall Street Journal* in 1889. As Mary Poovey has argued, financial journalism's most ambitious goal was to cultivate "an understanding of the new commercial economy that placed special trade opportunities within a larger social and political context, whose contours were mapped by the new science of political economy."[26] Besides popularizing the ideals of laissez-faire economics, the American financial press also delivered a heavy dose of boosterism.[27] Unlike much of the popular reportage previously discussed, financial journalism worked to legitimize Wall Street by emphasizing its key role in the nation's economic expansion and by drawing the line between normal investment practices and unsafe acts like speculation.

Financial writers invariably made a crucial distinction between "investing" in shares—that is, entrusting one's capital to some steady, safe business for the long term—and "speculating" in shares by buying and selling in the short term, in anticipation of a rising or falling market, to make a quick, spectacular profit. The passive nature of investment seemed especially appropriate for women, who would not have to dirty their hands in business but would receive a regular income by allowing men to manage their money for them. Speculation, on the other hand, was equated with gambling, with an overwhelming desire to get rich quick and to secure "unfair" profits at the expense of others. The distinction between investing and speculating was a technical one given a moral overlay by the Victorians.[28] As noted above, this distinction was not recognized by most social commentators of the Progressive Era. For the critics of Wall Street, either to invest or to speculate was to expect to get money without working for it. Both practices involved risk, and both ran contrary to the Protestant work ethic. Most financial writing, however, worked diligently to uphold the moral difference between investing and speculating.

The financial press was also much less hostile regarding women investors than mainstream journals or ladies' magazines but still urged caution and restraint. The *Financial Review of Reviews* maintained that "a real sense of responsibility as to the use of money should lead woman in the first place to avoid risky investments, and then to be careful to place her money in business concerns which are not only safe, but which will use her money . . . for the good of the community."[29] Women obviously needed assistance to make good investment decisions, and most financial writing assumed that they would be guided by male advisors, either relations (fathers, brothers, husbands) or professionals (lawyers, bankers, brokers). Women's vital contributions to national development were never doubted by the financial press, but it was more comfortable with women as passive suppliers of capital than as active agents in the marketplace.

Most financial writing assumed that women were ignorant about investment, but it usually countered the prevailing view that they were mentally or emotionally incapable of managing their own money. Women's incapacity was real enough, but it was socially constructed and could be remedied with proper education. In the second half of the nineteenth century, the first investment guides for women began to appear. These advice books are themselves a distinct genre of financial writing and provide another perspective on women's financial literacy and autonomy.

Financial guides for women shared certain assumptions, one of which was that women were woefully unprepared to handle money. One of the earliest works specifically targeting women, *A Guide to the Unprotected in Everyday Matters Related to Property and Income* (1863) by "A Banker's Daughter," assumed that its readers knew absolutely nothing about business, including how to perform such simple tasks as writing a check or withdrawing money from a bank. The book contained a wealth of practical information on basic business terms (*capital, interest*), banking, shareholding, and property law, and it included sample business letters suitable for buying and selling shares or requesting payment of one's dividends.[30] The book was still in print twenty years later, having gone through five editions, and its publishers continued to proclaim the business incapacity of even the most educated women.[31]

Women's ignorance may have been a constant theme of the guides, but it was one the publishers hoped to rectify, and over time they came to promote a more active and assertive body of female investors. In 1863 "A Banker's Daughter" assumed that only "unprotected" women, those who had lost their fathers or husbands, needed financial education. The book gave these unfortunate women basic information, but it also encouraged them to seek out new male protectors. They needed "a sensible and upright Friend, who is a good man of business" to advise them on safe investments. The readers were repeatedly urged to consult "respectable" bankers and brokers who could conduct their business for them. In any case, male advice was always preferable to female. One should "seldom consult ladies in business matters ... It is much like the blind leading the blind."[32] That the author only identified herself as "a banker's daughter" further suggests that there is something a bit immodest or improper in a woman setting herself up as a financial expert.

Later guides were less conservative and often argued that even young girls and married women should have a business education and that they should not be too dependent on their fathers and husbands. J. L. Nichols's *Safe Methods of Business*, first published in 1886 and still in print twenty years later, held that girls should be brought up conversant with basic business practices. He encouraged parents to buy their daughters "a little account book, and make them have an account of all the money they receive, and the disposition they make of it." If a man were wed to a woman ignorant of business principles, he needed to rectify the situation. Indeed, "every husband should teach his wife some of the more important ways of business." Women with greater financial literacy would be better helpmates, able to assist and advise their husbands, and capable of settling their estates when called upon.[33]

A constant theme in all guides for women investors is the need to be extremely cautious and conservative in the disposition of their money. *A Guide to the Unprotected* warned that a woman should never ask, "How can I invest my money so as to get the highest possible interest? Let her rather seek to place it where her *capital* will be *safest*." Women were advised to diversify their portfolios, favor bonds over stocks, and realize that anything promising more than 4% interest carried risk.[34] *The American Business Woman* insisted that women must avoid "schemes for the rapid making of fortunes" and instead focus on "legitimate and proper methods of managing property."[35] Most investment guides for women recommended government securities, railway bonds, public utilities, and mortgages on valuable real estate as the safest investments. Shares traded on the stock market should mostly be avoided, with the exception of established railway lines and large banks. Mining shares and the shares of new stock market flotations were condemned as especially risky. Speculation was never recommended for women.

An underlying tension that ran through most financial guides for women is that the qualities presumed necessary for success in business are rarely qualities associated with Victorian women. A successful businesswoman would thus need to cultivate masculine qualities that might render her less attractive to men. In the worst-case scenario, a woman who was too protective of her money might become, in the language of the day, "unsexed." J. H. Cromwell warned that, if she were not careful, she could emasculate her husband. He gave the example of "women of means" married to men with less property of their own. To husbands "possessed of proper manly spirits," this scenario would be a source of "constant humiliations." Sensitive wives should endeavor "to relieve their husbands of such disagreeable sensations" by avoiding public mention of their own property, and by letting their husbands receive their income, keep the accounts, and pay the bills.[36] Advice books sought to empower women by endowing them with financial knowledge, and yet these same guides conveyed a certain ambivalence about the propriety of women appearing too knowledgeable or acting too independently from men.

Financial Miscellanies: Inside Stories of Wall Street

Another genre of financial literature comprised works meant to entertain and amuse. These seriously understudied works were sometimes memoirs or journalism but often took the form of pastiches, combining anecdotes, jokes, poems, humorous stories, and reminiscences about Wall Street written by stockbrokers, businessmen, and financial journalists. I have christened these works "financial miscellanies." By the late nineteenth century, as David Itzkowitz has demonstrated, speculation on the stock market was "becoming a form of entertainment and was entering into the same raffish bohemian world that was described by sporting and theatrical journalists."[37] Humorous stories about the stock exchange helped to cultivate an image of it "as a distinct and charmingly idiosyncratic culture" with its own colorful characters (bulls and bears) and its own colorful lexicon (lame ducks, bucket shops, corners, and margins).[38] Some of this work was fictional, and much of it clearly fictionalized, but most of it purported to be the "real-life" stories of brokers and speculators. The narrators of this literature invariably presented a male point of view, and the risqué tone of much of it presumed a masculine readership. Women did figure heavily in these works, but almost always as objects of ridicule and as the butt of jokes.

Humorous and sarcastic stories about women predominated. In 1879, H. C. Percy published *Our Cashier's Scrap Book*, one of the first financial miscellanies. This book, subtitled "a portfolio of bank anecdotes and incidents, queer, curious, odd, ludicrous, touching," included several examples meant to illustrate women's ignorance in money matters. In a section called "Business and Beauty," Percy recalled the surprise of a friend, "a mercantile gentleman in search of a wife," when he learned about a young lady's financial illiteracy. She thought a "dividend was a sum in long division" and bullionists "were a religious sect," and she "had read about consuls—they were ancient Romans."[39] Over the years, much humor was derived from the stock figure of the dimwitted female holding forth about business.[40]

Comic anecdotes about women's inability to balance their checkbooks or keep proper accounts had remarkable staying power.[41] In his popular memoir of the 1880s, *Life with Father* (1920), Clarence Day recounted his stockbroker father's constant exasperation with his mother's inability to keep track of household expenses. Before her marriage, Mrs. Day had been a debutante and "had never laid eyes upon a ledger." She would "put down all sorts of little expenses, on backs of envelopes or on half-sheets of letter paper of different sizes, and she gave these to Father with many interlineations and much scratching out of other memoranda, and with mystifying omissions. He would pore over them, calling out to her to tell him what this was, or that, in a vain attempt to bring order out of feminine chaos."[42] In the 1920s, few people alleged that women were still like this, but popular works like Day's helped cement the idea that Victorian women had been financially incompetent.

A great deal of financial humor revolved around women attempting to play the market. In another miscellany, *The Sayings of Uncle Rufus* (1881), purportedly the musings of stockbroker Rufus Hatch, the protagonist was plagued by women who fancied themselves shrewd investors. At one point, Hatch received a letter from a woman in the country seeking his advice. Previously she had invested her capital in farm mortgages but now had "decided to speculate a little." Inspired by the example of Jay Gould, she thought she would try her luck with Texas Pacific stock. The sardonic stockbroker's reply was stern, echoing the guidebooks: "Invest your $5,000 in additional Jefferson County cheese and butter farms. By doing this you have the dowries of your two little girls always under your eyes." If she persisted in "the insane idea of becoming suddenly rich through the action of some unknown quantity," she had better be aware that ladies "who venture in Wall St." were regarded "as lambs to be fleeced."[43]

Other comic tales of Wall Street underscored the point that women customers were more trouble than they were worth. Edwin Lefevre endorsed this view in his story "A Woman and Her Bonds," from his financial miscellany *Wall Street Stories* (1901). The tale centered on a widow, Mrs. Hunt, who pestered her broker every time her electric company bonds fluctuated even slightly in value, despite his assurance that they were a safe investment. Finally, to calm her fears and be rid of an annoying client, the broker bought the bonds back from her. When the bonds later shot up in value, Mrs. Hunt demanded to buy them back, but at their original low price. The moral of the story was clear: women were awful clients—unbusinesslike, ignorant, and capricious. They didn't understand the rules of the marketplace and had no sense of personal responsibility.[44] This literature drew lines of inclusion and exclusion about who was a legitimate player, in the hopes of keeping Wall Street a male preserve.

Stockbrokers were frequently cited as the sources for jokes and colorful stories about women speculators, and their memoirs form a distinct subgenre of financial writings intended to entertain. Brokers certainly colluded in depicting Wall Street as an exotic and exciting world, as well as a vigorously male subculture where women ventured at their peril. The late-nineteenth-century autobiographies of two stockbrokers, William Fowler and Henry Clews, perpetuated myths about the fecklessness of women investors. Both men devoted substantial chapters to women, whom they treated with a mixture of chivalry, humor, and disdain. Fowler began by noting the incongruity of women dreaming of stocks and bonds when they should "sit embroidering golden bees and butterflies on black velvet." He claimed that during his visits to the fashionable resorts of Newport and Saratoga, all the "dowagers and damsels talk of little but the stock market." One group of these ladies pooled their resources, made a quick profit in railway shares, and then made "heavy investments in moiré antique, Mechlin lace, and India shawls." Fowler was amused by these women, who were not seriously interested in business matters, but in fashion and dress fabric. He was less charitable in his description of other women investors he had known, such as "Miss M"—a "strong minded" woman whose "face is that of a goshawk." Her preoccupation with the market had rendered her ruthless, predatory, and unfeminine.[45]

Henry Clews was less satirical than Fowler and more matter-of-fact in his assessment of women's financial acumen. He asserted categorically: "Women do not seem to have the mental qualities required to take in the varied points of the situation upon which success in speculation depends. They are, by nature, parasites as speculators . . . when obliged to go alone, they are like a ship at sea in a heavy gale without compass, anchor or rudder. They have no ballast apart from men, and are liable to perish when adversity arises." Clews believed that women were "too impulsive and impressionable" to make well-reasoned and thoughtful investment decisions on their own. He concluded that a woman's most successful "investment" was to marry a wealthy man: "It is probably only in the matrimonial line that women can become successful speculators."[46]

Fowler's and Clews's memoirs, like most financial writing, defended the honor of the stock market against the widespread calumnies found in much popular discourse. They also embodied a certain ambivalence about women investors that can be seen in other types of financial writing, such as financial journalism, investment guides, and financial miscellanies. On the one hand, women's capital was welcomed and women were encouraged to better educate themselves about financial opportunities and the management of their money. On the other hand, women were sometimes denigrated as too frivolous, indecisive, and temperamental to look after money. In some quarters, women's alleged financial incapacity was attributed to faulty education, but in others it was seen as evidence of certain inborn characteristics like emotionalism and compassion. These qualities were not inherently bad, as they fitted women for the domestic realm, but handicapped them in the more boisterous and cutthroat world of business.

Financial Fictions: Women and Wall Street in the American Novel

Representations of women and finance found their richest, most heightened, and darkest expression in the imaginative literature of the late nineteenth and early twentieth centuries. The novels and short stories of this era were especially fascinated with the workings of Wall Street, which they tended to present in a highly negative light. Many writers of the Gilded Age were harshly critical of capitalism and what they believed was its spirit of selfish materialism. As Wayne Westbrook argued in his pioneering study *Wall Street in the American Novel* (1980): "Instead of the straight and narrow way to wealth, riches, and the American Dream, Wall Street, in the popular mind as well as in literature, is a broad road that leads to destruction and ends in nightmare."[47]

Novelists often drew upon a deep-rooted Puritan faith in the work ethic, viewing speculation, like gambling, as lazy, reckless, and even sinful. As Caroline Walch argues in *Doctor Sphinx* (1898), "our whole American life is being pervaded by this restless desire of immediate unheard-of returns for a non-equivalent expenditure of honest labor."[48] In *The Lion's Share* (1907), Alice French maintains that workers and industrialists create wealth, while speculators only manipulate it. "Why should they have the lion's share?" French asks her readers. "The lion's share belongs to the lion. They are nothing but jackals."[49] Financiers are scavengers on a productive economy.

American novelists' condemnation of Wall Street also drew upon a rich British literary tradition that was critical of high finance and speculation. Some of the Victorian era's most celebrated novels—Thackeray's *The Newcomes* (1855), Dickens's *Little Dorrit* (1857), and Trollope's *The Way We Live Now* (1875)— detailed the colossal frauds of bankers, stockbrokers, and company promoters that epitomized a society obsessed with material success at any price. Themes of financial insecurity permeated Victorian fiction, including romantic novels, where a sudden fall in share prices could imperil domestic security. As an important body of recent scholarship has demonstrated, Victorian writers often employed financial plots as a way of engaging with issues of risk, indeterminacy, and social instability.[50] In the novels of the period, financial speculation is a sign of general economic and social disorder.

During the first decade of the twentieth century, American publishing saw a boom in novels about the stock market and high finance.[51] Among the nation's most celebrated novelists, Theodore Dreiser, Upton Sinclair, and Frank Norris all wrote about the financial world.[52] Scores of other writers, some well known in their day, most forgotten in ours, participated in this publishing craze. Although most of these writers shared a contempt for Wall Street, they often had little else in common, having arrived at their conclusions about American finance from a wide variety of ideological backgrounds. Dreiser, Sinclair, and Norris wrote squarely from a position in the Progressive Movement, which lashed out at economic and political corruption in America. Others, like Margaret Deland and Helen Campbell, criticized capitalism from a Christian, Social Gospel perspective or, like Caroline Walch, from a feminist point of view. Some popular middlebrow writers simply grafted financial themes onto their conventional romantic plots for added spice or to capitalize on the latest publishing trend.[53]

Novels about Wall Street sometimes assumed that the stock market was an exclusively male enclave in which women could play no active part. William

Hawley Smith's *The Promoters* (1904) centered on the male subculture of brokers, company promoters, and politicians plotting fantastic schemes in smoky offices and seedy boardinghouses. The book's subtitle, "A Novel Without a Woman," makes clear that the world of high finance is a purely masculine realm.[54] This work, however, is quite unique in its absence of women. Of the scores of popular novels about the stock market, most are packed with female characters. Although plentiful, these women seldom understand much about finance, and their purported ignorance only perpetuates the notion that the stock market is a male space.

Popular literature usually assumed that the woman's place was in the home, but this home was often maintained by investments in shares. In Frank Norris's *The Pit* (1902), the heroine, Laura Dearborn, is shocked to realize that her domestic comforts cannot be separated from the grubby workings of the stock exchange. One night, as she is returning from the opera, her carriage drives through Chicago's financial district and she is surprised to see the offices all illuminated. She is told that the brokers are working late, balancing their accounts in the aftermath of a plunge in share prices. "Laura looked, suddenly stupefied. Here it was, then, that other drama, that other tragedy, working on there furiously, fiercely through the night, while she and all those others had sat there in that atmosphere of flowers and perfume, listening to music."[55] Conservatives saw the home as a refuge from the tumultuous world of business, but this separation is seldom upheld in novels, where domestic tranquility is often threatened by financial problems.

Like Frank Norris, Edith Wharton also makes explicit the link between women's genteel lives uptown and men's sordid business dealings downtown, and she underscores women's vulnerability to this relationship.[56] In Wharton's last novel, *The Buccaneers*, a stockbroker's wife reflects on the material uncertainty of her life: "She knew that a gentleman's financial situation might at any moment necessitate compromises and concessions. All the ladies of her acquaintance were inured to them: up one day, down the next, as the secret gods of Wall Street decreed."[57] The ubiquity of financial danger in so much domestic fiction undermines a too-rigid imposition of separate spheres.

Women as victims of the stock market was a cliché of popular literature throughout the nineteenth century and into the twentieth. Common plot devices included male trustees gambling away women's inheritances on speculative shares and women being plunged into poverty by sudden downturns in the market. The specter of female victims added an extra pathos to financial novels. In *Doctor Sphinx* (1898), the heroine's own economic hardships had led her to work as a stenographer for a stockbroker, and she naturally empathized with other women's financial victimization. Whenever she saw men on Wall Street who had lost their fortunes, "she wondered what would become of their wives and daughters. The time must come, now, any day, when they too would be brought face to face with wretchedness and poverty."[58]

The predatory financier—the forecloser of mortgages, the despoiler of widows and orphans—was a favorite villain in Victorian melodrama, and unprotected females his chosen prey. Onstage he appeared as a menacing presence in a black cape and top hat, twirling his black mustachio with one hand and brandishing a notice of eviction with the other. He frequently used his economic clout to blackmail pretty women into marriage, or worse . . . This crudely drawn villain of the mid-Victorian stage had remarkable longevity in popular culture. He was still recognizable in the novels (and films) of later generations, continuing to embody a twin threat to feminine property and propriety.[59]

Villainous stockbrokers acquired attractive women like they acquired gilt-edged securities, by any means necessary. In Dreiser's *The Financier* (1912), the amoral protagonist, Frank Cowperwood, is utterly contemptuous of his society's reverence for womanhood. "There was a great deal of palaver about the sanctity of the home. It rolled off his mental sphere like water off the feathers of a duck."[60] Upton Sinclair's *The Moneychangers* (1908) chronicles the decline of Lucy Taylor, a young widow from Mississippi, who moves to New York, where she is menaced by a series of indecent Wall Street men. First, Dan Waterman, an eighty-year-old tycoon who controlled the steel trust, tries to rape her on his yacht. Narrowly escaping Waterman's clutches, Lucy later falls for Stanley Ryder, a disreputable stockbroker, who seduces her and inveigles her out of valuable railway shares. In the end, she poisons herself.[61]

The link between financial and sexual danger is probably given its most poignant expression by Edith Wharton in *The House of Mirth* (1905), which chronicles the economic and social decline of Lily Bart, a young beauty from a prominent but penniless family. Early in the novel Lily appeals to Gus Trenor, a family friend and stockbroker, for help in better investing her small capital: "I have a tiny income of my own, but I'm afraid its badly invested, for it seems to bring in less every year, and I am so ignorant of money matters that I don't know if my aunt's agent, who looks after it, is a good adviser."[62] The oily Trenor promises to increase Lily's income, as an act of friendship, but his business dealings for her become a source of gossip, even scandal, and he soon makes clear to her that he expects to be repaid sexually: "Why can't we go off somewhere on a little lark together . . ." When Trenor realizes that Lily has no intention of becoming his mistress, he confronts her, in a scene that comes perilously close to sexual assault: "That ain't playing fair: that's dodging the rules of the game. Of course I know now what you wanted—it wasn't my beautiful eyes you were after—but I tell you what, Miss Lily, you've got to pay up for making me think so."[63] Fleeing from Trenor, but disowned by her family and abandoned by her friends, Lily descends into the world of low-wage work and eventually commits suicide.[64]

Women's victimization by the stock market was never in doubt, but some writers blamed the victims, rather than the agents of the market, arguing that feminine gullibility and greed led women to their doom. In Ellen Warner Kirk's *Queen Money* (1888), women's desire for fashionable clothes, social advancement, or "a skilled cook and a third servant" leads them into reckless speculation. Brokers' warnings that "no woman should buy speculative stock" go unheeded. Indeed, one broker jokes that "no woman is satisfied with five per cent or six per cent; ten per cent is better, but what they want is fifty per cent."[65] In *Doctor Sphinx*, the heroine "realized that, in many respects, her own sex is most selfish" and that many families had been ruined in the stock market "to gratify the foolish desire for that meaningless display, which rules the lives of most of our American women."[66]

The most extended examination of a woman's addiction to stock speculation can be found in H. H. Boyesen's *A Daughter of the Philistines* (1883), the story of Alma Hampton, a banker's daughter from the West, whose family has recently moved to New York. Seduced by the city's lavish department stores, Alma runs through her allowance and then decides to get more money via the stock exchange: "She was well aware that ladies sometimes took flyers in stocks and no one seemed to think the less of them for it." She becomes entrapped by a sinister Jewish broker, Simon Loewenthal, until she is saved by a chivalrous young businessman, Harold Wallingford, whom she marries.[67] Unfortunately, Alma cannot give up "her dreams of Wall Street" and falls under the spell of a charismatic broker, Cunningham, who demands sexual favors as payment for his financial advice.

Weak and materialistic women were unable to resist the temptations of Wall Street, but virtuous women could. Indeed, some novelists saw women as the best bulwark against the evils of speculation. The innate moral qualities that Victorian culture usually assigned to women—compassion, nurturance, modesty, charity, honesty—would inoculate them against the selfish, ruthless, and competitive ways of businessmen. In many financial novels, women were the moral voice, speaking out against speculation and fighting to protect domestic space from the contaminating influence of the marketplace.

In several novels women were cast as moral redeemers, condemning speculation and steering men away from the stock market. In *Queen Money*

(1888), the heroine, Lucy, admonishes her sweetheart to abandon his work as a stockbroker: "I hate that wicked thirst for money—I hate that sordid materialistic view that money can give everything one wants in this world—I tell you, it brings disappointment, destruction, ruin."[68] In *Wall Street and the Woods, or Woman the Stronger* (1885), Emma Grandin has been brought up by her virtuous father to hate the ways of the stock market: "It is a mere game of chance they play, or, if skill has anything to do with it, the skill is that of swindlers and thieves." When Emma marries a wealthy speculator, William Wraxall, she makes him promise to "never gamble nor speculate to the value of a single cent." Wraxall is unable to resist the allure of speculation and, despite his promise, loses half his fortune "in the panic of an hour." Emma decides that "an immense change of scene" is necessary and takes her husband to the wilderness of western Ohio. There, the virtues of country life cleanse him of the corruption of Wall Street.[69]

Christian writers (mostly women) of the Social Gospel Movement especially hoped to promote kinder and gentler economic development as an alternative to the ruthless competition and materialism of industrial capitalism. In their works, women characters embodied the values of compassion, charity, and community. Helen Campbell's novel *Mrs. Herndon's Income* (1886), serialized in the *Christian Union*, chastises the rich for being ignorant about the source of their wealth. The heroine, a young widow with an immense income of $100,000 a year, is horrified to discover that her fortune is derived from squalid tenements and sweated labor. Like many women of her class, Mrs. Herndon relied on her husband's financial stewardship. "The money side of things I could never understand, and, like other foolish women before me, I asked no questions," she says. She now resolves to use her money to benefit others, and the novel details her quest for ethical investments.[70]

The great majority of literary depictions of finance and financial women was negative, but a minority counterdiscourse defended the integrity of the business world and could even imagine a space for (some) women in that world. One work that imagined a woman as a successful investor was "A Woman's Romance in Wall Street," a short story by Arthur Field that appeared in *Demorest's Family Magazine* in 1894. The protagonist, Elinor Alvis, is a young woman who "had played her part in the affairs of Wall Street and had come out with flying colors." The sudden death of Elinor's father forces her to settle his business affairs and to invest her inheritance to save the family home. Her investment choices, however, are not based on experience or on a rational assessment of market trends, but are "the result of a mere inspiration, like Joan of Arc's," which prompted her "in some indescribable manner to go to New York and do certain things with certain stocks." Elinor accomplishes her mission, but her experience is so unique that it could hardly serve as a blueprint for other women. Indeed, the story actually cautions women to avoid the stock market, which is best left in the more capable hands of men. The conclusion predicts that "it will be a long time before the average woman will make up successfully as a 'bull' or a 'bear.' The majority will be well content to let the Jasons go forth and do battle for the Golden Fleece."[71]

The most remarkable literary defense of the stock market and women investors is James Blanchard Clews's *Fortuna: A Story of Wall Street* (1898). The author was a stockbroker, who in his introduction laments all the "rubbish" written about the stock market: "One often hears a tirade of abuse directed against 'Wall Street' by persons who are ignorant of the methods employed there, or else willfully pervert the facts, in an effort to discredit it as much as possible." He also intends to counter the prejudice against women investors. According to Clews, "the growing importance of women in the business world has also led me to introduce that topic in my story, and I have no doubt that the majority of the female sex would be quite as capable of managing their business affairs as Miss Montague (the heroine of the book) did hers, if they would only go about it in the same manner."[72]

Fortuna chronicles a shipboard romance between a young stockbroker, Fred Tremaine, and an heiress, Helen Montague. Initially, the broker is hostile to Miss Montague managing her own money, arguing that in business matters women's "pretty heads get confused, and they are forced to depend on others for help." Helen concedes that "the average woman displays a woeful ignorance where business is concerned" but insists that this is the result of faulty education. She counters that if women "had received the same business training that a man does . . . they would be quite competent to take charge of their own affairs."[73] Won over by Helen's logic and determination, Fred immediately agrees to tutor her in the basic principles of sound investment. By the novel's end, Helen has learned enough about financial matters to manage her own fortune.[74]

Fortuna's author, James Blanchard Clews, was the nephew and business associate of the legendary stockbroker Henry Clews, whose memoir *Twenty-Eight Years in Wall Street* (1888) is discussed above. A mere decade separated the two men's books, but they were eons apart in their attitudes toward women investors. The elder Clews embodied the values of the Victorian patriarchy. He argued that women required male protection and guidance. They are too emotional and capricious to operate successfully in Wall Street. In 1888 Henry Clews was looking back over a long career that had begun before the Civil War. In 1898 the younger Clews was instead looking ahead to a new century, and he welcomed the "New Woman"—more independent and self-reliant than her Victorian mother. Nonetheless, James Clews's heroine achieves her independence only under the tutelage of a male financial expert.

Whether novelists were optimistic or pessimistic about women's financial abilities, most could agree that women were destined to play supporting roles. Imaginative accounts of women on Wall Street treated the very idea of a woman stockbroker as a joke or impossibility. A 1912 Broadway musical, *The Wall Street Girl*, depicted the escapades of a woman broker as a comic diversion. The play was a lighthearted romp in which a "brokeress" saves her father from bankruptcy through a lucky investment and then happily gives up the stock exchange to marry her sweetheart.[75] Frederick Bartlett's 1916 novel, also titled *The Wall Street Girl*, follows the adventures of Sally, the most intelligent clerk in a broker's office. When she assists a young male employee, far less savvy than herself, to master the business, her reward is a marriage proposal. That she could become a broker herself is never contemplated.[76]

By the second decade of the twentieth century, popular hostility to the stock market was fast receding. Financial writers and even mainstream journalists recognized that it was better to advise Americans how best to invest their money than to demonize all financial transactions. The government's aggressive marketing of savings bonds during World War I further familiarized Americans with new investment opportunities and

Figure 2. Postcard advertising Broadway musical *The Wall Street Girl*, 1912. (Collection of the author)

helped legitimate the securities market. By the 1920s, an unprecedented growth in the stock market led to an even greater expansion of shareholding among ordinary Americans, including women. The Roaring Twenties seemed fueled by stock speculation as much as by jazz and bootleg liquor. Long-standing literary condemnations of Wall Street evaporated.

Stockbrokers were no longer exotic or sinister figures in literature, but were now as unobjectionable and "all-American" as cowboys, athletes, and aviators.[77] Most novelists of the 1920s, however, were far less interested in exploring the world of finance than were the writers of the Progressive Era. In a 1920s essay on the novel, Willa Cather wondered whether "the banking system and the Stock Exchange [are] worth being written about at all? Have such things any proper place in imaginative art?" Not much, according to Cather, who championed novels about people's inner lives.[78] As speculation became less controversial, it may have lost some of its attraction for writers.

In a half century of American literary depictions of Wall Street, from the 1880s until the 1920s, most popular fiction expressed a general disdain for financial activity. American novels and short stories often reflected the critiques of muckraking journalists, Progressive Era reformers, and Christian idealists from the Social Gospel Movement. Writers' attacks on the stock market might draw upon a long-standing religious opposition to gambling and might reflect the prejudices of the professional middle class against the "moneygrubbing" ways of businessmen.

Opposition to women's participation in financial activities was also fairly consistent in the imaginative literature of the period, but the depictions of women's relations with the stock market were multivalent. Some writers upheld an image of women as unsophisticated and naive "lambs" who were no match for the "wolves" of Wall Street. Other writers portrayed women as greedy and hysterical stock gamblers who longed for sudden riches but were too emotional to manage the market in a rational manner. Still others idealized women as guardians of domestic security, who shrank instinctively from speculation and used moral suasion to guide men away from the market. As inconsistent as these fictional versions of women's financial agency were, they could all agree on one thing: women investors should proceed with caution and male guidance.

Wall Street Women in Popular Culture

Images of women and finance pervaded popular culture far beyond the bounds of literary expression. The newest genre to depict the stock market, though not the most modern ideologically, was film. By 1910, motion pictures had become a mass entertainment in America and were reaching audiences far larger than even best-selling novelists could dream of.[79] These films, silent, and initially short and simple, but growing increasingly long and complex, dealt with many of the same economic concerns found in the novels of the period: the problems of poverty, the struggle between capital and labor, and the stock market's impact on the lives of ordinary people.[80]

The stock market's corrupting influence on women was dramatized in *The Price of the Necklace* (1914), a film directed by Charles Brabin for the Edison Film Company. Mrs. Lyons, a stockbroker's wife, desires a pearl necklace costing $80,000. When her husband hesitates to grant her wish, she stamps her foot with impatience. "How stupid!" she exclaims. "Can't you make the market do something or other, and get it for me that way?" Mr. Lyons agrees, and he makes a windfall by manipulating railroad shares to a great height and then unloading them on a bank, which collapses, bringing ruin to thousands of people. Later, Mrs. Lyons is giving a magnificent party, when a poor woman asks to see her. She is one of the thousands wiped out in the crash—all for a pearl necklace. "With sudden horror," Mrs. Lyons realizes "what it cost the world to keep her in luxury."[81] The idea that pampered society women turned to speculation "to buy new gowns, hats, and jewels" was widespread at the time. An article from the *New York Times* in 1909 told how speculators bought their wives "pearl necklaces" with profits from their share deals.[82]

Another cinematic melodrama that centered on the perils of speculation for women was *The Cheat* (1915), an early film by Cecil B. DeMille, later famous for his biblical epics. The film tells the story of Edith Hardy, a stockbroker's wife and Long Island socialite, who is living beyond her means through extravagant consumption of jewelry and clothes. When her husband tries to curb her reckless spending by limiting her allowance, she attempts to increase her funds by playing the stock market. As the treasurer of the local Red Cross, Edith "borrows" $10,000 meant for Belgian war refugees and loses it in a reckless speculation. Desperate to conceal her embezzlement, she turns to a neighbor, Hishuru Tori, a Japanese businessman, who loans her the money to cover her losses but later demands sexual favors as repayment of the debt.[83]

The Cheat is a melodrama about the dangers of the libidinous "Oriental," but the villain would never have had his chance had Mrs. Hardy not been extravagant, not flouted her husband's authority, and not taken a flyer on Wall Street. The film features many of the elements from literary treatments of women speculators. Like *A Daughter of the Philistines* (1883), it portrays a shopping addict seeking funds in the stock market and turning to a sinister financier, coded as "other." In the film the villain is Asian, in the novel, more typically, Jewish. Like *The House of Mirth* (1905), the film also features a woman sexually blackmailed for financial favors. The film may have borrowed from these literary sources, or the novels and the film may have drawn from the same melodramatic pool of helpless women, villainous financiers, and stock plotlines about the uncertainties of the market that had permeated so much Victorian literature.

Other novel forms of popular entertainment also came to incorporate financial themes in unexpected ways. In the 1880s, for example, a new type of board game emerged whereby players achieved success through competitive capitalist behavior. In "Bulls and Bears," players moved tokens around the board as they speculated on the rise and fall of shares. In the card game "Commerce," players attempted to corner the market in certain commodities by yelling out bids to other players. Parker Brothers created a board game called "The Pit," clearly based on Frank Norris's novel about grain speculation and advertised as "exciting fun for everyone."[84]

That some of these games were marketed to women can be seen in the box cover for "Commerce," which depicts a pretty, stylishly dressed "Gibson girl" energetically raising her arms in a "commodities deal." The games certainly raise questions about how seriously the general public took the Progressive Era's condemnation of Wall Street. For muckraking journalists and novelists like Norris, a corner in wheat was no game, but an evil and deadly act, imperiling the lives and livelihoods of the nation's most vulnerable citizens. It seems unlikely that American families who played "Commerce" or "The Pit," allowing their daughters to act out speculative corners, shared Norris's zealous commitment to reform. They might in fact have admired the financial machinations of a Vanderbilt or a Carnegie. At the very least, they saw no real harm in letting girls pretend to be brokers, if only for fun, and if only in the seclusion of their homes.

The allure of the stock exchange also inspired W. Duke Sons & Company to launch "Preferred Stock" cigarettes in 1886, sold in packets picturing a stock ticker. Targeting businessmen and the economically ambitious, Duke's Preferred Stock included as a premium "Histories of Poor Boys"—a series of small booklets detailing the rags-to-riches stories of wealthy men. Advertisements for the brand typically featured attractive women posing in a stockbroker's office. As tobacco was marketed exclusively to men at the time, ads frequently employed beautiful women and sexual innuendo. Turkish cigarette posters often depicted scantily clad "harem girls," and Spanish cigar boxes might include an image of a tempestuous gypsy—à la Carmen. The models promoting Preferred Stock cigarettes were fully, and fashionably, dressed. They smiled demurely or heartily as they gazed at the stock tape, no doubt overjoyed at their earnings. The figure of the woman speculator had long been regarded as transgressive and was as easily eroticized as the odalisques and gypsies usually featured in tobacco advertisements.

Figure 3. Advertising card for
Preferred Stock Cigarettes,
W. Duke Sons & Co., c. 1890.
(Courtesy of the Museum of
American Finance, New York)

*   *   *

Women's participation in the American securities market was the subject of extensive commentary from the moment of Wall Street's extraordinary expansion following the Civil War until the stock market crash of 1929. This period of a burgeoning and largely unregulated share market coincided with intense debates over women's nature and their proper role in society, as well as witnessing the birth of an organized women's movement that sought legal equality, greater political participation, and new educational and economic opportunities. Not surprisingly, much of the public discourse regarding women's financial activities was bound up with anxieties about women's changing roles and fears of declining patriarchal control.

As we have seen, there were numerous warnings to women about the potential dangers of the marketplace in all manner of writings: journalism, advice books, humor, and novels. Although these narratives about women and investment had many similarities, there were also differences peculiar to genres or to the ideological perspectives of writers. Fictional accounts of women speculators were colored by a general disdain for financial activity and were more prone than other kinds of writing to depict women's interactions with the stock market as wholly undesirable. Novels and other fictional representations, like short stories and films, employed narrative conventions that led to exaggeration and distortion for dramatic effect. They tended to regard female economic players in the starkest terms: as victims of male financial skullduggery or as saviors of men from speculative mania.

Financial journalists and business writers vigorously defended the stock market against the libelous attacks of novelists but were more ambivalent in their advocacy of women's economic empowerment. A few financial writers championed women investors and strove to educate them to better manage their own money. Others accepted women investors as a fact of life, pleasant or unpleasant as the case may be, but sought to limit their autonomy and guide their capital into certain safe and accepted channels. Many financial writers and brokers, even as they welcomed women's capital and pocketed commissions from women clients, belittled their female customers through jokes and humorous stories about the frivolity and financial incapacity of "the fair sex."

So long as women entrusted their wealth to the stewardship of their male protectors and advisors, they received public approbation and were likewise fitting objects of pity when their trust was betrayed by unscrupulous financiers. On the other hand, whenever women were seen as too actively or enthusiastically seeking their own fortunes on the stock market, they became the objects of scorn and ridicule, and their financial losses were seen as just deserts for having abandoned their modesty and domestic responsibilities. When, for example, Elizabeth Barrett Browning's friend Mary Trepsack lost money in a financial investment, Robert Browning declared that this "should be a lesson to women not to take the administration of their affairs into their own hands."[85]

Did any of the cautionary tales of novelists, journalists, and financial writers detailed in this chapter deter women in the least from investing in the stock market? Were women really unprepared to make their own financial decisions? Were they victimized by the market any more than men? Sifting out the reality of women's economic lives from the mass of prescriptive literature, journalistic hyperbole, and dramatic license is no easy task, but it lies at the heart of this project. The next chapter will begin the process of excavation and recovery.

2 Engendering Finance

Women and Wall Street

> "There is no more patent sign of the times than the fact that
> woman is attracting the attention of the financial world, and that
> her large property interests are being recognized as an integral part
> of the so-called 'Woman Question.'"
> —Ellen Henrotin, "The Financial Independence of Women" (1894)

For most of the twentieth century, American women's long-standing participation in financial activities remained hidden from history. Most studies of Wall Street and the stock market never mention women at all. Others do so in passing, with an occasional reference to Victoria Woodhull or Hetty Green. Cedric Cowing's pioneering social history of speculation, *Populists, Plungers, and Progressives* (1964), mentions women only briefly in relation to the 1920s stock mania, as if this were the first moment that women ventured into Wall Street in large numbers. In Charles Geisst's *Wall Street* (1997), women are not referred to until the chapter on the 1940s, when the New York Stock Exchange hired some female clerks to replace men who entered the military. Steve Fraser's monumental six-hundred-page cultural history of Wall Street, *Every Man a Speculator* (2005), includes around ten pages about women.[1]

Unlike so many historians of Wall Street, nineteenth-century Americans were well aware of women's activities as investors. The phenomenon was the subject of frequent, if not always favorable, commentary. Journalists and financiers had noted the presence of women at the nation's stock exchanges since the 1870s. The woman's-rights advocate Victoria Woodhull had a brief but spectacular career as a stockbroker in the early 1870s. (See Chapter 4.) In January 1875, the *San Francisco Chronicle* reported that "the number of female operators is increasing daily, and the lucky ones, with smiling faces, may be seen at all hours of the day dodging into brokers' offices to give orders and receive reports."[2] The New York stockbroker William Fowler noted in 1880, "On almost any bright day, when stocks are rising, a dozen or so showy carriages may be seen drawn up in front of the offices of prominent brokerage houses, waiting for the gorgeous dames who ride in them to come out, when they have transacted their business with their brokers."[3] In September 1882, the *New York Times* observed that "Wall Street is overrun with women—women who are old, and women who are young; women who are poorly clad, and women in rich attire . . . women attractive and women repulsive—all with an eye single to gain. Old operators in the Street say that there has been a big change in this matter within the past few years."[4] While these reports often poked fun at women investors, they also clearly acknowledged their presence.

Women's "invasion" of Wall Street coincided with the tremendous expansion of the American securities market following the Civil War. From 1875 to 1880, the number of shares sold on the New York Stock Exchange in a given year rose from 54 million to 98 million, and the collective value of those shares more than doubled, from $2.8 billion to $6.8 billion. Most of this increase was accounted for by railroad securities. The nation's railway mileage doubled between 1865 and 1873, and this massive construction was financed by publicly floated stocks and bonds, which became an important investment outlet for wealthy, and even middle-class, Americans, women as well as men.[5]

Most large public companies sold their shares through the New York Stock Exchange, the nation's most important and prestigious securities market. Exchange membership was limited to 1,100 men, whose seats cost as much as $20,000 in the 1880s, an immense sum at a time when the average working man made $400 a year. Brokerage firms with seats on the New York Stock Exchange served the elite of big business and the plutocracy. They normally dealt in large blocks of shares and expected their customers to put large amounts of cash up front. The grandest firms had lavish offices near Wall Street, employing several brokers and dozens of clerks and messenger boys.[6]

A national securities market spread out from Wall Street and reached down the social ladder. For modest investors, there were several hundred brokers' offices crammed into the narrow streets of lower Manhattan. Most of them were little more than cubbyholes with a desk or counter, employing one or two men. They dealt in small lots of shares and allowed customers to buy on credit, with margins as low as 10%. Several stock exchanges existed outside of New York City, most notably in Boston, Philadelphia, Chicago, Denver, and San Francisco. They mostly dealt in local securities for local customers.[7] The invention of the stock ticker in 1867 meant that share prices were now available nationwide, transmitted instantaneously and continuously via the telegraph wires. Telephones appeared on Wall Street as early as 1878 and, like the ticker, served to decentralize buying and selling.[8]

From the outset, brokers high and low sought women's business. A *New York Times* article from 1882 nicely captures the wide variety of financial intermediaries available for women:

> The demand for opportunities to speculate upon the part of women has caused the erection of many tickers in the fashionable parts of the City. Some of them are connected with establishments of somewhat unsavory repute, but there are others where all the proprieties are observed . . . As a rule these places are not well known to the public. They have a profitable clientage and seek no notoriety. Ultra respectable ladies have the entrée, and intoxicated with the Wall-street atmosphere they remain the day through hovering over the tickers . . . just as their pantalooned prototypes do down town. There are other establishments where the lady's margin is accepted which are conducted on far less aristocratic principles. One such advertising firm has located in the centre of the shopping district, and in big, bold letters informed the public that it boasts
> AN OFFICE EXCLUSIVELY FOR LADIES
> Within the past twelve months many of the best firms in Wall-street have opened branches up town.[9]

Clearly, large numbers of women had money to invest, and large numbers of brokers, reputable and sleazy, were eager for these women's business. The article also contrasts wealthy women, who could afford risky but potentially lucrative speculation, with poorer women, who were more vulnerable to the vicissitudes of the market. The *Times*'s tone, like much of the commentary on women investors discussed in the previous chapter, was sarcastic and condescending.

This chapter seeks to separate the known realities of women's finances— how women invested, their level of expertise, their sources of information, their attitudes about money, and the nature of their interactions with male financial advisers and gatekeepers—from the often censorious judgments of commentators. This is no easy task, since we have an abundance of widely accessible literary sources detailing nineteenth-century attitudes regarding the marketplace and women's proper roles, but much less material detailing how individual women managed money or interacted with the securities markets. The surviving sources are few and fragmentary, scattered among numerous scholarly and business archives.

Women Investors in the Gilded Age

What follows is a unique reconstruction of middle- and upper-class women's investment portfolios during the Gilded Age, based on private financial documents and the records of New York stockbrokers. In some cases, valuable information about women's financial holdings has survived by chance, as in the following marriage settlement between Virginia Woodbury and Gustavus Vasa Fox, which lists the property each of them possessed at the date of their wedding, October 29, 1855:

Fox's Property	Value	Interest
10 shares, Merchant's Bank, Boston	$1,000	8%
7 shares, Boston & Maine RR	$700	6%
3 shares, Commonwealth Ins. Co.	$300	12%
228 shares, NY & MI Mining Co.	$456	none
Real Estate, Lawrence, MA	$1,537.20	
	$3,993.20	yields $158 p/a

Woodbury's Property	Value	Interest
6 bonds, St. Louis	$6,896	6%
4 bonds, Cincinnati	$4,000	6%
3 bonds, Louisville	$3,000	6%
4 bonds, New Orleans	$4,000	6%
2 bonds, Holmes Co., OH	$500	6%
6 shares, Eastern RR	$600	none
5 shares, Merchant's Bank, Boston	$500	8%
14 shares, Penn. Coal Co.	$700	10%
Deposit Portsmouth Savings Bank	$362.40	
	$20,558.40	yields $1,213 p/a

An ordinary middle-class couple like the Foxes does not usually leave financial data for the benefit of future historians. This document has survived only because of Fox's subsequent celebrated career as assistant secretary of the navy during the Civil War.[10]

We can see that the bride brought five times more capital to the marriage than the groom and that her money earned almost eight times more than his. On the other hand, he would bring additional money to the marriage through his salary as a naval officer and later as a lawyer—economic opportunities that were closed to women. These figures corroborate Davidoff and Hall's claim about the greater importance of investment income for women as well as their argument that women's capital played a vital role in launching a family's business or a husband's career.[11]

Virginia Woodbury's money was also better invested than her husband's, mostly in municipal bonds, which guaranteed a safe and steady return of 6%. Her investments were consistent with the conservative advice given to women and women's trustees. Gustavus Fox's investments were less secure and, as it transpired, were ill chosen. Two of the four companies in which he had invested subsequently failed—the Commonwealth Insurance Company and the New York and Michigan Mining Company. These were the very sorts of securities that investment manuals warned against: mining companies were seen as highly speculative, and companies with very high profits (like the insurance company, with its 12% dividend) were linked to high risk. A man, with other sources of income, might be able to take such chances, but a woman who was dependent on her investment income could not.

Gustavus Fox signed a wedding contract that enabled his wife to retain control of her own property after their marriage. By the 1850s, some states had granted a measure of protection for married women's property, but a prenuptial agreement was even more thorough. The Foxes subsequently expanded their stock portfolio quite considerably, primarily with municipal bonds and railroad company shares that increased their investment income from $5,200 in 1870 to $16,000 in 1880. Perhaps Fox learned from his earlier mistakes, as the later investments were more in line with his wife's more conservative holdings. Sometimes shares and bonds were purchased in her name, sometimes in his. Their investments don't appear to have been managed separately, and the total income seems to have been treated as a joint family asset. We do not know who made the investment decisions.[12]

In 1874, Virginia Fox inherited the estate of her mother, Olivia Woodbury, whose property holdings are thus fortuitously preserved among the Fox papers, providing a rare glimpse at the investment portfolio of a comfortable, but far from wealthy, widow:

Securities	Value	Interest
2 bonds, New York & Hartford RR	$2,000	7%
1 bond, Northern Missouri RR	$1,000	7%
1 bond, St. Louis & Iron Mt. RR	$1,000	7%
2 bonds, Casco National Bank	$1,800	10%
3 bonds, Boston & Albany RR	$3,600	5%
1 bond, Erie RR	$1,000	5%
1 bond, Portland, Saco & Portsmouth RR	$1,000	5%
1 bond, Fitchburg RR	$700	5%
2 bonds, State of Maine	$2,000	6%
2 bonds, City of Portland	$2,000	6%
4 bonds, City of Portland	$2,000	5%
2 bonds, City of St. Louis	$2,000	6%
1 bond, State of Alabama	$1,000	5%
1 bond, City of Chicago	$1,000	6%
1 bond, City of Chicago	$1,000	7%
	$23,100	yields $1,415 p/a

Mrs. Woodbury's money had been invested very conservatively in a wide assortment of government and railway bonds. She, or her financial advisers, had followed the conventional wisdom of diversifying her portfolio and favoring bonds over shares. Her estate contained an additional $23,000 that had come from the sale of unspecified securities as well as mortgages and money deposited in savings banks. Altogether, her securities totaled some $40,000, yielding her an annual income of more than $2,000 a year, a tidy sum for a middle-class widow.[13]

The investments of another widow from the period, Jane C. Smith, have survived among the correspondence of her banker.[14] After her death he drew up a complete listing of her estate on November 13, 1880:

Securities	Value
13 shares, New York, New Haven & Hartford RR	$2,067
100 shares, Chicago, Burlington & Quincy RR	$14,600
34 shares, Western Union	$3,587
50 bonds, Long Dock Co.	$5,700
Cash with Morton, Bliss & Co.	$1,800
Cash with New Haven County Bank	$1,367.86
Gold watch	$100
Wearing Apparel	$50
	$29,271.86

Jane Smith had little to her name apart from her securities. Depending on interest rates and dividends, her investments could be expected to earn her between $1,000 and $1,400 a year, rendering her rather less secure than Olivia Woodbury. Her portfolio was also less diversified than Woodbury's, with almost half her capital in the Chicago, Burlington & Quincy Railroad. Smith also had more in shares than in bonds, which was not recommended for women, but established railway lines were still considered relatively safe investments. Perhaps she had other sources of income, such as a pension from her late husband or support from her children. Or she might have been looking to enhance her modest income through higher-yield, though riskier, shares—a constant temptation for widows of slender means.

Important, and previously underutilized, sources for understanding women's investment decisions are the archives of two firms of stockbrokers held by the New York Historical Society. The records for Morton, Bliss & Company cover the period from the 1870s to the 1880s and include detailed accounts of securities deals for women clients and an extensive correspondence with these women. Similar records exist for George P. Butler & Brother for the first decade of the twentieth century.[15] Together, these materials constitute an invaluable record of how middle- and upper-class American women invested their money, how active they were in overseeing their investments, how they arrived at their decisions, and how they interacted with their brokers. They can serve as a powerful corrective to the prescriptive literature of the period, as well as to the often censorious literary depictions of women speculators.

Morton, Bliss & Company was one of the most important and well-connected merchant banks of Gilded Age America. The firm was founded in 1869 through the partnership of Levi P. Morton and George Bliss. Both men were important power brokers in the Republican Party. Morton served as U.S. vice president under Benjamin Harrison and later as governor of New York. The firm's clients included leading Republican politicians, such as Roscoe Conkling and James G. Blaine. Morton, Bliss & Company also served as the American agents for numerous foreign businessmen. In addition to their banking business, the partners acted as stockbrokers for many of their clients. A large number of women did business with the firm.[16]

In 1886–87, Morton, Bliss & Company had 188 clients, 45 of which, or 24%, were women. The ledger for those years provides individual account balances along with a detailed record of securities bought and sold. We can also see how much income the firm's clients earned in a given year from their investments. A detailed analysis of this ledger provides in-depth and hitherto unknown information about how American women invested their money during the 1880s. Most of the customers of Morton, Bliss & Company held only bank accounts with the firm. This was especially true of the men, many of whom were merchants and businessmen. A third of the bank's customers in 1886–87, that is 63 persons, also held investment accounts, buying and selling shares through the firm. Of these investors, 24 (38%) were women, while 39 (62%) were men. Another way to look at it is that only 27% of the firm's male customers had investment accounts, while 53% of its female customers did. Most of the men plowed their wealth back into their own businesses. Most of the women did not have another way to make money, which confirms the great importance investment income held for middle-class women at this time.[17]

The 24 women with investment accounts had a total balance of some $324,000, which averaged out to around $13,000 per woman. The 39 men had a total balance of around $2,600,000, or about $67,000 per man. This gave the men five times the invested wealth of the women. If, however, we eliminate the two wealthiest men, whose assets of $1 million and $500,000 are vastly out of line with the other men's, the average male account would be approximately $25,000, not quite double the average woman's $13,000. Similar figures can be derived by comparing annual income from stocks and bonds.[18] The average man earned $4,350 from his securities in 1886–87, the average woman $2,600, or 60% of the man's earnings.[19] If the very wealthiest man's securities income is omitted, as it was far in excess of all others, the male average plummets to $2,900 per annum, scarcely more than the female average of $2,600. Again, these figures underscore the comparative importance of investment income for women, as the $2,600 would represent most, if not all, of an unmarried woman customer's income, while the $2,900 was a smaller part, in some cases even a minor part, of a male customer's income. For a married woman, $2,600 was a great deal of "pin money." Most of the female clients of Morton, Bliss were married but held investment accounts in their own names. By the 1880s, most states had enacted married women's property laws that allowed them to do so.

While the average woman investor at Morton, Bliss & Company did not earn significantly less than the average man, her capital was certainly invested in very different ways. Of greatest significance was the proportion of money invested in stocks or bonds. The female customers of the firm received 70% of their securities income from bonds, 30% from shares. For male customers, it was almost the exact opposite: 73% from shares, only 27% from bonds. Shares, or stock, represented a corporation's capital, that is, the money with which it operated. Shares paid investors dividends, or a portion of the corporation's profits, but only during periods when the business was profitable, and only once outstanding debts had first been paid. Bonds were securities issued by corporations or governments to secure loans. Bonds, unlike shares, did not raise money for normal operating expenses, but for some special purpose; a municipality might issue bonds to build a school, while a railroad company might issue them to finance a new branch line. Corporate bonds were usually backed by tangible assets or mortgages, and government bonds by the credit of the city, state, or nation issuing them, including its power of taxation. Bonds thus held greater security than shares. Bonds were also considered safe and conservative investments, since corporations paid bondholders before they paid shareholders. Unlike shares, bonds guaranteed regular interest payments, usually 5% or 6% during the 1880s. Shares were considered riskier investments, since they depended on a corporation's profitability. One year shares might pay fabulous dividends—8% or more on an investment—but another year they might pay nothing at all. The conventional wisdom, as reflected in advice books and the financial press, saw bonds as more suitable for women, shares for men. My findings confirm the work of Jannette Rutterford and Josephine Maltby on nineteenth-century British women investors, who were also more risk-averse than men.[20]

As we have seen, the customers of Morton, Bliss and Company conformed to the gender expectations of the Gilded Age regarding investment choices.

Not only did women customers earn 70% of their investment income from bonds, but half of these women owned no shares at all, but only bonds. The most conservative accounts were trusts, where the women received interest from securities chosen by their trustees, who were usually bankers or lawyers. A father might place his daughter's inheritance in a trust if he were uncertain of her financial acumen, or if he wished to protect her money from possible depredations by her husband.[21] In 1886, Elizabeth Sanford's trust fund was invested as follows by her trustee, George Bliss:

Securities	Income
20 bonds, Chicago, Milwaukee & St. Paul RR	$100
30 bonds, Milwaukee, Lake Share & Western RR	$180
30 bonds, Columbus, Hocking Valley & Toledo RR	$150
30 bonds, Minneapolis & St. Louis RR	$180
40 bonds, Northern Illinois RR	$200
	$810 p/a

Sanford's capital was all invested in railway bonds, a favorite choice of trustees, and risks were further minimized by dividing her investments fairly evenly among five different corporations.[22]

A more affluent woman with a trust account, Mrs. M. M. Grinnell, had her money similarly invested in five railway securities in 1886 by Levi Morton:

Securities	Income
100 bonds, St. Louis & Iron Mountain RR	$500
100 bonds, Iowa Loan and Trust Company	$500
150 bonds, Columbus, Hocking Valley & Toledo RR	$750
150 bonds, Chesapeake & Ohio RR	$450
200 bonds, Indiana, Bloomington & Western RR	$1,000
200 shares, Long Island RR	$200
	$3,400 p/a

Grinnell's capital was spread out over five different railroads and a trust company.[23] In addition to the usual bonds, Morton also purchased 200 shares in the Long Island Railroad. As Grinnell was wealthier than Sanford, some shares were certainly acceptable. Shares in established railroads and banks, with a history of healthy dividends, were considered relatively safe investments for women, so long as they were outnumbered by bonds.

Few of the 24 women in this sample bought and sold securities with much vigor. Most of them were passive investors who maintained fairly regular investment accounts for the sake of a steady income. A typical example would be Mary Sanford, whose portfolio of 68% bond income and 32% share income earned her around $1,200 in 1886:

Securities	Income
50 bonds, Milwaukee, Lake Shore & Western RR	$300
50 bonds, Chicago, Milwaukee & St. Paul RR	$250
40 bonds, Iowa Loan & Trust Company	$100
30 bonds, Minneapolis & St. Louis RR	$180
50 shares, Chicago, Milwaukee & St. Paul RR	$350
16 shares, Chicago, Rock Island & Pacific RR	$28
6 shares, Chicago & Northwestern RR	$18
4 shares, Delaware, Lackawanna & Western RR	$3.50
	$1,229.50

Sanford held a typical assortment of railroad securities. Her only account activity for the year was to sell some government bonds and to purchase the Iowa Trust Company bonds.[24]

For most of the women who invested with Morton, Bliss, buying and selling was confined to exchanging one type of security for another. For example, Mrs. M. H. Morton sold 60 Minneapolis and St. Louis Railroad bonds in 1886, and then purchased 60 bonds of the Indiana, Bloomington & Western Railroad. Mrs. E. F. Minot diversified her portfolio by selling 100 bonds of the East Tennessee, Virginia & Georgia Railroad, and replacing them with 100 bonds from three different railroads: 10 from the Indiana, Bloomington & Western, 40 from the Chesapeake & Ohio, and 50 from the Columbus, Hocking Valley & Toledo.[25]

Few women seriously engaged in speculation. One of them, Jeannette Bliss, made 30 trades in 1886, buying numerous securities for some $27,000 and selling them for more than $54,000. The profits she realized from these transactions were an astonishing $27,824.92. Her investment income that year was a mere $210, as she rarely held securities long enough to collect interest.[26] Jeannette was clearly benefiting from her connection to George Bliss, her father-in-law and a partner in the firm, who could capitalize on the most up-to-date and privileged stock market information. Most women's attempts at speculation were rarely so successful. Elizabeth Fogg, for instance, tried to speculate in Consolidated Gas Company shares, with disastrous consequences. While trading 400 shares, she lost $8,525.[27] Luckily she was a wealthy woman, for such an enormous loss would have ruined most of the firm's female clients.

Most of the male clients of Morton, Bliss, like the females, bought securities for the income they generated, but speculation was more common among the men, and some of them engaged in it on a massive scale. Edward C. Billings made $11,812 in profits from securities trades in 1886, and M. E. Ingalls made more than $76,000. Both men had dividend/interest incomes of around $3,000 from their securities—significant sums, but ones that paled next to their speculative profits. Billings speculated in railway, canal, bridge, and trust company bonds. Ingalls, the president of the Chesapeake & Ohio Railroad, dealt exclusively in railway shares, probably benefiting from inside information, a source unavailable to most women.[28]

There were significant differences in the types of securities held by women and men in the 1880s. At that time, the vast majority of stocks and bonds issued in the United States were associated with railroad companies. In 1885, railway securities represented 81% of the New York Stock Exchange's business.[29] At Morton, Bliss, 84% of women's investment income was derived from railroad securities, mostly bonds. The other 16% was mostly derived from U.S. government bonds, foreign government bonds, and trust company bonds, followed in importance by bank shares and utility company shares. A few women had bridge and canal company bonds. None owned industrial securities. In other words, the women conformed to the conservative investment advice that recommended railroad and government bonds.

Male investors at Morton, Bliss were far more daring and adventurous than the women, favoring shares over bonds and committing less exclusively to railway securities. Half the firm's female clients held railway securities exclusively, but only a quarter of the men did. While the women received only 16% of their investment income from nonrailway securities, nonrailroad income for men averaged 24%, significantly higher than for women. After railroad securities, the men received their largest portion of investment income from industrial, telegraph, and import companies—businesses in which the women did not hold shares. Other types of investments found only among the men included mortgage companies, state and municipal bonds, insurance companies, and mining companies. Men's more widespread involvement with the business world familiarized them with a greater variety of investment possibilities than was available to most women, and their greater financial resources allowed them to take chances on risky, but potentially lucrative, industrial securities.

Another measure of women's more cautious investment strategies was their tendency to spread risk by diversifying their holdings. They were less likely than men to place all their eggs in one basket. Only one woman from the sample received all her income from a single security: Mrs. A. L. Morton earned $1,200 annually from 200 Indiana, Bloomington & Western Railroad bonds.[30] None of the other women had more than 50% of their capital in a single security. Most were very highly diversified. Mary Byrne, for example, divided her investments almost equally among six different corporate bonds:[31]

Securities	Income
50 bonds, Chicago, Milwaukee & St. Paul RR	$250
50 bonds, Chicago, Milwaukee & St. Paul RR—Southern Minnesota Extension	$300
50 bonds, Chicago & Northwestern RR	$250
50 bonds, Minneapolis & St. Louis RR	$300
50 bonds, Burlington, Cedar Rapids & Northern RR	$250
50 bonds, Iowa Loan & Trust Company	$250
	$1,600

Among the wealthiest women investors, Cornelia Smith was certainly the most diversified. She earned more than $8,000 annually from her investments, which were divided among twenty-two different securities: fourteen kinds of bonds and eight kinds of shares.[32]

The men, on the other hand, spread their risks more thinly. Several from my sample received the great majority of their investment income from a single type of security. John Barker got 78% of his $1,215 annual securities income from 945 shares of the American Contango & Dredging Company. Rufus Cowing got 70% of his $1,436 investment income from his Iowa Loan & Trust Company bonds.[33] As noted, men often had other sources of wealth from their professions or businesses. They could afford to be more careless, or enterprising, than women by concentrating their investment capital into fewer areas.

Women's relative conservatism and caution as investors can be explained by a number of different factors. They may have been following the advice of their brokers and of investment guides. Their exclusion from privileged sources of financial information also narrowed their investment choices, and their more modest capital probably made them risk-averse, as well. Certainly, the average woman's subordinate economic position was disabling, as it inhibited her from taking risks that might have made her wealthy.

Morton, Bliss's share ledgers document how women invested their money during the 1880s. Further insights into how women made investment decisions and how well or confidently they managed their money can be gleaned from their correspondence with their brokers. George Bliss's letter books have survived for the period 1876–91 and document a great deal of the broker's interactions with female clients. Unfortunately, the women's letters were not kept, so that only the outgoing correspondence has survived. Although written in a fairly dry business style, the letters still capture the concerns and queries of the women to whom they were addressed. Bliss's forceful character comes through, but the personalities and idiosyncratic styles of the women are harder to recover.

Bliss did far more than advise clients on investments or execute trading orders. His letters reveal that he acted as a banker, lender, and general financial factotum for many of the women who had accounts with his firm. Women's paper bonds and share certificates were kept safe in the firm's vaults. Bliss collected dividends and interest payments for his clients, recorded their securities trades in the share ledger, and mailed checks to them when their profits were due. He paid interest of between 3% and 6% for money left on deposit. He was also called upon for all manner of advice, and his letters convey the varying levels of financial literacy among women at the time.

Among the women investing with Morton, Bliss & Company were a wide range of types. Some women were very uncomfortable about managing their own money and might have known very little about how that money was invested. For example, client Mary Orton, a widow, was the beneficiary of a small trust, set up by her father, that was meant to give her $1,000 a year in quarterly payments of $250. In her correspondence with her broker, George Bliss, it was apparent that Orton had no idea how her money had been invested (in farm mortgages). She appears to be the classic passive investor who depended on dividend payments, but who left the management of her money to others. Unfortunately, Orton's trust was poorly managed and Bliss frequently acted as her advocate, writing a series of letters to her trustee, Morris Seymour, chastising him for nonpayment or late or incomplete payment of her trust money. He rebuked Seymour in a letter of October 9, 1879, "Mrs. Orton has called my attention to it several times, and I have no doubt needs her money promptly."[34]

Other women turned to Bliss for problems big and small. On December 24, 1878, Bliss told Mrs. S. M. Gist how to cash a postal money order, and in July 1879 he assisted another client, Jane Smith, in tracking down missing interest payments from government bonds.[35] On May 17, 1881, Bliss responded to Carrie Kingman's request for advice on the management of her invalid husband's property holdings. She should probably hire a lawyer or estate agent, Bliss suggested, but only if her husband was not expected to live much longer. "If he should live four or five years this plan might be unfortunate, as the expense of the legal adviser and the real estate agent would be considerable."[36] In April 1882, another distressed woman, Mrs. Easton, wrote from Hannibal, Missouri, concerning the business affairs of her late husband, a banker. His bank was being wound up, and she feared there would be shortfalls, for which the estate would be sued. Bliss advised her to hold on to the house, which was protected under her dower rights. If she sold it to raise funds, the bank's creditors might try to seize the money.

He concluded, "I know how difficult it is for a lady situated as you are to attend to business of this sort."[37]

As detailed in the previous chapter, Victorian stockbrokers and financial writers frequently complained that female clients "pestered" them too much over minor matters and panicked at the slightest financial predicament. A stock market exposé from 1877 claimed that "Lady-clients give much more trouble, require more consultation, and never seem to think you have any other fish to fry."[38] This caricature is not substantiated in George Bliss's correspondence. Some women customers expressed concern over their investments or financial problems, but there was no sense of helplessness or panic.

Many of Bliss's female clients played a very active role in overseeing their investments. They were well informed about market trends, quick to notice downturns, and eagle-eyed with regard to the proper payment of their dividends. Miss S. E. Forbes, for example, wrote to Bliss in February 1879 since she had not been paid interest commensurate with her brokerage account and the profits generated from recent stock transactions. He acknowledged the error (or delay, as he preferred to characterize it) and promised to rectify the situation.[39] This is clear evidence of Forbes's knowledge about her investments and active stewardship of her account. Another case can be seen in the continual flow of correspondence during the spring and summer of 1878 between Bliss and Miss C. Nash concerning Delaware & Hudson Railroad shares—whether the price was rising or falling, how long they should be held, and at what price sold. Nash was paying close attention to her investments, and Bliss was careful to consult her before making any transactions. As he wrote her on May 15, 1878, "I incline to expect higher prices for the next two or three months, but do not like to advise you too confidently. Shall I sell if the price advances one or two percent? Or wait longer, till you give me definite instructions?"[40] Single women like Miss Forbes and Miss Nash would have had greater latitude in managing their own money, but I have found many cases of married women taking a leading role in directing their families' finances. For example, in May 1878, Mrs. Wicks, rather than her husband, wrote to Bliss attempting to secure a loan to forestall a foreclosure on their farm.[41]

One of the best examples of a dynamic woman investor is Emily Billings, the wife of a Louisiana judge and the beneficiary of a lucrative family trust worth more than $850,000. The trust was managed by her brother, Charles Sanford, a New York businessman, until he was incapacitated by a stroke in 1879. Emily then moved quickly and decisively to dissolve the trust and to place the investments under her own control and her own name—rather than her husband's. She was not satisfied with the interest being earned and worked closely with George Bliss to reinvest her money in railroad shares, coal mines, mortgages, and New York real estate. As Bliss wrote her in January 1882, "I shall not lose sight of your wishes in reference to investments which I approve of and that will pay satisfactory income." Since Emily Billings lived most of the year in New Orleans, she gave Bliss power of attorney to transact business for her, but despite the distance they maintained a steady correspondence about her investments. He made no important decisions without her consent.[42]

Confident and well-informed investors like Emily Billings have been largely forgotten by history. In their place we find the hapless literary victims of the stock market—Miss Matty from Elizabeth Gaskell's *Cranford* or Lily Bart from Edith Wharton's *The House of Mirth*. My archival sources may have a built-in bias toward more knowledgeable and active investors, who would be the women most likely to keep in close touch with their brokers. The more passive and uninformed investor would simply collect her interest payments and seldom write to her broker. The archive would, however, include letters from the pesky, worrywart lady investor who was supposedly so common, and I have found no evidence of this type.

Bliss's correspondence also furnishes valuable data about women's sources of financial information, as well as the kinds of advice offered by financial experts. During the nineteenth century, women were excluded from certain important vehicles for transferring financial information—coffee shops, gentlemen's clubs, professional organizations—but did have access to the financial press, which seems to have been the basis for many investment decisions.[43] In December 1887, Elizabeth Fogg wrote to Bliss because she had seen a newspaper advertisement for the Omaha Loan & Trust Company and was interested in buying some shares. The broker, ever cautious, was skeptical of a new company pushing its securities in the press. He advised against the purchase, telling her that she was better off with her 5% bonds of "the old and well established company at Des Moines [Iowa Loan & Trust Co.] of which you already have a few."[44]

Companies also mailed out mass advertising circulars for their securities. In June 1890, Mrs. E. C. Hobson received such a circular from the New Hampshire Investment Company and wrote to Bliss about the possibility of buying its bonds, which offered a tempting 8% interest. Bliss had never heard of the business and was again dubious. As he warned Hobson, "I think a Trust Company that will issue 8% debentures at par will not continue long in good credit."[45] The Morton, Bliss archive demonstrates that financial advertisements and circulars were often effective in reaching out to women investors. Probably many women bought securities on the strength of such promotional materials, especially if they did not have the advantage of professional advice.

Some corporations also hired agents to travel around the country promoting their securities. They were often little better than hucksters who preyed on the unsophisticated. In October 1883, an agent for a finance company dazzled Mary Orton with the prospect of big profits from mortgages in western states. She wrote to Bliss with the idea of placing her money in this concern. He was horrified, suspecting fraud, and told Orton that she should be happy with the steady 6% that her Midwest farm mortgages provided. "I can tell you that very many of those who loan money at the West never receive back their money."[46]

Of course, for Bliss's clients, their most important source of financial information was the broker himself. By the time his surviving correspondence begins, George Bliss had been a banker and broker for more than ten years. Before that he had made a fortune as a dry-goods entrepreneur. He was very well connected politically and had many important contacts in business, banking, and stock market circles. He did not, however, use his inside information to encourage speculation among his clients. With women customers in particular, Bliss urged caution, repeatedly emphasizing a preference for modest but steady profits over high but risky returns. When, in January 1880, Emily Billings pressed Bliss to buy her higher-yield securities, he countered with a salutary example gleaned from the press: "Perhaps you would notice the sale of $200,000 four percents of the New Haven Shore Line the other day, which were sold at $1/4$ or $3/8$ per cent above par! This shows you how small a rate of interest some people are content to receive, if they secure a favorite investment."[47] Bliss repeated this lesson many times over the years. In December 1886, he wrangled with Maria Bliss over the purchase of new bonds. She wanted 6%, but he disliked the available bonds that paid that amount. He offered several 5% bonds "that I am sure are perfectly good and safe."[48]

When advising women about securities purchases, Bliss favored the bonds of certain established and well-run railroads, as well as government securities. If women inquired after securities with which he was unfamiliar, he would make a careful investigation. In June 1886, Elizabeth Fogg suggested the purchase of Sciota Valley Railroad bonds, and Bliss consulted another broker who actively dealt in those bonds. His colleague "would not advise any lady to purchase them for investment." The next year Mrs. Fogg, who clearly was on the lookout for profitable investments, asked about Memphis & Charleston

Railroad bonds. This time Bliss consulted Poor's *Manual of Railroads* and concluded that the company's prospects were "exceedingly unfavorable." The railroad already had too much debt, and its recent earnings were sluggish.[49]

The ledgers and letter books of Morton, Bliss & Company offer a unique window into the investment patterns of women in Gilded Age America. They confirm that women were in fact more cautious and moderate in their investment choices than men, and that women mostly avoided high-yield risky shares in favor of steadier and more secure investments like railroad bonds, government securities, and public utilities. Here, women's behavior conformed to the conservative advice offered up by investment manuals, the financial press, and popular literature. However, the Morton, Bliss archive does not validate the popular stereotype of the woman investor as unbusinesslike, impatient, ignorant, and capricious. Most of the firm's female clients were effective custodians of their own wealth. They were well informed about market trends, realistic about potential profits, and resourceful in soliciting information and advice from their brokers. Women were far more successful in navigating the securities market than the cautionary and censorious literature of the period has led us to believe.

Women and Wall Street: New Century, New Opportunities

The Morton, Bliss archive provides a snapshot of American investment during the 1880s, the period in which the stock market experienced its most tremendous growth spurt to date and in which Wall Street first burst onto the national stage. During the next twenty years, the nation's securities market underwent even more profound growth and expansion. Greater numbers of Americans were now buying an even greater variety of stocks and bonds. Wall Street was becoming more accepted as a key component of the American economy, and popular hostility to the market was becoming more muted. Women investors, however, continued to garner negative press and were even banned from the offices of some Wall Street firms.

By the early twentieth century, New York had consolidated its position as the nation's financial capital. In 1910, two-thirds of the stock trading in the United States was conducted by the New York Stock Exchange (NYSE), and 90% of bonds sold in the country were went through the exchange. Regional stock exchanges greatly diminished in importance, but this in no way hindered Americans' access to securities in the hinterlands, as 23% of New York Stock Exchange members either had branches outside of New York or were members of firms located elsewhere. Even when regional brokers had no direct connection to the NYSE, they could easily transact business with it via telephone.[50]

As the securities market became more concentrated in New York City, it further diversified its offerings. In 1885, 81% of stocks traded on the NYSE were railroad shares. Twenty years later, in 1905, railroad shares accounted for only 49% of trading activity. Industrial shares had grown from only 16% of stocks traded in 1885, to 41% in 1905. The surge in industrial securities was the result of the trust movement, which created massive conglomerates like Standard Oil, U.S. Steel, and Amalgamated Copper. By 1913, industrial and utility shares dominated the stock market.[51]

The volume of stock exchange business more than doubled in the 1890s, and the number of Americans trading in securities continued to rise. In 1930, Gardiner Means estimated that there were approximately 4.4 million shareholders in the U.S. in 1900.[52] Unlike many of the people who have subsequently cited this figure, Means was careful to point out that these were "book stockholders," not individual stockholders.[53] He derived the figure by adding up all the stockholders listed on the books of the nation's major corporations. Of course, many people held shares in several different companies and thus would be counted multiple times. A more realistic estimate for individual U.S. shareholders in 1900 would be closer to 1 million, though one scholar has put the figure at around 500,000.[54] Whichever number one chooses, given that the U.S. population stood at 76 million in 1900, shareholders were members of a rather exclusive club.

Most women investors were certainly middle- and upper-class, though there is some evidence that lower-middle-class and even working-class women sometimes bought securities. In 1894 the *Cleveland Plain Dealer* reported that women telegraph operators played the market, as they had easy access to the latest stock quotations as well as "private advices and orders that are continually passing along the wire." In 1911 the *Colorado Springs Gazette* referred to local "shop girls" who had purchased shares in copper mines. There was even a term among stockbrokers—*mudhen*—for women of modest means who dabbled in the stock market. According to the *Omaha World Herald*, "some of them have hardly enough clothing on their backs to keep them warm, yet every cent they get goes into stocks." It is unlikely that very many poor women speculated, but the appeal of the market was far-reaching and contagious.[55]

Whether many African American women invested in securities is especially difficult to assess, but Lynn M. Hudson has documented one such investor, Mary Ellen Pleasant, from nineteenth-century San Francisco. Born a free person in Philadelphia in 1814, Pleasant migrated to California at the time of the 1849 gold rush. She operated laundries and boardinghouses, the profits from which she used to purchase rental properties. By 1870 she owned $30,000 worth of real estate in the Bay Area. As Pleasant's capital grew, she invested heavily in silver mines, banks, and government securities. She was a major shareholder in the Bank of California, and in 1884 the *San Francisco Examiner* reported that Pleasant owned $100,000 of U.S. bonds.[56]

How many of the nation's total shareholders were women is impossible to say. Certainly not half, but based on the available, and admittedly scanty, evidence, a reasonable guess would be around 20–25% in 1910.[57] In any case, women continued to invest heavily in certain key sectors of the economy, especially railroads and banks. A *New York Times* article from 1909 reported that almost half of the 50,000 shareholders of the Pennsylvania Railroad, the nation's largest corporation, were women, and that for many leading railroads, women shareholders averaged 40 to 50%. Bank stock was another favorite investment; the 1909 Report of National Banks revealed that out of 330,000 shareholders, 104,000, or nearly a third, were women.[58] Women's shareholdings in major corporations were also increasing dramatically at this time.[59]

Women's growing significance as shareholders did not necessarily translate into greater public approbation. As documented in the previous chapter, journalistic and literary critiques of women investors continued apace, and even members of the Stock Exchange expressed some hostility. A *New York Times* article from July 13, 1902, detailed "a movement among brokers in New York to exclude women" from their offices. According to the article, brokers had long considered women undesirable clients for "a multitude of reasons": they were ignorant of finance, too emotional, and bad losers. "During the past fortnight the opposition has crystallized and several prominent firms have taken a bold, determined stand to ostracize those members of the fair sex whose gaming instincts and desire to get rich quick prompt them to speculate on the markets." The *Times* included a copy of a letter—with the firm's name and location removed—from "a well-known firm of stock brokers . . . not unlike letters that have been sent out recently by other firms":

New York, July 7, 1902
Dear Madame:
    We regret to inform you that in future we shall be unable to afford you the privilege of calling at our office on Blank Street.
    We find that some of our best customers find it undignified for women to frequent brokers' offices, and for that reason beg to ask that in future you will kindly communicate with us only by letter or telephone.
    In this matter we have used no discrimination. Every woman who has an

account or has done business with us will receive similar notice by the same mail.

Yours very truly,

A broker from another office confirmed, "we have done all in our power to discourage their patronizing us, and I am going to take particular pains to see that my instructions that women be kept out of our offices are carried out."[60]

It is difficult to know how to read this act of hostility against women investors, or even how seriously to take it. In part it was probably a contest over public space and public visibility. Some men didn't want to *see* women on Wall Street or in business offices. The number of women investors had grown significantly by 1900, attracting more attention. There was a backlash against women becoming too "conspicuous," making a "spectacle" of themselves, and invading masculine space. The ban from brokers' offices was temporary and far from universal. It was not remarked on in later years. In any case, it was purely cosmetic, as women could phone in their orders from home, and much business continued to be conducted by post and telegram.[61]

Later years brought occasional reports of brokerage houses hostile to women customers or to certain types of securities business by women. In 1906, a stockbroker informed *The Independent* that "we do not like women customers, and execute orders for them only when we cannot, for one reason or another, refuse them, as they are usually very bad speculators and troublesome as clients."[62] The main commodities trading firms in Chicago would not accept women customers, arguing that futures trading in grain and livestock was inappropriate for women.[63] Other firms merely refused to assist women in "speculation," buying and selling shares for a quick profit. As noted in the previous chapter, speculation was frequently equated with gambling and was seen as especially unsuitable for women. In 1909 the *New York Times* reported that "many stock exchange houses try their best to keep women's speculative accounts out of their offices."[64] A magazine article on women investors from 1913 agreed that most reputable brokerage houses would not offer to women clients "highly speculative securities, in which either the profit or the loss is likely to be large." The article endorsed this paternalistic policy, saying that most women "know nothing of the science of investment."[65] Turning away women's business was not just about shoring up separate spheres, but about maintaining male economic privilege, as women were excluded from certain potentially lucrative investment opportunities.

Some of the criticism of women speculators by brokers was also a public-relations strategy. As Chapter 3 will make clear, by the early twentieth century there was an increasingly influential Progressive push to regulate securities markets. One way to counter this move was for financiers to shift the blame for market volatility onto ignorant and inexperienced speculators, such as women. Banning women from brokers' offices or barring them from certain kinds of securities trades was in part a defensive strategy to fend off government oversight.

While some Wall Street firms may have been hostile to women customers, this attitude was never universal. Furthermore, whatever resistance women encountered in some quarters was more than offset by the explosion of outside brokerage firms, often referred to as "bucket shops," in the 1890s and early 1900s. Bucket shops were brokerage houses unconnected to the official stock and commodities exchanges. The name, of uncertain derivation, originated in England and was rather elastic in its application in America.[66] Most bucket shops were seen as disreputable and marginal. They dealt in small lots of securities, for small margins and small commissions. The worst examples were gambling dens, pure and simple. Customers dealt in shares simply on the basis of changing prices. No shares or commodities ever changed hands, even momentarily.[67]

However louche their general reputation, bucket shops held many attractions for small investors. They were conveniently located in cities and towns across America and kept longer hours than most established stockbrokers. While brokers dealt in minimum lots of 100 securities and expected customers to put up a margin of at least 10%, bucket shops would trade in lots of ten or twenty shares for margins as low as 1%. Brokers usually charged a commission of $1/8$% for every transaction, whereas bucket shops might charge $1/16$% or even less.[68] The biggest advantage of bucket shops over brokers' offices was that they automatically closed out stock trades once a customer's margin was exhausted. As Edwin Lefevre acutely observed, "you couldn't get stung for more than you had put up."[69]

Bucket shops democratized stock trading, attracting many modest investors who could not afford to operate on Wall Street. They were especially welcoming to women. A bucket shop would often maintain a "ladies-room" with a "manageress." By the 1890s, numerous bucket shops solely for women had sprung up in New York. According to the *Watertown Daily Times*, "there are thirty odd concerns in the city which cater especially to women. Most of these have offices uptown, on or near Broadway, between Twenty-third and Forty-second streets. These offices are in charge of women, and are furnished with particular regard to the comfort of feminine clients."[70] Arthur Field visited one such establishment in 1894, describing it as "a spacious office supplied with tickers, messengers, clerks . . . even the board of quotations.

Figure 4. "A Bucket Shop for Women," *Demorest's Family Magazine* (January 1894): 157. (Collection of the author)

A number of women were present, all of whom wore a decidedly business-like air, consulting the tickers and board frequently, and giving orders to the messengers with promptness when ready to make a transaction."[71]

Several uptown bucket shops catered exclusively to wealthy women. Mrs. Finley Anderson visited one of these establishments in 1899 and reported: "Its appointments were superb . . . a maid in black gown and white apron and cap waited upon the ladies. A dainty luncheon was served and the buffet was stocked with liquors."[72] Both observers were rather disapproving. Field described the female habitués of the bucket shop as sloppy and unladylike, exhibiting "a lack of attention to their toilets." Anderson felt that "women age rapidly in this atmosphere."[73]

Bucket shops diverted money from the "legitimate" brokerage houses and gave them a bad name by association. The official stock and commodities exchanges mounted a vigorous campaign against bucket shops. In 1896 the Chicago Board of Trade launched a series of investigations against the illicit practices of bucket shops. Exchanges attempted to prevent bucket shops from receiving price quotations via the stock ticker, and a Supreme Court decision in 1905 affirmed their right to do so. In 1909 the U.S. Attorney General appointed a special agent, Bruce Bielaski, to investigate and indict the major bucket-shop chains. By the eve of World War I, most of the nation's bucket shops were out of business.[74]

Women Investors in the Early Twentieth Century

The types of investments made by American women in the early twentieth century can be gauged from the records of George P. Butler & Brother, a firm of New York stockbrokers. The firm, which existed from 1898 until 1911, was founded by George Butler, a banker, and his brother Arthur Butler, a member of the New York Stock Exchange. The brothers came from a family of distinguished and influential jurists. Their father was president of the U.S. Bar Association, and their grandfather was attorney general under Andrew Jackson and Martin Van Buren.[75] Butler Brothers' ledgers and letter books are an important, and hitherto unexamined, source for studying women's investment behavior during the first decade of the twentieth century. What follows is an analysis of the firm's ledger for 1908–9. This will provide a snapshot of women's investment portfolios at a given moment, as well as a point of comparison with the Morton, Bliss stock portfolios from 1886–87, a generation earlier.

In 1908, Butler Brothers had 90 clients, 25 of whom, or 28%, were women. This represents a slight increase from 1886, when 24% of Morton, Bliss clients were women. The average account balance for the 1908 women was $24,000, almost double the average of $13,000 for the women in 1886. As the intervening years were a period of low inflation, even deflation, this represents a real and significant gain. Male investors, however, were also increasing their balances, and they continued to hold much greater value in securities than women. In 1908 the average account balance for a male client of Butler Brothers was $113,000, or five times the female average. If, however, one eliminates the two millionaires from the sample, the average male balance was $46,000, not quite twice the female average. Most of the Butlers' women clients were married, and, like the Morton, Bliss women twenty years earlier, kept their accounts in their own names.[76]

Women continued to prefer bonds over stocks. The women clients of Butler Brothers on average held 96% of their securities in bonds and only 4% in shares. This was even more conservative than in 1886, when the women clients of Morton, Bliss derived 70% of their securities income from bonds, 30% from shares. In 1908 only one woman, Emily Coaney, had a significant amount of her capital (24%) in shares, but this amounted to only $933. By contrast, 30% of the men were heavily invested in shares.[77]

In 1908, women's investment portfolios were far less dominated by railway securities than in 1886, when 84% of women's investment income came from railway stocks and bonds. Railway securities still accounted for the largest percentage of women's invested capital in 1908, at 41%, but the majority of women's investments was now in other areas: 27% in government bonds, 25%

in industrial securities, 4% in tobacco, and 2% in public utilities. Government bonds continued to be the second most important investment for women, but while women at Morton, Bliss mostly bought U.S. government bonds in 1886, by 1908, women at Butler Brothers were more heavily invested in municipal bonds, especially those of New York City. The biggest change from 1886 to 1908 was the growing importance of industrial securities for women. While no women in the Morton, Bliss sample owned industrials, the women at Butler Brothers had 25% of their capital in industrial corporations, with the most popular choices being Colorado Industrials, Allis-Chalmers Manufacturing, U.S. Rubber, and AT&T.[78]

A sampling of Butler Brothers' investment portfolios will give some sense of how American women were investing their capital in the early twentieth century. In 1909, Margaret Munn, a middle-class widow, owned the following securities:

Securities	Value
U.S. Rubber 6% bonds	$3,000
U.S. Steel 5% bonds	$3,000
Western Maryland RR 4% bonds	$3,000
Colorado Fuel & Iron 5% bonds	$2,000
Wheeling & Lake Erie RR 4% bonds	$1,000
	$12,000

As a widow, Munn's capital was conservatively invested exclusively in bonds.[79] She further minimized her risks by dividing her investments fairly evenly among five different corporations. Yet with 2/3 of her capital in industrial securities and only 1/3 in railroad bonds, Munn looked very different than a widow of the 1880s, like Jane Smith (see page 45).

In 1909, Mrs. M. A. Corning had more than three times the capital of Margaret Munn invested with Butler Brothers:

Securities	Value
Pittsburgh, Shawmut & Northern RR 4% bonds	$20,000
Havana Tobacco Company 5% bonds	$10,000
Coney Island & Brooklyn RR 4% bonds	$5,000
Guanajuato RR 8% bonds	$2,000
American Steel Foundry Co. 4% bonds	$2,000
Bailey-Cobalt Mining Co. shares	$1,000
Guanajuato RR shares	$600
U.S. Light & Heating Co. shares	$500
Manhattan RR shares	$100
	$41,200

With 67% of her capital in railway securities, Mrs. Corning was more old-fashioned than most of the women clients of the Butler Brothers, but her tobacco securities (24%) represented a new avenue of investment.[80] Her money was also conservatively invested in bonds (95%), with only a smattering of shares. Her portfolio, however, was far from diversified, with almost half her capital invested in a single corporation, the Pittsburgh, Shawmut & Northern Railroad. This level of concentration was not advised and, in this particular case, proved foolhardy. The Pittsburgh, Shawmut & Northern went bankrupt early in its existence and remained in receivership for decades.

The letter books of George P. Butler & Brother provide further insights into women's investment behavior and document the professionalization of business practices during the early twentieth century. While George Bliss's correspondence from the 1880s was handwritten and often expressed his personality, the Butlers' letters were typed, carbon-copied, and constructed of impersonal, boilerplate business phraseology. Butler Brothers, unlike Morton, Bliss, also preserved incoming correspondence. A happy result of this practice is the preservation of the distinct voices of women investors.

Most women's letters to their brokers, like most men's, were brief and businesslike. Fortunately, occasional spectacular standouts among these letters capture the unique financial concerns of individual women. In December 1909, for example, Margaret Munn requested her broker to sell certain railway shares for her, but what might otherwise have been a routine trading order in this case became a more personal and philosophic reflection:

> I am told that Southern R.R. stock is again going down and that it would be better for me to sell the remaining 16 shares and invest it in something else that would pay!
>
> My play is soon to be published and as published plays are not usually a success Dodd and Mead expect me to pay $350 toward the 600 required for publication. My moving expenses and repairing of furniture, etc. require $150 more. This makes $500. If the stock could be sold for 1000 or 1100 I could take 500 for my investment in my play and 100 for the settling of my home and have five hundred for (if possible) a 6 percent investment or a 5 percent investment. So if you can sell the stock I will be glad and also if you can invest the remaining $500. Pardon this long explanation. I do not spend my capital—this is only the second time in my life that I have done so. The first time was a small legacy which bought my *trousseau*, but my home and my play could not be consummated without some sacrifice and both are in the nature of *investments*![81]

Recently widowed, Munn needed a bit of cash to settle her affairs and to advance her own literary career.[82] She probably felt the need to justify dipping into capital, and her chatty missive might be construed as unprofessional.

Munn, however, was no foolish female client of the sort constructed by financial writers. She was well informed about market trends and share prices; her shares were in fact sold for $1,100, the very figure she mentioned in her letter.[83] Her letter also included a playful take on "investment," which can be found elsewhere in women's writings from the period. For instance, Anna Dickinson's 1876 social critique *A Paying Investment* contrasted men's investment in stocks and bonds with women's investment in their children and homes.[84]

The Butlers' women customers exhibited a wide range of abilities and varying levels of commitment to managing their investments. Some women held shares in their own names, but their husbands made investment decisions. For example, Mrs. Eleanor Boyd of Harrisburg, Pennsylvania, had her money managed by the Butlers, but investment decisions were made by John Y. Boyd, her husband. In 1910, William Stanley invested $13,000 on behalf of his wife, Elizabeth.[85] Other women sometimes made their own investment decisions and sometimes had their husbands act for them. Such a couple were the Greenes of Philadelphia. In May 1909, for instance, the Reverend Greene sold some of his wife's U.S. Steel shares. A few days later, Louise Greene bought $3,000 of International Pump shares and had them registered in her name.[86]

Some women simply sent money to their brokers, asking that it be invested as they saw fit. For example, in 1909 Margaret Munn sent Butler & Brother a check for $3,000, asking the firm to "please invest the whole for me at as high a rate of interest as you safely can."[87] A Miss Baumgartner sent the firm one of her calling cards, on which she had written, "Dear Mr. Butler: will you kindly use this money for the purchase of bonds or stocks which you consider to be favorable."[88]

As in the 1880s at Morton, Bliss, the Butlers also had women clients who were active stewards of their own money and extremely conversant about market trends. In August 1909, Mary Gould gave the firm detailed instructions for the sale of certain securities:

> I have almost lost my faith in the speculative possibilities of steel and as an investment its yield is too small. So unless it does the unexpected and sails up with a bound I would just as soon get out of it around 79 . . . I do not feel nervous at all about rubber and will take a good profit on it in this rise or wait for the next . . . I want to get out of Steel and Smelters on the upward movement . . . You can sell whenever you think it is time to get out from under and I will be perfectly satisfied with your judgment.[89]

Gould frequently asked her brokers for information and advice about specific securities, such as Sloss-Sheffield, which they informed her was "the largest independent maker of pig iron in the country" and which "has great speculative possibilities even yet."[90] She always made the final investment decisions herself.

The Butlers' most remarkable female client was probably Hannah Mynderse, a Brooklyn widow who was indefatigable in managing her money. Mynderse wrote to her brokers in a large, strong hand. Her trading orders were scrawled across postcards and hotel stationery from many different cities. She employed a terse, no-nonsense prose:

> Dear Sirs,
>   I gave you an order for ten (10) shrs. steel common at 86. I will pay 86½ no more—and sell at 92.[91]

Nothing escaped her eagle eye, as when she found an error in a purchase order sent her for twenty shares of U.S. Steel at 109¼. As she immediately wrote back, the correct price was 111.[92] She was constantly on the lookout for good investments and maintained a steady stream of correspondence with her brokers concerning new possibilities. "I notice in today's paper," she wrote in June 1909, "that there is a good deal of activity in Inter-Borough Metropolitan 4½ %s. What do you think of this security and would you advise me to purchase five of these bonds?"[93]

This brief analysis of the investment portfolios and correspondence of Butler Brothers' female clients from the early 1900s offers remarkable similarities to the data in Morton, Bliss & Company's share ledgers and letter books from the 1880s. In both periods, women overwhelmingly favored railroad and government bonds. By the 1900s, women were also investing heavily in industrial securities, but at a much lower rate than men. Women's long-standing adherence to more conservative investment strategies than those chosen by men reflected their more limited financial resources and their lack of access to alternative sources of income. Across both periods we can find women who relied on male intermediaries to manage their capital for them, as well as women who took a very active and energetic role in overseeing their own finances. In neither archive do we find examples of the helpless and pathetic woman investor who was so common in the popular literature of the day.

The diversity of these women investors should caution us against the censorious generalizations of contemporaries and the homogenizing tendencies of historians. Women investors were not a monolithic group, and class distinctions are especially important. Some women investors were wealthy and privileged, and they embraced capitalism's profit-making possibilities with gusto. They longed to participate in the stock market as full-fledged members of an investing elite and as part of their right as citizens. In many cases, wealthy women investors had more in common with elite male investors than with women less well situated. Wealthy women like Emily Billings and Hannah Mynderse worked on their stock portfolios like men did. Their brokers treated them with respect, and their social and economic positions enabled them to take risks that their humbler sisters could only dream about. Morton, Bliss & Company's wealthiest women clients invested their capital more like men than like other, less affluent women. For example, Mrs. S. W. G. d'Hauteville earned 76% of her princely annual investment income of $4,600 from shares rather than from the safer but less lucrative bonds favored by most of the firm's female clients. Her investments were more in line with those of the Morton, Bliss men, who on average derived 73% of their investment income from shares.[94]

World War I and the Expansion of the Securities Market

The most significant expansion in the number of American shareholders occurred during World War I, 1914–18, and the decade immediately following the war, 1918–28. Book stockholders grew from 4.4 million in 1900, to 7.5 million in 1913, to 12 million in 1920, to 18 million by 1928.[95] The stock market enthusiasm of the 1920s is well known, but the wartime increase in securities holders much less so. During both periods, women's importance as investors continued apace. Indeed, brokers and corporations became much more conscious of women's financial significance and much more aggressive in marketing securities to them.

Most historians have rightly emphasized the tremendous wartime sales of government bonds as key to the expansion of the U.S. securities market, but certain pre-war developments helped lay the groundwork for this expansion. As David Hochfelder has argued, the destruction of the nation's bucket shops on the eve of World War I freed up significant capital that could then be invested in the stock exchange. Most bucket-shop transactions had been time bargains, in which no actual shares changed hands, but they did educate a wide public in the "mechanics of trading on margin" and the potential profits from shareholding. A *New York Times* article from April 1916 noted that thousands of former bucket-shop customers had now "opened accounts with branches of Stock Exchange houses."[96]

In the years just before the war, employee stockholder plans also contributed to the expansion of share ownership among the general public. A number of large corporations, such as U.S. Steel, General Electric, DuPont, and AT&T, created these stockholder plans as a means of improving labor relations and counteracting the prevailing view that they were heartless monopolies. The more shareholders a company had, the more its interests could be aligned with that of "the public." By 1928, there were more than

800,000 employee shareholders in the United States.[97] That many of these shareholders were women only helped companies convey the impression that their "owners" were "modest housewives or needy widows." As early as 1917, AT&T noted that "about half" its shareholders were women.[98] Women quickly became the iconic shareholders in the company's advertising illustrations, as exemplified in a 1919 ad titled "Our Stockholders," which depicted a young widow opening her dividend check as her two children look on.[99]

Our Stockholders

There are over 135,000 stockholders who own the American Telephone and Telegraph Company. This great body of people, larger than the entire population of such cities as Albany, Dayton or Tacoma, share the earnings produced by the Bell System.

More than 45,000 of these partners are workers in the telephone organization. They are linemen, switch board operators, clerks, mechanics, electricians.

The vast property of the Bell System represents the savings of these thousands of people, in many cases *all* their savings.

In the truest sense of the word this big public service corporation belongs to the people. The people own it and the people receive the profits. More than 93% of its stock is owned by persons holding, each, less than one-ninth of one per cent.

The Bell System is a real industrial democracy. On its economic operation depends the future independence of many citizens of small means, as well as the profitable employment of thousands of other men and women.

  AMERICAN TELEPHONE AND TELEGRAPH COMPANY
AND ASSOCIATED COMPANIES

One Policy   *One System*   *Universal Service*

Figure 5. "Our Stockholders." AT&T advertisement, 1919. (Collection of the author)

The creation of a federal income tax in 1913 was another spur to the ownership of securities. Government bonds were tax-exempt, and dividends were taxed at a lower rate than earned income. Securities earnings were also easier to hide than salaries. From 1917, heavy wartime surtaxes on the top incomes led to even more bond and share purchases.[100]

A perusal of Eleanor Roosevelt's 1919 securities portfolio illustrates the importance of government bonds for wealthy wartime investors:

Income from Personal Investments, 1919	
Chemical National Bank	525.00
New York Life Insurance & Trust Co.	450.00
Central & South American Telegraph Co.	923.00
Broadway Improvement Co.	600.00
City & Suburban Home Co.	21.25
Government Bonds	1,125.00
	3,644.25

Approximately 40% of Eleanor Roosevelt's money was invested in industrial securities, 30% in banks and trust companies, and 30% in government securities. Government bonds constituted her single largest source of income at this time. As the wife of a government official (Franklin was then assistant secretary of the navy), Eleanor may have had political and patriotic motivations to purchase treasury bonds and war bonds, but her choice had the added benefit of reducing her taxable income by a third.[101]

The war itself was a key factor in expanding American securities holdings. Strapped for cash in war-torn Europe, foreign investors liquidated their American securities, transferring many of these assets into American hands. In 1915 alone, European investors sold almost $1 billion of American railway securities, often at big discounts, to be snapped up by eager U.S. investors.[102]

With American entry into the conflict in 1917, Congress authorized a series of "Liberty Loans" to finance the war. At this time, bankers estimated that the U.S. bond market comprised around 350,000 people, and they were skeptical that the government could sell all the bonds it needed to. The securities market, however, was more robust than imagined, for reasons suggested above, and by 1919, more than 11 million Americans had purchased war bonds worth $21 billion. The nation's twelve regional Federal Reserve Banks created Liberty Loan Committees to market war bonds. They enlisted the aid of bankers and brokers, as well as community organizations. As Edwin Lefevre noted at the time, "every reputable stockbroker in the United States automatically became a government bond broker." No sales commissions were charged, as brokers sold bonds out of both patriotism and the realization that they might thereby acquire new customers.[103]

Women were extremely active in bond drives. Woodrow Wilson's daughter Eleanor chaired the National Woman's Liberty Loan Committee. Almost a million women served as sales agents for the committee, constituting American women's biggest contribution to war work. Traditional women's charity organizations and church groups sold bonds. Even the Girl Scouts took part. Popular movie star Mary Pickford, "America's Sweetheart," appeared at a series of mass rallies in 1918, raising millions in bond sales.[104]

War bonds were actively marketed to women via widespread propaganda campaigns. Posters targeting women were found on every conceivable surface: billboards, fences, shop windows, buses, and trolleys. As men were away in the military, fighting for their country, women could take a leading role in raising money for the war. One Liberty Loan poster for the spring 1918 bond drive featured a smiling, attractive young woman handing a loan coupon directly to the viewer.[105] Another popular poster depicted a girl clad in shining armor, along with the caption "Joan of Arc Saved France—Women of America Save Your Country—Buy War Savings Stamps." A woman's purchase of government bonds was thus equated with military service. Women made up almost one-third of the subscribers to the First Liberty Loan campaign in 1917. By the time of the Third Liberty Loan drive in 1918, women constituted 40% of bond purchasers.[106]

Bonds were issued in $50 and $100 units, making them affordable to all classes and introducing millions of Americans to the concept of "intangible property." As Benjamin Ginzburg pointed out in the 1930s, war bonds taught the nation "that money could be made by the simple process of holding paper securities until they went up in value."[107] Two female journalists, writing in 1917, predicted that women in particular would build upon their wartime experience as bondholders:

> The War loans have brought to the individual notice of women sound schemes for the investment of their money, the prospectuses of which . . . were simply and clearly written, with the particular aim of interesting and attracting the embryo investor. Indeed, many women received their first lesson in investment from the prospectuses, which patriotism compelled them to study, and the interest thus aroused will not entirely disappear after the War.[108]

Bond sales helped set the stage for the stock market boom of the 1920s.

Even before the war's end, some commentators noted that women were playing an active part in speculation, seduced by a buoyant market and the desire to "get rich quick." An article in the *Forum* from January 1918 commented disapprovingly on idle women who had taken up the stock market as "a game much more fascinating than auction bridge." Apparently, fashionable women now kept "Wall Street secretaries," decorative and polite young men who placed trading orders for them and kept them company "in the lounge or tea rooms of uptown hotels." Some brokerage firms cultivated a female clientele by setting up "women's rooms, cozy, soft-cushioned lay-outs where cigarettes and drinks are to be had. These are places where women with more money than brains can loll back, watch the quotation board and write out their buying and selling orders on cute leather pads." Typically, the writer regarded women "stock gamblers" with a mixture of moral disapproval and condescension. Unlike similar commentary from earlier periods, however, the proposed solution was not to banish women from Wall Street.[109]

Stock exchange firms wanted women's business. The wartime expansion of the securities market had brought forth even more women with capital, and brokers eagerly competed for this clientele. The *Forum* article mocked ignorant women, but it reserved its greatest condemnation for unscrupulous brokers who preyed on their ignorance. Women could be educated, and the "reliable" stock exchange firms now planned to do this. According to the article, "legitimate houses of Wall Street have declared war on women throwing their money away." In a bid for women's business, one established firm, Henry L. Doherty & Company, offered securities on an installment plan. Conservative securities would be sold to women for 20% down and 10% per month. While women were paying off the installments, any interest earned would be credited to their accounts. In this way, the firm hoped to secure women's business. As one of Doherty & Company's brokers affirmed, "We are after the confidence of these women. We are going to meet them more than half way." Gone were the days of stock exchange firms spurning women clients or downplaying their significance.[110]

Some brokerage firms began establishing separate women's departments "to capitalize on the investment needs of women, some of whom were both independent and well-heeled."[111] Women were frequently hired to staff these departments, creating new opportunities for careers in finance. In 1914, Alice Carpenter, a Smith graduate who was active in the suffrage movement and settlement work, became the first woman to manage a women's department at a brokerage house, William P. Bonbright & Company in New York. So successful was this endeavor that Bonbright opened another women's department in Boston in 1916, under the direction of Margaret Stackpole, a Radcliffe graduate.[112]

Class clearly matters here. These pioneering women brokers, like early women bankers, had access to higher education and family connections that enabled them to enter business. Such career advancement was denied to the thousands of working-class women employed in clerical positions by banks and brokerage houses. Whenever such firms wanted to cultivate a female clientele, they never promoted an experienced woman secretary, teller, or bookkeeper from within to head their women's departments, preferring women with social prestige and connections who could project a gracious and assured demeanor and attract the business of other society women.[113] The 1920 census lists 376 women stockbrokers. As a cohort, they were mostly young and single: 79% were unmarried, and 61% fell between the ages of 25 and 44. All were white.[114]

Women and Wall Street in the Roaring Twenties

By the 1920s, women's importance as shareholders was taken for granted. *Barron's* surveyed over a hundred corporations in 1927, many of which reported that the majority of their shareholders were women. Women owned 50.4% of Pennsylvania Railroad stock, and the number of female shareholders in that railroad (known as "the ladies' line") had grown from 49,492 in 1917 to 71,479 by 1927, an increase of 31% in ten years. Women also owned the majority of stock in Westinghouse and AT&T. They owned 46% of the Southern Pacific Railroad, 43% of DuPont, and 40% of U.S. Steel. Many companies were unable to supply *Barron's* with a breakdown of their shareholders by gender, but most had noted a marked increase in women shareholders over the past decade. A 1925 shareholder listing from the Insurance Company of North America (INA) also reveals that women made up the majority of individual shareholders and held 49% of such stock. Among INA's more than three thousand women shareholders was Eleanor Roosevelt, who owned 175 shares.[115] Julia Ott has cited a 1928 study by the Financial Advertisers Association that found women purchased some 20% of new securities issues. By 1929, some financial experts estimated that women constituted 35% of the nation's shareholders. This percentage continued to grow during the 1930s and 1940s, as the New York Stock Exchange's first shareholder census in 1952 found that women made up half the nation's shareholders.[116]

The social composition of women investors had broadened considerably since the nineteenth century, when shareholding was primarily an elite phenomenon. A *New York Times* article from February 1927 proclaimed, "Housewives Big Stock Buyers." According to the paper, "the transfer books of the corporations show that it is the middle-class woman—mainly the housewives, who from their tidy savings from the household budget, build up a second family income by stock purchases—that form the vast bulk of women security purchasers."[117] During the height of the share mania, "the professional slang of Wall Street" was said to have invaded the domestic realm. One husband recalled that his wife began "talking like the ticker and *The Wall Street Journal*." When asked how the children were, she replied that "the boys were bearish on oatmeal at breakfast time, but there was strong support for hot dogs at lunch . . . Offerings of shares in dishwashing and general housework brought little response."[118]

Businesswomen were another new and important category of female investors, probably more significant than housewives. In his 1930s study of a New York brokerage house, economist Paul Wendt found that two-thirds of its women customers were employed. A 1929 article from the *North American Review* highlighted this new class of women investors—"buyers for department stores, small shop owners, advertising writers. Some of them are earning $15,000 a year, living on half, and investing the rest. Often they buy stock in the companies for which they work, or in others whose soundness they know from first-hand experience."[119] Career women pioneered investment clubs in which a group of them pooled their resources and knowledge to buy securities. In March 1925, the *Magazine of Wall Street* profiled one such club, consisting of twenty women from a town in New England. Through the purchase of "high grade bonds" and AT&T stock, members earned $80 for each $525 club share they held. The members saw themselves as "able business women . . . who are in a position to keep in touch with the financial news."[120]

Women shareholders could even be found farther down the social scale. Commentators frequently referred to secretaries, waitresses, shop assistants, and beauticians as taking part in speculation, though they usually mentioned working-class women only in passing, as a way of dramatizing how pervasive stock buying had become by the late 1920s. Such women probably owned very few stocks, which they doubtless bought on margin like so many speculators at the height of the mania. Indeed, the presence of "scrub-women" and "gum-chewing blondes" in brokers' offices was often cited as evidence of just how out of control stock gambling had become.[121] No one's business was refused, and the financial press even promoted fanciful investment schemes for working girls. In October 1925, the *Magazine of Wall Street* published a plan for a stenographer making $125–150 per month. She should place $2 a month in a state-regulated building-and-loan society that payed 6–7% interest. When she had accumulated $400, she should buy government bonds, or corporate shares such as U.S. Steel or AT&T.[122]

As greater numbers of women became shareholders, the nature of their investments diverged less from those of men than had been the case in earlier periods. A broker in 1929 claimed that there were no longer "such things as 'women's bonds' or 'women's stocks.'"[123] Other observers, however, still discerned certain preferences among women investors. A 1930 article from *Nation's Business* argued that "corporations which come directly in contact with the daily lives of women, such as chain stores, department stores, light, power and gas companies show, in most instances, a continual gain in the percentage of women stockholders over men." Women typically held 50–60% of the shares in such companies.[124] They were, after all, the principal shoppers and knew better than men "the relative crush of customers at the five-and-ten cent stores, in the various chain grocery and drug stores whose stocks are offered on the market." As consumers, women might also have been drawn to food companies; they owned more shares than men in the American Sugar Company and the National Biscuit Company.[125]

During the 1920s, there was heavy competition for women's investment business. While this was not entirely a new phenomenon, writers at the time believed that it was. The *New York Sun* and the *Saturday Evening Post* both insisted that until a few years prior, brokers did not want female clients. The *North American Review* claimed that "stock market operators for the first time in history are actually bidding for feminine favor."[126] The types of advertising available in the 1920s—billboards, magazines, radio, flyers, film—reached many more women than in the past. Radio in particular was credited by many brokers "for advertising stock trading to the home woman and the farm woman who never before thought of Wall Street . . . The review of the market for the day and Wall Street closing prices come over the loud speaker in the leisure hours of her afternoon, after the dinner dishes are washed and before she has to go out into the kitchen again to get supper."[127]

Much financial advertising was targeted specifically at women. For example, in March 1925, Baird & Warner, a Chicago investment firm, placed a quarter-page ad in the *Magazine of Wall Street*. In boldface type, the firm announced that the "Baird & Warner Plan will protect the inexperienced investor." That such an investor was presumed to be a woman was underscored by an illustration of a woman customer sitting in an office, gazing at a man behind a desk who is presenting her with securities. The text promised "a simple plan of investment, which, if conscientiously followed, assures financial independence in the years to come."[128]

In bidding for women's business, the number of brokerage firms maintaining "women's rooms" greatly expanded. In 1928 the *Literary Digest* noted that Wall Street houses "now have uptown branch offices bearing the sign 'Woman Customers Only,' and the rooms are generally filled when the market opens." In 1929 the *New York Sun* reported that "New York is dotted with trading rooms for women. There are all kinds of rooms. Some of them are merely little cubby holes, plainly furnished, with a couple of tickers chittering away, while others are big, elaborate board rooms, with half a dozen" women brokers.[129]

One of the more lavish women's trading rooms was described in loving, though rather snide, detail by Eunice Fuller Barnard in 1929. Nestled "among the smart specialty shops" of Fifth Avenue, "it might almost have been a club. The same discreet lighting, the cavernous davenports, an occasional bronze. In the deep Florentine armchairs a dozen women lounged and smoked." A "sprucely tailored woman manager" supervised a cadre of "young assistants, smartly turned out as so many mannequins," while "at the blackboard two blue-smocked girls, their leather belts bulging with cardboard checks, sprang nimbly about, changing the posted stock prices." A beauty salon was attached to the room, "to raise the spirits in time of loss." A woman broker defended the separate trading facilities for women: "'Men do not want us in their board rooms. And I am sure,' she added, surveying her interior-decorated domain, 'we do not want a lot of men smoking cheap cigars in here.'"[130]

Some women investors eschewed the flashier brokerage firms in favor of more established banks and trust companies. An "old money" investor like Eleanor Roosevelt relied on her family's numerous banking connections. Her trust funds were managed by the private bank Roosevelt & Son and by trustees like Douglas Robinson, a prominent financier married to Teddy Roosevelt's sister. By the late 1920s, Eleanor was earning far more money from her radio broadcasts, newspaper columns, and magazine articles than she received from her trust funds. This considerable personal income was invested for her by the Bank of New York & Trust Company, which kept Eleanor carefully informed of its securities choices for her account, often seeking her approval before making major purchases.[131]

By the late 1920s, at the height of the speculative mania, many more stock exchange firms hired women, some of whom were "rated as among the best brokers in Wall Street," according to the *New York Times*. By 1929, at least twenty-two New York brokerage houses had women partners. That same year, financial writer Eunice Fuller Barnard profiled the women of Wall Street for the *Times*. She noted that "saleswomen's desks are ranged indiscriminately, if still sparsely, among the desks of 'the boys' in many a big investment house." Experienced women brokers were said to earn as much as $20,000 a year, while beginners might make $6,000. Barnard praised these brokers as "women of intelligence, ambition and tact," many of whom were also "college graduates."[132]

One such woman, Mrs. Irma Eggleston, set a national sales record by selling $30 billion worth of bonds for C. F. Childs & Company by 1927. The

New York Times celebrated her achievement, although its story concluded with the statement, "She has no children." Despite her business success, or because of it, she had failed in her most vital duty. In 1928 the *Times* profiled another woman broker, Marjorie Sweet, who had been hired by the Wall Street firm of Throckmorton & Company to recruit women customers in New Jersey. In her first year, Sweet acquired 150 new accounts from "working girls" in the Garden State. As she matter-of-factly explained, "I have a little car and I drive around nights after the girls get home from work and talk securities to them." This "petite, blue-eyed" broker with "bobbed hair" was depicted as a kind of Wall Street flapper.[133]

The number of women stockbrokers more than quadrupled during the 1920s, from 376 to 1,793, but represented only 2.5% of the nation's brokers. In 1930, more than 160,000 American women were employed in banking and brokerage services, although 92.5% of them were engaged in clerical work.[134] Whatever modest inroads some women had made on Wall Street, the New York Stock Exchange remained an exclusively male club, its floor "better protected against women members than that of Congress." No official rule barred women from membership, but the sexist traditions of the exchange were not easy to overcome. In January 1927, the press reported that negotiations were underway by a brokerage firm to purchase a seat on the exchange for a woman. Neither the firm nor the woman was named, and no formal application was ever made to the stock exchange's Admissions Committee.[135] The story might have been circulated to test the waters as to whether the committee was receptive to a woman's application. If so, the answer must have been negative, as no woman was to join the exchange until 1967.

Perhaps the most dramatic sea change of the 1920s was a much more positive assessment of women's financial abilities on the part of brokers. The popular press still repeated some of the old clichés about women's incapacity to manage money, but stockbrokers rarely played along. For example, in a 1926 *New York Times* article, "Women Learn to Invest on Big Scale," Wall Street specialists cited cases of women who carefully investigated companies before investing.[136] Likewise, "a dozen bank officials and brokers interviewed" in 1929 for the *North American Review* saw little difference between men and women as investors. One banker concluded that women "can be as good handlers of securities as men." A broker believed that "it is all a matter of individual temperament"—some women were emotionally too nervous to speculate, but then so were some men.[137] Another broker, interviewed elsewhere, developed this theme more fully: "Trading, after all, is not a function of sex; it is a function of the brain. There are cool men and cool women; panicky, emotional men and panicky, emotional women . . . And I should like to say that most business men are little better educated as regards operations in the stock market than women."[138]

Stockbrokers now countered the long-standing stereotype of women investors as emotional, pesky, and bad losers. One broker insisted that "they don't nag, blow up emotionally or make scenes in their market transactions." Another observer argued that "the woman speculator takes her loss 'like a man,' and says nothing."[139] After interviewing several brokers in 1929, a reporter for the *New York Sun* concluded, "The truth seems to be that a large and increasing number of women are playing the market without displaying any of the so-called 'feminine' traits, and who have proved that they are just as stable and dependable in their dealings as men customers."[140]

*   *   *

For the half century from 1870 to 1920, the popular image of women investors was shaped by journalistic and literary portrayals that reflected the sexist stereotypes of the day. Women were meant to be wives and mothers. They supposedly lacked the stamina, intelligence, and emotional equanimity necessary for success in the business world. While financiers were happy to pocket women's commissions, they frequently mocked their financial knowledge and acumen. Popular hostility to Wall Street during the Progressive Era further underscored the inappropriateness of women partaking in the supposedly sordid business of stock gambling.

Later generations inherited this rather warped view but rarely challenged the caricature of the incompetent woman investor. In fact, writers of the 1920s who championed a more active political and economic role for women inadvertently reinforced the myth that earlier generations of American women were financially incapable. Eunice Barnard, for one, celebrated in 1929 the achievements of women investors who, for the first time in history, she asserted, "financially became people." She contrasted economically liberated modern women with "the fainting females of the reign of Victoria" whose "inability even to draw a check was a standing joke." Barnard and others accepted the jokes of an earlier era as true.[141]

More recently, historians have undermined too rigid an imposition of separate-spheres ideology by documenting Victorian women's economic importance as shopkeepers, consumers, laborers, and household managers. Excavating women's financial activities, especially as investors and shareholders, has proven more difficult due to a paucity of surviving evidence.

This chapter has initiated a process of recovery whereby the actual behavior and investment choices of American women have been set against the largely negative judgments of their contemporaries. Company records, stock portfolios, shareholder ledgers, and business correspondence from the late nineteenth and early twentieth centuries paint a very different picture of women investors. These sources depict women who were resourceful and capable. Whether they oversaw their investments themselves or entrusted their capital to the management of others, these women constructed stable and diverse securities portfolios that embodied the best financial thinking of the time.

Popular images of women investors as ignorant, capricious, and emotionally unstable are not borne out in the financial records consulted for this study. Nor did the cautionary tales about the evils of speculation appear to deter women from investing in securities. It seems likely that the images of female incompetence and the tales of financial danger spun about the stock market were designed in part to preserve a male enclave of wealth and power from too-easy access by women. In this case, separate spheres might be less a descriptive account of restrictions on women than, in the words of Amanda Vickery, "a conservative response to an unprecedented *expansion* in the opportunities, ambitions and experiences" of Victorian women.[142]

3 Lambs to be Fleeced and Petticoated Sharks

Women and Financial Fraud

"Bogus securities are most easily foisted upon women. That is a
fundamental rule of dishonest promoters."
—*Forum*, 1918

The exposure of financial frauds perpetrated against women—as well as by
women—highlighted the danger, uncertainty, and corruption associated with
certain forms of investment, and with Wall Street in general. Speculative
securities were condemned as too risky and vulnerable to fraudulent
manipulation, and the volatility of the share market was supposedly too
stressful for the feminine constitution. Stock gambling attracted the wrong
sort of woman, usually characterized as a thrill-seeking adventuress, but
it potentially could corrupt and coarsen all women drawn into its sleazy
practices. As the conservative writer Henry Norman argued in 1920, when a
woman "determines to succeed in business at any cost, the qualities for which
men love and respect her become wholly subservient to her ambition and to
such an exaggerated degree as to make her almost repulsive."[1]

American historians have had little to say about women as either the
victims or perpetrators of financial fraud.[2] The corporate victimization of
women has been taken up by some criminologists, but their work fails to
acknowledge the deep historical roots of the phenomenon in the Industrial
Revolution and the tremendous expansion of the securities market associated
with nineteenth-century railroad building.[3] As we have seen, the industrial
economy transformed business relations and capital formation in ways that
enabled greater female participation. Unfortunately, many of these new
economic opportunities for women also included greater risks for fraud
and embezzlement. As Harold Perkin noted, "the investing public was

compulsorily educated in a whole new world and vocabulary of ingenious crime, which could only be perpetrated by business men, and by large, prominent, wealthy or at least credit-worthy business men at that."[4]

The expansion of big business and the complexity of the corporate form created a world of new opportunities for criminal exploitation. Company organization increased the distance between the nominal owners, the shareholders, and the active directors, and heightened the impersonality of this relationship. Thus, directors were more open to the temptation to subject the investments of the faceless thousands to a wide variety of manipulations. Brokers, bankers, and trustees also had great latitude in how they managed other people's money. Investors usually lacked the financial know-how to protect themselves from fraud and received little assistance from the government.[5]

Laissez-faire economics reigned supreme in nineteenth-century America. Common law enshrined the principles of caveat emptor, placing few obstacles in the paths of white-collar criminals. Legal requirements concerning accounting and audits were inchoate and ambiguous. The guidelines for prospectuses and advertisements were equally vague, so that the public had little information on which to base its investment decisions. Although all investors suffered under this regime, women were seen as especially vulnerable to its abuses, as they were usually less knowledgeable about business matters than men and often had less access to good sources of financial information.[6]

Ironically, the same freebooting financial system that offered women investors little protection also allowed a few enterprising women to operate at its margins. It was sometimes possible for women to manage banks or to act as brokers. Not all of them were honest. Female financial criminals were exceptionally rare, but they attracted widespread attention and received condemnation out of all proportion to their numbers. Contemporaries preferred to see women as victims of fraud rather than as perpetrators, as this was more consistent with prevailing gender stereotypes of women's innocence and passivity.

The financial victimization of women loomed large in debates over social and economic reform. Populists and progressives cited women's exploitation by an unregulated share market as justification for greater state intervention and oversight. Financiers countered that market instability was mostly the fault of ignorant and inexperienced speculators, like women, who should be barred from commodities and stock exchanges. Financial fraud was invoked by both conservatives, who cited it as evidence that the business world was too dangerous for women, and progressives, who used it to justify a program of economic reform and regulation to better protect women.

Wall Street Wrecks

Critics of high finance and speculation frequently warned women against entrusting their savings to stockbrokers. In his Wall Street guide *Bulls and Bears of New York* (1875), M. H. Smith characterized most stock market business as essentially fraudulent: "The moral sense is so low that the temptation to commit wrong is very great, and the disgrace and punishment slight. Dishonesty is known as shrewdness, and fraud is regarded as being sharp."[7] An 1878 article from the *Christian Union*, "Wall Street Wrecks," detailed the countless victims of the stock market's sins: "they are scattered all up and down our broad land: some shut up in asylums, crazed by their misfortunes; others living out crushed, aimless lives—mental paralytics dazed by the magnitude of their sorrows."[8]

Journalists and financial writers depicted women as especially vulnerable to financial fraud, and their assessment of female investors changed little from the 1880s to the 1920s. Women were presumably too trusting and gullible to resist the "soft ways and smooth palaver" of brokers, who were "wolves in sheep's clothing," according to an account from 1887.[9] In her 1893 lecture "Woman as an Investor," the insurance executive Louise Starkweather warned that "women left with money are looked upon as legitimate prey by a class of men who have over their office door the word 'Investments.'"[10] Women's ignorance of business matters was frequently cited as a reason for their entrapment. In his guidebook *The American Business Woman* (1900), John Howard Cromwell lamented that "many a woman who ought to have been in independent circumstances during her lifetime, has come to an old age of poverty because of her inability to protect herself against that army of sharks and rascals which, unfortunately, must be permitted to exist, and to which a defenseless woman of means presents a golden opportunity."[11] A 1918 article in *Forum* still saw women as easy marks for the wolves and sharks of Wall Street: "Bogus securities are most easily foisted upon women. That is a fundamental rule of dishonest promoters."[12]

Single women were seen as especially at risk in investment matters, as they were "unprotected" by men and likely to be tempted by risky schemes promising them big returns for their modest capitals. Such women were not necessarily greedy, but they might be desperate, as all that stood between them and economic ruin could be a small annuity or the interest from stocks and bonds. In 1881 the *Independent* published a letter from a Mississippi widow with a few thousand dollars who was "extremely anxious to make a few more thousands" on Wall Street. The paper believed that such women almost encouraged fraud because of their ignorance and naiveté. They "had better keep their money out of Wall Street, and buy some safe security for investment, even if they cannot get more than 3% interest for it. Be it known to them that, if they put it there for stock speculation, the chances are overwhelming that they will never see it again."[13] In 1899 the millionaire businesswoman Hetty Green condemned financial frauds, but she also chided American women for falling victim to get-rich-quick schemes that promised them outlandish profits. Green insisted that "the only way to get rich is the Bible way," through the sweat of one's brow, and that "the good old virtues of thrift and prudence and carefulness should be cultivated more than they are."[14]

Some corporations, like the Prudential Insurance Company, capitalized on stereotypes of the vulnerable female investor to market their securities. A 1909 Prudential advertisement from *Harper's Weekly* warned: "Investing money is usually a difficult matter for women. Where shall they put money to bring them a good income? Where shall they put it to be absolutely free from loss? Did you ever think that your wife may some day have two, five, or ten thousand dollars of life insurance money handed to her? Where do you suppose she will put it to produce the best income?"[15]

Prudential was marketing a new type of policy that paid out benefits in monthly installments over several years. The company, which would benefit from delayed payment, played upon male fears of women's inability to safeguard their money. Husbands could thus protect their wives from future exploitation by purchasing an annuity.

The Economics of Victimization

Women's vulnerability to financial fraud was taken for granted in the nineteenth century, and pathetic and sensational cases frequently appeared in the newspapers and journals of the day. Women's magazines often printed warnings to their readers about business frauds directed against women. During the 1870s, the American suffragist Victoria Woodhull's publication, the *Weekly*, exposed numerous fraudulent business schemes aimed at unwary women investors. An article from 1871 warned readers against "Bogus Bankers and Brokers." That same year the paper condemned "a persistent disregard of the rights of the widow" by life insurance companies intent on fraudulently refusing claims.[16]

The press imagined women, especially widows, as the archetypal victims of financial failures and frauds. Stories about absconding brokers and bankrupt corporations frequently noted that women would bear the brunt of these financial catastrophes. On May 4, 1878, *Harper's Weekly* published an illustration by S. G. McCutchin depicting the aftermath of a bank failure.

Figure 6. S. B. McCutchin, "Trust Betrayed—A Broken Savings Bank," *Harper's Weekly* (May 4, 1878): 353. (Collection of the author)

Titled "Trust Betrayed—A Broken Savings Bank," the image showed a crowd of worried depositors gathered outside the bank. The crowd contained several women, including at least two in widow's weeds.

Women of modest means were often targeted by swindlers, who well understood their vulnerability. Such women not only lacked business experience and acumen, but were ill-placed to fight men in court. Many could not afford to pay for a prosecution, and others were too ashamed to have their business failings publicized. Bucket shops especially catered to modest women investors, and some of the establishments were outright frauds. In April 1893, Stephen H. Sprague was arrested for running a crooked bucket shop at 1212 Broadway. "His customers were almost all women," who were unaware that "Sprague doctored the ticker to mislead" them.[17] The *New York Times* reported on a similar bucket shop for women in 1902. In this case, a fake telephone was used to deceive customers. The manager could push a button, causing his phone to ring. He would then answer it and pretend to take down the latest stock quotations. He boasted to a friend that "it was 'easy money'—just like taking money from a child."[18]

Brokers had great latitude in manipulating their clients' capital, as some women learned, to their cost. In 1875, Silvia Livingston, "a maiden lady who moves in good society," met a stockbroker, Henry Hoffman, "on the back piazza of the United States Hotel at Saratoga." She gave him $1,000 to invest for her but was shocked when, a year later, he presented her with a bill for $4,000, most of which represented his commissions for stock trades. As it transpired, "in many cases the stock bought in the morning was sold in the afternoon at the same price, so that there was neither loss nor gain in the transaction by itself, but as the commission was regularly charged, Miss Livingston was a loser to the tune of about $50 a day." Needless to say, she refused to pay, as "she had no idea that she was indulging in the luxury of paying a broker $50 a day for the mere gratification of losing her money." Hoffman sued her in the Superior Court, winning his case in 1878. Livingston appealed to the New York Supreme Court, where her lawyer argued that Hoffman had a "plain duty to let her know that he was making money out of her daily, while she was losing all the time." The Supreme Court ruled in Silvia Livingston's favor, but the case dramatized just how dependent some women were on the honesty of the men who managed their money.[19]

Dishonest trustees were the bane of women investors, who were not expected to be active economic agents and might have little detailed knowledge about their own property. Men often established trust funds to safeguard the inheritance of their wives and daughters, but there was little protection from the depredations of trustees.[20] Louis Therasson, lawyer and Sunday school teacher, acted as trustee for a widow, Maria Titus, for more than twenty years. "Such was her confidence in him that she never asked for an accounting." Upon her death in 1876, it was discovered that Therasson had embezzled more than $130,000 from her estate.[21] In 1884, Samuel Walker, "a capitalist" and trustee for Maggie Flagg, made off with the bulk of her estate, some $220,000. So long as the trustee paid her the accustomed income, a woman had little reason to suspect that her capital was being wasted.[22]

Before trust laws were tightened in the twentieth century and before the emergence of professional trust companies, many trustees did their work badly, though more problems were caused by careless and sloppy management than by outright fraud. Another issue usually downplayed by Victorian commentators was the fact that a woman's trustees were usually her own relatives—uncles, brothers, sons—who were just as likely to misappropriate trust funds as lawyers, bankers, or brokers. Most writers, however, preferred to scapegoat villainous financiers rather than question the power dynamics of the patriarchal family.[23]

While some stockbrokers spurned women's business, others regarded women clients merely as lambs to be fleeced. One firm of Chicago brokers, consisting of four brothers, specialized in defrauding "unprotected" women.

After the firm's failure in 1893, one of the brothers admitted that "his duties in the transactions of the firm's business was to look up widows and women of means, and by a system of flattery and attention gain their confidence and a full statement of finances." Apparently all that was required to secure "the management of the woman's property" was "a few lunches, a theater party, a ride or other attentions of like nature." Once the brokers had access to a woman's money, they could spend it as they liked, telling her it had been lost during a downturn in the market.[24]

Once money had been handed over to a fiduciary agent, tracing its path was no easy task. In 1897 a particularly bold stock swindle was perpetrated against a woman by the brokerage firm of Tobin, Troy & Company, 11 Broadway. The brokers took $1,300 cash and 60 Philadelphia & Reading Railroad shares from Mrs. F. N. Wheaton, a boardinghouse keeper, promising to invest it in stocks "making vast profits." Instead they pocketed her money, planning "at the first convenient opportunity" to inform her "according to the market reports of the day, the loss of the investment." Two months later, when sugar futures plummeted, Wheaton "was notified that her money and stock had been invested in sugar certificates, and had been lost, and that she owed the firm" an additional $1,000. The fraud was discovered only because Mrs. Wheaton complained so vigorously and persistently that one of the partners panicked, turning state's evidence. During the initial hearing, the judge became so enraged at the cheating of a poor widow that "he suddenly broke out with a fierce denunciation of the accused men, declaring their transaction to be the worst and most shameful outrage and most barefaced swindle he had ever heard of."[25]

Other brokers foisted worthless stock on women, whom they assumed to be easy marks. In 1905, Thomas Condon, a broker of 88 Beaver Street, sold Cora Barnes and Anna Bliss 500 shares of the Fireproofine Company for $30,000, knowing the stock to be "valueless."[26] In 1908 the brokerage firm of Henry T. Rodman & Company, at Thirty-Third Street and Fifth Avenue, was found to have sold to numerous women shares in the bankrupt Lynwood Gold and Copper Company. It later transpired that the "throngs of gullible women" were induced to invest with Rodman & Co. by a Svengali-like fortune-teller, "Yogi" William F. Garnett. In this case, there was less sympathy for the victims, who were portrayed as frivolous and superstitious society women with more money than brains.[27]

The upswing in the securities market during and after World War I also created immense opportunities for fraud. A flurry of newspaper stories in the early 1920s reported fraudulent stock scams, many of which were directed at women. Crusading journalists alleged that some wartime bond salesmen had compiled "suckers lists," which they later used to unload worthless stock.[28] In December 1922, the *Buffalo Commercial* reported that a local woman tried to commit suicide because she had lost everything her late husband left her in a crooked share deal. According to the paper, "such tragedies as a woman's attempt to take her own life when she finds herself penniless from investing in fly-by-night schemes are only too common nowadays."[29]

The frequent exposure of financial crimes might have been intended to warn women about the dangers associated with certain types of investment, but it also helped to perpetuate an image of women as gullible and helpless. Some women who lost money in the stock market or in other investments embraced the role of victim, as this afforded them a measure of public sympathy and absolved them of responsibility for bad financial decisions. Women and their lawyers capitalized on the assumption that women did not understand finance and were easily hoodwinked.[30] In 1905, Cassie Chadwick's lawyer tried to excuse his client's reckless borrowing by asserting her incapacity as a woman: She "belongs to the class of people which, in the eyes of the law, is coupled with convicts and idiots. She has nothing to say about the making of laws because she is a woman. She was not informed regarding the laws of banks."[31] In 1907, Jennie L. Briggs of Taunton, Massachusetts, sued her broker, Augustus Barnard, when she lost $15,000 in a stock speculation. She claimed that she "ought not to be considered a 'business woman'" and that she knew "nothing about the market, only what Barnard told her."[32] When making financial claims, women were more likely than men to stress their needs and vulnerability. In remonstrating with her broker over stock losses in 1882, Sophia Mattern pleaded poverty: "You know I am a poor woman and have only what I work for daily . . . I am really suffering for necessities."[33] In 1910 a group of widows who had been defrauded in an investment scam made a pathetic spectacle by parading into a New York court "heavily veiled" and in deepest mourning.[34]

Women as victims of financial fraud became a cliché of popular fiction as well as the press. Writers of domestic fiction frequently emphasized how women's lives were shaped by the vicissitudes of the market and economic forces over which they had little control. Their plots often dealt with domestic happiness threatened by financial problems and commercial impropriety. Women as victims of the financial system remained a common literary theme throughout the nineteenth century and into the twentieth (see Chapter 1). In Thomas Stewart Denison's *An Iron Crown* (1885), a young man, having lost his own fortune in speculation, takes his sister's money without her knowledge and loses it, as well. Upon learning of her destitution the sister laments: "To think it should come to this, that men will steal bread from their wives and children and sisters. God certainly will curse such things."[35] Women were usually portrayed as defenseless against the machinations of financial swindlers, who were invariably assumed to be men.

Literary depictions of women's financial exploitation, like the press exposés of real-life frauds, simultaneously served to indict a corrupt capitalist system and to warn women away from the market economy and speculative investments. In the novels of the period, the female victims of financial fraud ran the gamut from naive and innocent ingénues to selfish and willful adventuresses. None of these types, however, were suited to manage their own money or to navigate the treacherous waters of high finance. Perhaps the less women had to do with such things, the better.

A Victorian "Ponzi Scheme": The Women's Bank of Boston

Women's financial victimization was so well established that commentators were hard-pressed to explain cases where women themselves committed fraud. Such cases were quite rare in the nineteenth century, but they usually received the harshest criticism and a disproportionate amount of attention from the popular press, which often depicted female frauds as monstrous and sexually depraved.[36] Active engagement with the masculine cutthroat world of high finance supposedly rendered the gentler sex ruthless, predatory, and unfeminine. Crime and depravity were sure to follow.

A forgotten but remarkable example of a female fraud was the Ladies Deposit Company, a savings bank in Boston run "by women for women," supposedly the first institution of its kind. It was, in fact, a Ponzi scheme.[37] The bank, established by Sarah Howe in 1878, accepted deposits only from "unprotected females," while guaranteeing astronomical returns of 8% interest per month. A $100 deposit would apparently yield $96 in interest by year's end, almost doubling in value. As an additional inducement, depositors were paid the first three months' interest in advance. News of the bank's fabulous profits quickly spread among Boston's domestic servants and schoolteachers, who hurried to deposit their meager savings. When skeptics voiced doubts about any bank doubling money within a year, Howe and her accomplices floated the rumor that their depository was no ordinary bank, but a "charity" for working women supported by Quaker philanthropists.[38]

Skeptics were not appeased, and the *Boston Daily Advertiser* began a campaign against the bank. The newspaper was especially dubious of Howe, whose previous career as a psychic did not suggest financial genius: "Who can believe for a moment that this woman, who a few years ago was picking up a living by clairvoyance and fortune-telling, is now the almoner of one of the greatest charities in the country?"[39] A correspondent versed in finance sent a detailed diagram to the paper explaining how the scheme worked, by paying depositors with their own money or with money paid by later depositors, and he theorized that such a scheme could probably last for three years at the most before it exhausted its resources.[40] The bank's survival was aided, it later transpired, by a number of women reinvesting their "profits." Still, Howe must have been reaching the outer limits of her scheme's existence, as she was contemplating opening branches in Philadelphia and New York to bring in new money.[41]

A run on the bank led to its collapse in October 1880. In the subsequent trial, Howe was found guilty of obtaining money on false pretenses and sentenced to three years' imprisonment. Around eight hundred women came forward with claims of more than $250,000 against the Ladies' Deposit Company. The losses were probably much greater, as many women were too humiliated to admit they had been duped.[42]

Sarah Howe's trial and the press commentary at the time provide remarkable insights into nineteenth-century constructions of women and finance, as well as beliefs about female criminality. The case was widely seen as a vindication of "separate spheres," warning women about the dangers inherent in investing their own money without male guidance. Many commentators blamed the victims of Howe's fraud for being so foolish as to entrust their money to a woman or to believe that any business could pay 8% monthly interest. According to *The Banker's Magazine*, "all sane persons" knew the bank's ruin "to be inevitable."[43] Nor were contemporaries surprised by Howe's embezzlements, since, having abandoned her proper role as wife and mother to pursue riches, corruption and crime were sure to follow.

That a woman swindler preyed upon other women surprised no one, since only women would be foolish enough to fall for such an obvious confidence game. Most observers believed that women's willingness to place their money in the Ladies' Deposit Company simply illustrated their economic incapacity, general ignorance, and even superstition. Some women, for instance, were alleged to have invested in Howe's bank because of messages from the spirit world.[44] One letter to the editor of the *Boston Daily Advertiser* concluded that "we must despair of teaching the female sex business principles."[45]

Who better to exploit women's ignorance and inexperience than another woman? The *New York Times* concluded that Sarah Howe's "intimate knowledge of the mental workings of her own sex puts male swindlers and male novelists to shame."[46] The public was more familiar with, and doubtless more comfortable with, women as victims of frauds than as perpetrators. *The Bankers Magazine* facetiously noted "that as females are so often the victims of financial frauds, it is no more than fair that they should occasionally profit by committing frauds themselves."[47] Another sarcastic observer trumpeted Howe's career as confirmation of "the suffragist claim that on every field of industry . . . woman needs only the opportunity to prove her full equality with the lords of creation."[48]

One mystery about the case that puzzled contemporaries was how news about the bank had circulated, since "a very large proportion of the deposits which have been received appear to have come by mail, and to a considerable extent from distant places." Women had in fact invested in the Ladies' Deposit Company from as far afield as Buffalo, Chicago, Pittsburgh, Baltimore, and Washington. And yet "no advertising by newspapers has been done, no circulars, so far as known, have been sent out, nor has any public announcement of the affair been made," reported Boston newspapers.[49] The bank's long-distance depositors pointed to the existence of a woman's investment network whereby women in one part of the nation (in this case, Boston) wrote to friends and relations in other cities, who in turn wrote to additional acquaintances elsewhere. This broadcasting of investment opportunities was further encouraged by a system of financial incentives. Some women received five dollars for every woman they induced to become a depositor. "One industrious young woman" recruited 150 people.[50] While contemporaries were quick to accuse women of financial ignorance, they failed to grasp the significance of women sharing investment opportunities with one another over great distances. Excluded from male sources of investment information like business clubs and fraternal lodges, women created their own information networks, amounting to a kind of "grassroots capitalism," which complicates our understanding of Victorian women as financial agents.

As the press and the courts grappled with the frauds at the Boston Ladies' Deposit Company, they also struggled to come to terms with Sarah Howe. In a culture like Victorian America, where women were idealized as emblems of purity and innocence, the criminal woman posed special ideological problems. How could one explain her anomalous behavior? Nineteenth-century newspapers and criminological works tended to portray female crime as more heinous and abnormal than male crime.[51] The press represented Howe as a graceless bumpkin. According to *The Bankers Magazine*, she was "short, fat, very ugly, and so illiterate as to be unable to write an English sentence, or to speak without making shameful blunders."[52] The *Boston Herald* claimed she was cross-eyed and "nearly as deaf as a post." She "dresses richly yet unbecomingly, uses execrable English and can scarcely write her own name legibly."[53] Apparently her criminal nature was written on her body.

The press quickly manufactured for Howe a criminal genealogy worthy of a sensation novel by Mary Elizabeth Braddon or Wilkie Collins. *The Bankers Magazine* reported that she had "been at different times a thief, a procuress, a swindler, a lunatic, and always a desperate adventuress."[54] The *Boston Herald* provided an especially detailed and lurid biography. According to that paper, she had been born out of wedlock in Providence, Rhode Island, around 1820. At fifteen she ran away to Massachusetts and married James Solomon, an "Indian physician." After thirteen years "with her dark-skinned Othello," Sarah left him and entered into a bigamous union with William Lane, a housepainter in Providence. Upon his death she married another painter, Florimund Howe, in Manchester, New Hampshire. After the Civil War they moved to Boston, where Sarah cast horoscopes and told fortunes with cards. She supposedly spent time in prison for fraud and in an asylum for depression following the death of a child. With added zest, the newspaper reported that she tried to procure a young girl into prostitution.[55]

How much of this dime-novel narrative was accurate is difficult to say. Much of it was unsubstantiated and based on gossip or testimony by persons hostile to Howe. In any case, the veracity of the biography is almost beside the point. There was a pressing cultural need to vilify Howe and to explain her crimes in a manner consistent with Victorian beliefs about gender and social class. She *had* to be ugly, vulgar, and immoral. The *Herald's* overdetermined narrative provided so many building blocks for a criminal life that one could fit Howe into either of the principal criminological paradigms vying for legitimacy in the late nineteenth century. She might have been a quintessential "born criminal" out of the pages of Lombroso—deformed, illegitimate, and mentally ill.[56] Or she could also be constructed as a "degenerate" worthy of Krafft-Ebing—her own perverse lifestyle (interracial and bigamous marriage, prostitution) leading inexorably to crime.[57]

Only one contemporary attempted a defense of Howe, the writer and women's-rights advocate Gail Hamilton.[58] She wrote a letter to the *Boston Daily Advertiser* on October 4, 1880, a few days before the bank's collapse, protesting against the personal attacks on Howe, which she dismissed as a sensational "novel of houses and husbands, jails and lunatic asylums." Hamilton did not insist on Howe's innocence, but she decried the double standard by which a woman's sexual character was judged more harshly than a man's. There were plenty of fraudulent businessmen, but their personal lives were not dragged through the press. Hamilton was almost unique for the period in questioning connections between a woman's private character and public behavior.[59]

Sarah Howe's punishment—three years' imprisonment—seems rather light for one who had defrauded hundreds of women of more than a quarter million dollars. In part, this probably reflected a degree of hostility toward her victims, who were characterized as foolish, greedy, and dangerously independent. While some sympathy was extended to the poor and ignorant among Howe's victims, it was pointed out that quite a few of the depositors were middle-class and educated—a number of them were schoolteachers. *They* "should have known better than to place confidence in the stability of a scheme so manifestly unsound and dishonest." How could women "who can translate Homer, Corneille and Schiller, who can do examples in calculus and draw a plan of the heaven's sphere" have failed to see "that no speculation of any kind has a solid bottom, that one only takes his [*sic*] chances."[60] Such women were blinded by their greed. In his defense of Sarah Howe, attorney William Towne argued that the depositors were the real criminals: "They were so avaricious that they wanted to defraud each other, and were using her as a conduit and means to do it."[61]

Especially shocking was Sarah Howe's subsequent career, for upon her release from prison in 1884 she opened the Woman's Bank "in elegantly furnished apartments on West Concord Street." This time around she offered depositors 7% interest per month, three months' interest payable in advance. Her assistant in this enterprise was Mrs. J. C. Ewell, a "magnetic physician."[62] Howe kept her second Ponzi scheme afloat for two years "before a single complaint was made against her." By April 1887, however, newspaper exposure and threatened prosecution caused her to flee the city. As no indictment or trial followed the second collapse, no figures tell us how many women entrusted their money to Howe, or the extent of her defalcations, but some estimated the amount to be around $50,000.[63]

Howe eventually made her way to Chicago, where in November 1887 she attempted to open yet another women's bank, the Ladies Provident Aid, on Superior Street under the name S. E. Elmer. Her identity discovered, she returned to Boston, where she was arrested on an outstanding warrant. The case against her collapsed from her victims' unwillingness to prosecute, and she was released from jail in March 1889. Thereafter she eked out a living "reading astrology" for twenty-five cents a visit. She died penniless in 1892, still living in Boston and still protesting her innocence.[64]

That Howe apparently had "no difficulty in finding dupes" called for some explanation. The *New York Times* was incredulous "that a woman with whose swindling operations all Boston, and especially all female Boston, had become familiar, should be enabled to repeat the same game, under the same name, in the same town." Some saw Howe's second career as evidence for "the trustfulness of woman," others for "the inexhaustible gullibility . . . of the female sex." There was even less sympathy for Howe's victims the second time around. The *Advertiser* sniffed that anyone who put money in her bank "ought to lose it."[65]

The history of the Ladies' Depository gave rise to an abundance of criticism—directed scattershot at the "preposterous" Sarah Howe and her "pathetic" female victims. Conspicuously absent from inclusion in the blame game was a laissez-faire economic system that allowed a penurious fortune-teller to establish a bank, promise 96% yearly interest, and collect deposits totaling hundreds of thousands of dollars. Howe's "Ponzi scheme" would never have been possible with even a modicum of government regulation of business in nineteenth-century America. The well-entrenched defenders of economic liberalism resisted all attempts at greater state supervision, arguing that this would actually result in more fraud by instilling in investors a false sense of security.[66] The individual investor, free traders argued, must be held responsible for her actions. This Victorian emphasis on individualism meant that financial fraud was usually viewed in personal rather than structural terms. Jurists and journalists alike opted to personify evil, castigating individual villains rather than the freebooting finance system that fostered their crimes. Scapegoating Sarah Howe deflected attention from larger issues of corporate corruption and social and gender inequality.

The Shady Lady Broker

Howe's career seemed to confirm the conservative view that women were unsuited to business and, indeed, that any woman who claimed to possess financial expertise was almost certainly a fraud. Sarah Howe's downfall drew attention to other women financiers, however few in number, who had impertinently invaded the male bastion of finance.[67] The most notable exposure was that of Marion Warren, a thirty-six-year-old stockbroker who operated the Ladies Mining and Stock Exchange at 23 Union Square in New York City. Mrs. Warren was described as attractive; her offices were elegantly furnished. "Stock indicators and telephones connecting with the offices of stock brokers were obtained, and patronage was solicited by extensive advertising," the *New York Times* reported. Warren claimed that "she had a large sum of money at her command and an extended experience with the intricacies of stock speculation." Her method of business was somewhat unorthodox, but it promised immense returns. Clients agreed to entrust a given sum of money to her "for a certain number of days, with the understanding that she could invest it or not according as her judgment dictated." She promised 25% profits and guaranteed that none of the principal would ever be lost. In reality she operated along Ponzi lines, paying profits to clients out of their own money or that of other clients.[68]

Sarah Howe's exposure in Boston in October 1880 excited suspicion of Warren, and she issued a statement that she did no business with Howe's firm. When some of her customers attempted to withdraw their capital, she stalled for time, telling them to return the following week. Kate O'Reilly, who had given Warren $2,500, later discovered that the Union Square offices had been abandoned and the broker had decamped. Creditors had already descended upon the property, seizing whatever assets remained. Marion Warren had converted several thousand dollars of clients' money to her own use. According to the press, "several of the victims were in moderate circumstances, their investments representing the savings of years."[69]

A year later, in December 1881, Marion Dow, "the only lady broker in Philadelphia," was arrested for stock fraud. It soon transpired that she was none other than Marion Warren. Having fled New York, she reestablished her brokerage business on an even grander scale in the city of brotherly love. Her Girard Street offices were "furnished in sumptuous style, and equipped with all the requirements of a large brokerage business. A woman was employed especially to record the quotations as they were given by the 'ticker.'" Dow was also assisted by a sporting gentleman, Royal Latouche, "whose style of dress and conspicuous mustache would mark him in a throng." Her clients now "ranked from the middle class to the richest and most fashionable. Some of the most distinguished ladies socially in the city were her constant customers." Many of these women lost thousands of dollars through their dealings with Dow. However, distinguishing losses due to bad investments from outright embezzlements was no easy task, which often frustrated clients' attempts to prosecute dishonest brokers like Marion Dow.[70]

In early 1882, Dow and Latouche fled to New Jersey to escape criminal indictment. At this time the press began to unravel the lady broker's lengthy and convoluted criminal past. She had been born Marion Gratz in New Brunswick, Canada. In 1870 she was living in Boston, involved in a series of confidence games with her first husband, Mr. Warren. Upon his death she married a Mr. Dow but was soon widowed again. Around 1873 she altered a certificate for a single share of Central Michigan Railroad stock to read 60 shares and attempted to sell the bogus securities. When her forgery was discovered, she fled to Canada to avoid arrest. In 1875 she was living in Chicago as Marion Ware but later had to leave that city for forging checks. At some point she abandoned her petty swindles and reinvented herself as a stockbroker, first as Marion Warren in New York and later as Marion Dow in Philadelphia.[71]

By October 1882, Marion Warren/Dow was back in New York, acting as a broker on West Thirty-Seventh Street, under the name Carrie Morse. By this point she could no longer afford fancy office space, and the Stock Telegraph Company, regarding her with suspicion, refused to supply her with a stock ticker. She soon disappeared when two of her clients, Annie Linton and Mary Brink, sued her for the recovery of money she "invested" for them.[72]

During much of 1883 and 1884, Marion Dow engaged in a series of minor stock frauds in New York, under a string of new aliases: Minnie West, Cassie Moss, Mrs. MacDonald, and Mrs. Weeks. Operating out of shabby rooms on Thirtieth Street, grandly styled the Ladies Investment Bureau, she was frequently sued by disgruntled clients. After years of arrests and indictments, she was finally convicted for a petty swindle, defrauding her own clerk, Hattie Herder, out of a $600 security. Arrested and tried, she was sentenced to two years' imprisonment in June 1884.[73]

Upon her release in 1886, she once more operated as a stockbroker, this time on Twenty-Third Street under the name Marianne Latouche. At some point she had wed her old accomplice Royal Latouche. He, however, failed to dissolve a previous marriage and was imprisoned for bigamy. In December 1887, Madame Latouche, as she grandly styled herself, was again charged with defrauding several women, but the cases were later dismissed for lack of evidence. At this point she disappears from the historical record, at least under her previous names.[74]

Like Sarah Howe before her, Marion Dow generated considerable commentary regarding her criminal career and, by extension, women's financial competency. Dow's seemingly endless ability to hoodwink women investors was taken as further evidence of women's incapacity to safeguard their own money. According to the New York Times, "every man" who saw Dow's circulars "knew at once that she was a fraud, but she snared a great many women."[75] In one case, her victims were ridiculed as "a score of silly women" who were easily duped. At other times her clients were denounced as avaricious, hungering after a delusional promise of 25% profits.[76]

Unlike Howe, who was constructed as vulgar and unattractive, Dow was depicted as beautiful and charming. The older woman was monstrous, the younger woman seductive; both of them had their morality linked to their bodies. Dow was variously described as "a well-built blonde" and "a pretty and fascinating brunette."[77] (Perhaps she changed hair color like she changed names.) One reporter noted that "her step was light, and her bearing graceful and composed," while another praised her "large and expressive blue eyes."[78] Like Howe, Dow's criminal nature was linked to sexual irregularity. She employed her charms to accumulate a string of husbands and accomplices, most notably the playboy Royal Latouche, her onetime "secretary" and later bigamous husband. Some believed that Dow evaded indictments for many years by dazzling police, lawyers, and juries. At her May 1884 trial for fraud, the *New York Times* accused Dow of using her hypnotic eyes "with telling effect upon some of the more sensitive jurymen, now gazing at one in mute appeal and then casting melting glances at another." The paper attributed the subsequent hung jury and mistrial to her flirtatious behavior.[79]

It seems unlikely that Dow evaded justice by charming juries, but she was adept at exploiting the license granted by an unregulated financial system. Criminal proceedings for fraud were difficult to sustain by the necessary evidence, and the volatility of stock market speculation made it almost impossible to distinguish between fraud and misfortune. Dow left no "paper trails" and insisted that her clients' losses were due to unfortunate downturns in the market rather than any malfeasance on her part. The very expense and difficulty of prosecutions also favored brokers like Dow rather than her victims. Some women could not afford to mount a prosecution, and others were so ashamed "they would rather pocket their losses than face the exposure of a police court."[80] As a last resort, Dow could simply cross state and national borders, change her name, and start her bogus brokerage business all over again. According to one of her creditors, she "had gone under 13 aliases in as many months."[81] Before fingerprinting, reliable forms of identification, and the easy sharing of records between police forces in different cities, Dow's frequent reinvention of herself was fatally easy.[82]

Confidence Women

Sarah Howe and Marion Dow received extensive coverage because of the scope and audacity of their criminal activity, but they were hardly typical of female frauds. After all, few women worked as bankers or brokers. Most female swindlers operated at much more modest levels and were just as likely to target men. The police and press occasionally alerted the public to the operations of "confidence women," like Bertha Heyman, who posed as wealthy and well-connected individuals to obtain money by false pretenses. New York detective Thomas Byrnes featured Heyman, the "confidence queen," in his 1886 handbook *Professional Criminals of America.*

Among Heyman's most impressive achievements was her swindling of Saunders and Hoffman, stockbrokers, out of cash in exchange for "a sealed package of worthless papers which she pretended were securities worth $87,000." She was able to deceive supposedly shrewd businessmen by dressing expensively and staying at the leading hotels, always "attended by a maid or man servant." Above all, she was "an excellent talker," glibly chatting "about her dear friends, always men well known for their wealth and social position."[83]

Confidence women were also thought to trade on their sexual allure in advancing financial schemes. Thomas Byrnes detailed the operations of one such "adventuress," who "in the evenings" received calls "from numerous bankers, brokers and others, whom she elegantly and pleasantly entertains, and meanwhile 'talks them' into, wheedles or coaxes or argues them into favorable notice of any scheme she may have at the time a pecuniary interest in."[84] In 1914, authorities in Pittsburgh uncovered a similar operation run by a woman and her "two very beautiful daughters" in "the fashionable district of the city." The women nightly entertained "many of the wealthy men of the industrial centre," inducing them to purchase "worthless stock" in a railway company.[85]

Associations among women, financial chicanery, and sexual impropriety converged with particular force in an 1888 scandal involving the death of a New York stockbroker, Nathaniel Hatch. In the early morning of May 8, 1888, Hatch fell to his death from a second-floor window of a house on West Twenty-Fourth Street belonging to Lillian Scofield, a forty-year-old former actress turned avid stock market speculator. As the case unfolded, the papers revealed especially unsavory details regarding Scofield's private life and financial dealings. She was a longtime and frequent speculator who "went downtown every day." Although married to a railroad contractor, she was intimately involved with two stockbrokers: David Ferris, whom she had known for twenty years, and Hatch, a new acquaintance. On the night of May 8, Scofield and Hatch had been dining late at Madame Fanny's, a restaurant near her home. Unbeknownst to the couple, a private detective was shadowing them. The detective had been hired by Ferris, who probably feared that Hatch was replacing him as Scofield's lover and financial advisor. Around midnight, Scofield and Hatch retired to her house, where they were surprised by her husband. Hatch tried to escape from an upstairs window and fell to his death.[86]

Although the coroner's jury ruled Hatch's death accidental, most commentators were sure this verdict concealed "dark secrets." Some assumed that "Broker Hatch was decoyed to his death by the woman's wiles" and that David Ferris was her partner in crime. The fifty-six-year-old Ferris was described as a "mature Don Juan," who "at an age when many men are grandfathers, still disports himself like a young man about town." Some members of the coroner's jury believed that Scofield and Ferris were in league "to inveigle wealthy men into their schemes."[87]

Almost everyone assumed that Lillian Scofield, the "actress," was a wicked woman who seduced wealthy businessmen and stockbrokers in order to acquire privileged information regarding securities deals.[88] In an editorial about the "Petticoated Sharks" of Wall Street, Oscar Willoughby Riggs denounced Lillian Scofield in the most extravagant language, as "one of the champagne-drinking, late-dining, loud-talking, stock-gambling Circes of New York, a daring adventuress in society and a studiously seductive Cleopatra in Wall Street, with more than one fool to play Anthony in his turn. She is one of those women in whom the suggestion of sex is uppermost, one of the full-lipped, thick-necked, big-veined sort in whom a tell-tale casualty is disclosed in every outward sign and to whom the door to spirituality seems inexorably closed."[89] Stock gambling had coarsened Scofield and her fellow women speculators, rendering them excessively carnal and unwomanly.

The Hatch case led some stockbrokers to complain that Scofield was far from unique and that a number of immoral women had laid siege to Wall Street. One broker claimed that he frequently received cards "from strange women requesting him to call." Another broker told how he was once blackmailed by a female customer with "a hard, cat-like look." As he discussed shares with her in his office, she demanded money, saying, "I want a thousand dollars or I will make an outcry and disgrace you before your clerks and customers and drive you from society." Apparently, many brokers had become so fearful of such ploys that they refused "to see a woman alone in their offices under any circumstances."[90] In this rather absurd scenario, the normally predatory brokers had become the prey of the "stock-gambling Circes."

The press continued to entertain the public with the high jinks of confidence women.[91] In the early twentieth century two remarkable cases—of Marie Josephine Eastwick and Cassie Chadwick—stood out both for the scale of the crimes and for the prominent status of the perpetrators. Unlike most confidence women, who fooled their marks into believing they were wealthy and well connected, Eastwick and Chadwick really were women of substance. They didn't need to steal to live well but did so for less obvious reasons. Contemporaries attributed their financial frauds to mental illness, believing that the women had become unhinged by their unnatural desire for business success. As one writer explained women's white-collar crimes: "once they determine to 'get on,' neither moral, business nor ethical considerations stand in the way of their 'success.'"[92]

Marie Josephine Eastwick was a thirty-six-year-old woman from Philadelphia living in London. She was in comfortable circumstances, residing at the Waldorf Astoria, but was short of funds due to reckless stock market speculations. In August 1901, she sought to purchase 1,000 shares of U.S. Steel through a London stockbroker, sending him a certificate for 1,000 shares of Canadian Pacific Railway stock, valued at $500,000, as security for the transaction. The broker's clerk noticed that the document bore only a shilling revenue stamp, instead of one for £10, which a certificate for 1,000 shares would carry. Closer inspection revealed that a certificate for 5 shares had been altered to read "one thousand." According to the *New York Times*, "this was skillfully done, three kinds of type and ink being used, showing considerable preparation" and presumably professional assistance.[93]

Miss Eastwick was committed to trial at the Old Bailey in October 1901 on charges of fraud. Her broker, Mr. Beeton, testified that she "impressed him as being a woman of wealth and position." She told him that J. P. Morgan advised her on investments, and that while she was in Russia the tsar placed a private train at her disposal. Eastwick's family argued that she was insane and had been under the care of the famous Philadelphia alienist Weir Mitchell, who specialized in the treatment of hysteria. She supposedly suffered from the delusion "that she was an immensely wealthy woman and destined to make her mark as a financier." The court proved skeptical of this defense, as Miss Eastwick had a rational motive—she was heavily in debt. The forgery also required considerable care and premeditation, inconsistent with hysterical impulse. She was convicted and served six months' imprisonment at Wormwood Scrubs, where she performed "light housework."[94]

A far more audacious and successful fraud was perpetrated the following year by Cassie Chadwick, a forty-two-year-old doctor's wife from Cleveland. Representing herself as the illegitimate but beloved daughter of Andrew Carnegie, she entrusted to Iri Reynolds, the cashier of the Wade Park Bank of Cleveland, several promissory notes amounting to more than $7 million, on which she had forged Carnegie's signature. Reynolds gave her a receipt for these notes, on the strength of which she borrowed almost $2 million from several Ohio banks as well as wealthy businessmen. When Chadwick was unable to repay some of the loans in 1904, her creditors began suing her and the National Bank examiners exposed her forgeries. A number of Ohio banks suffered serious losses, and one, the Citizens' National Bank of Oberlin, collapsed, ruining many of its depositors. Cassie Chadwick was convicted of fraud in 1905 and sentenced to ten years' imprisonment. She died at the Ohio Penitentiary in 1907.[95]

Forgotten today, the Chadwick case once excited considerable commentary. Ohio's lieutenant governor, Warren G. Harding, joked that "one of Ohio's daughters taught Wall Street that it was not the only-only." For a time, to be cheated was to be "Cassied," and a Cleveland drugstore sold a "Cassie Chadwick Nerve Tonic."[96] There was also considerable mystery about where the money went. It was no easy feat in those days to spend $2 million in two years. Some people assumed it had been lost in stock market speculations. Conspicuous consumption certainly played a role. Cassie Chadwick appears to have been something of a hoarder. When her possessions were auctioned off, "the Chadwick home was found to be crowded from cellar to garret with goods that were still in their original packings."[97]

Most embarrassingly, Chadwick's victims were not naive and gullible women, but experienced businessmen who should have known better. Some of them were now prosecuted for the reckless way in which they loaned money to "a woman not in business and not known to be possessed of tangible assets." Had it never occurred to the Ohio bankers that if Andrew Carnegie wanted to provide for his natural daughter, he had plenty of cash on hand and would hardly resort to credit instruments? Would a woman who actually possessed valuable securities from one of the world's richest men have "been reduced to the necessity of hawking her paper through the small towns of the Middle West?" None of the bankers involved actually examined the alleged promissory notes from Carnegie. Nor did they investigate Mrs. Chadwick's background. Had they done so, they would have discovered that before her marriage to Dr. Leroy Chadwick, "a man of good family," she had told fortunes in Toledo as Madame DeVere and served time in prison for forgery.[98]

One perplexed commentator jokingly suggested that Cassie Chadwick must have been a hypnotist. Others believed that she was the front person for a gang of criminal men. Such was the opinion of Hetty Green, millionaire businesswoman, who suggested that "some of these big bankers and lawyers have been behind her, using her to get money . . . All the crooked bankers ain't in jail yet, and the Lord knows there's enough of them there."[99] *The Nation* came closer to the mark, attributing "genius" to Chadwick for realizing that bankers and businessmen worshipped legendary financiers like Carnegie to such an extent that they allowed "romantic snobbery" to prevail "over the impersonal laws of business." Her brilliance lay in "choosing a legend that nobody would want to puncture or even dare to probe."[100]

The trust movement and the boom in new industrial company flotations in the early twentieth century created a world of new possibilities for financial fraud. Dummy corporations were promoted for the sole purpose of enriching the promoters. During this upswing in the securities market, disreputable businesses found it easy to hide themselves among the crowded field of new companies. The better the market, the easier it was to foist trash upon the public, and fraudsters were quick to take advantage of this situation. That some of these disreputable promoters were women seemed especially shocking to contemporaries.

In 1905, Sophia Beck was revealed as "the brains" behind the Storey Cotton Company and the Provident Investment Company, two bogus stock market flotations that had bilked the investing public out of some $5 million. Beck and her associates, Frank Marrin, Ewart Storey, and Henry "Handsome Harry" Lattimer, had been involved in numerous petty confidence games for years before they hit upon the idea of reinventing themselves as company promoters. In 1903 the gang launched the Storey Cotton Company, which "pretended to deal in cotton, but never bought or sold a bale, even on margins," and the Provident Investment Company, which "pretended to deal in wheat." The companies peddled their shares through the mails, sending out glossy flyers that promised investors sudden riches.[101]

Beck's official position with the Storey Company was stenographer, but her real talent was in concocting the firm's extravagant "get-rich-quick" publicity campaign. According to the *Cleveland Plain-Dealer*, "she understood better than anybody else how to write circulars that would bring patrons and their savings to the company. Complaints of people worried over the delay in their dividends were turned over to her and she dictated replies that not only soothed the fears of the investors but coaxed bigger sums from them." The firm paid their stenographer well; her weekly salary of $500 was as much as some typists made in a year.[102]

When the postal authorities closed in on the Storey syndicate in 1905 for "conspiracy to defraud through the mails," Sophia Beck decamped to Europe with $1 million in cash. The press was amazed by the ability of a "sweet-faced girl" in her twenties to manage a million-dollar swindle and dubbed Beck the "Queen of Confidence Women." She was "beautiful," but also "the slyest of all" the conspirators, and eluded capture for nearly five years. By 1910, most of her confederates were in prison, and Ewart Storey had "died in an insane asylum in France." Beck was finally brought to trial in Philadelphia in July 1910, but the authorities had difficulty pinning responsibility for a gigantic fraud on the company stenographer. In the end, she was merely fined $500 for "using the mails to defraud."[103]

Sophia Beck's only rival as queen of confidence games was Agnes Skelly, head of the American Steel Car Company, another stock-exchange swindle. Skelly peddled her company in Chicago, where she managed to hook a couple of the city's prominent businessmen. The concern was supposed to manufacture a new lightweight freight car and was represented as having $10 million in capital. Skelly claimed that eastern money interests were backing her, including Hetty Green and E. H. Harriman. The press lauded Skelly as "the wizardess of finance" and "million dollar Agnes." It soon transpired, however, that the "company" had never been incorporated and that its only tangible assets were a pile of blueprints and prospectuses.[104]

Agnes Skelly, like Sophia Beck, was represented as beautiful and charming. It was widely assumed that both women used their seductive powers to entrap male investors. A lurid illustration from the *Salt Lake Herald Republican* in 1909 represented one of Beck's victims caught in a gigantic spiderweb. The "Confidence Queen" lorded it over him, clad in a filmy gown and perched atop an ermine cape. Empty champagne bottles sat nearby.[105] Skelly's chief dupe

Figure 7. "Sophia Beck: 'Confidence Queen,'" *The Salt Lake Herald-Republican*, October 24, 1909. (Courtesy of the Library of Congress)

was an elderly Chicago architect, John Armstrong, referred to as Sampson to her Delilah. Apparently Armstrong was "at the beck and call of the young woman promoter." An article from the *Boston Herald* in 1911 claimed that many financial frauds depended upon good-looking women wheedling money out of investors: "Of course as bait for suckers a woman far surpasses a man."[106]

Protecting Women from Fraud

The seeming ubiquity of financial fraud eventually generated a backlash against a capitalist system regarded by many as hopelessly corrupt. If women—the weakest and most vulnerable members of society—were so easily and frequently exploited by swindlers and unscrupulous financiers, then the financial system itself was probably in need of reform.

Before the twentieth century, the defenders of the free market had always circumvented state regulation by arguing that the market was self-regulating and that good business would drive out bad. The government could not, so the argument ran, make people honest by act of Congress. Financial regulation was even held to be counterproductive, as it would "confuse" the public with a welter of new laws, at the same time begetting a false sense of security and extinguishing the habit of self-protection. As Henry Havemeyer, president of the American Sugar Refining Company, told a congressional commission in 1899, "You cannot wet-nurse people from the time they are born until the day they die. They have got to wade in and get stuck and that is the way men are educated and cultivated."[107] Whether women were well served by this brutal philosophy was another question.

Laissez-faire was increasingly hard to defend in the face of widespread fraud and in relation to a highly complex international securities market. Adam Smith had formulated his theories on the assumption that buyers and sellers were on an equal footing and had accurate information about one another. By the late nineteenth century, however, most people were passive investors. They lent their money to governments or corporations over which they had no control and about which they had little knowledge. The investing public also depended on the expertise and honesty of "professional" financial intermediaries—bankers and brokers—who were, in fact, subject to no uniform professional standards, examinations, or oversight. In most cases, financial transparency was a farce.

Public companies were barely accountable to the public. As David Hawkins has demonstrated, "during much of the nineteenth century the amount of financial data revealed by business corporations to the American public, including stockholders, depended upon the whim of the managers." Some corporations provided no financial information whatsoever. From 1897 to 1905, Westinghouse, one of the nation's biggest companies, neither published annual reports nor held annual meetings for its shareholders. Few companies released balance sheets detailing assets and liabilities, and even fewer issued auditors' reports. Only about half of U.S. states required companies to provide any financial information to shareholders. Even when states required an annual report, they seldom specified the contents of the report, or how and when the report was to be made available. There were no penalties for noncompliance.[108]

Newspapers drew attention to financial scandals and pushed for greater state oversight and regulation of Wall Street. In the early twentieth century, muckraking journalists and progressive politicians worked hand in hand in bringing to account a freebooting financial system. In 1904, Thomas Lawson wrote a series of articles for *Everybody's Magazine* titled "Frenzied Finance." The articles, later published as a book, detailed a sleazy system of stock market manipulation, fraud, and bribery associated with the flotation of the Amalgamated Copper Company. Lawson castigated "the brutal code of modern dollar-making," which he believed converted ordinary people "into beasts of prey, and put to shame the denizens of the deep which devour their kind that they may live."[109]

Politicians increased scrutiny of Wall Street. Following the Financial Panic of 1907, the reforming governor of New York, Charles Evans Hughes, appointed a commission to investigate stock market practices. The Hughes Report, published in 1909, recommended that the New York Stock Exchange curb reckless speculation by tightening its control over price quotations and raising margin requirements.[110] A number of scandals involving fraudulent oil and mining stock being peddled door-to-door led to the passage of the first "blue sky law" in Kansas in 1911, which aimed for greater transparency in financial dealings. Henceforth, a government commission would have to approve all securities sold in the state. Over the next two years, twenty-three western and southern states enacted similar laws.[111] In 1913 the House Banking and Currency Committee, under the chairmanship of Arsène Pujo of Louisiana, launched an investigation into whether a "money trust" was controlling American finance. The Pujo Report concluded that an interrelation among financial institutions was endangering free enterprise.[112] Based on the report, the lawyer and reformer Louis Brandeis wrote for *Harper's Weekly* a series of articles later published as the book *Other People's Money and How the Bankers Use It* (1914). According to Brandeis, lack of competition in the financial industry permitted high brokerage commissions, overpriced securities, and insider trading.[113]

Politicians and journalists emphasized that women were especially victimized by financial fraud. In 1918 the journal *The World's Work* revealed how Louis Edward Baumeister and his associates lured "a widow to part with $17,000 on the promise that they were going 'to let her in on a good thing.'" In 1922, Congressmen Edward Denison of Illinois maintained that con men were "fleecing" widows of their bonds by sending the women "lurid literature

describing their fraudulent offerings in glowing colors and promising fabulous returns."[114] As more ordinary Americans purchased securities, especially
war bonds, it became increasingly difficult to imagine stock-market investors
as a privileged and wealthy minority who could look out for themselves. In
concluding the series "Pirates of Promotion" for the journal *World's Work*,
Louis Guenther argued that "the Government which has had the united
support of the people in financing the war, must now protect those people"
from fraud.[115]

Nineteenth-century criticisms of women investors as ignorant or greedy
gave way to more sympathetic treatments from the war onward. In these
later accounts, women were still seen as naive and helpless, but they were not
blamed for their bad financial decisions. The fault now lay squarely with the
unscrupulous men who took advantage of their innocence and incapacity. The
press and other commentators remained insensitive to the class inflections of
fraud cases. They tended to depict all women as potential victims of white-
collar crime, eliding the greater vulnerability of poorer women, who were
more likely to patronize bucket shops or to be solicited by confidence men.
Affluent women had access to more established banks and brokerage houses,
as well as a far greater range of investment options to choose from. If a well-
heeled woman was occasionally entrapped by a fraudster, she was also much
less likely to be beggared by the experience than a woman of slender means.

A number of popular accounts began depicting swindlers as sexual
predators who sought out lonely women, especially widows. In a 1917 article
from *Forum* on "Male Vampires," Shirley Burns narrated several tragic tales
of women charmed out of their fortunes by "well-educated, well-dressed,
well-bred" frauds. In one story, a widow is courted by a "vampire" who makes
"violent love to her . . . not a day passed that he did not send a telegram
expressing his ardent devotion; and as for his letters—it was a wonder they
didn't burn holes through the mail sacks!" In the end she handed over to
the financier "every cent she had in the world—thirty thousand dollars in
cash, *and without security!*" Left destitute, her only explanation was: "He
has magnetism—perfectly wonderful magnetism!"[116] In a 1924 piece from
Outlook, George Witten warned of fake company promoters who employed
handsome young men to secure women clients. One such gigolo/broker
"cultivated a neat little mustache, . . . wore spats, carried a cane, and talked
with a languid drawl."[117] As Elizabeth Frazer explained to readers of the
Saturday Evening Post, "It is very easy to take advantage of women on their
vulnerable side, and that vulnerable side is man, from whose rib they sprang
. . . He makes love to a woman to induce her to invest her earnings in some
worthless company."[118]

The "luring" of women into speculation and the cheating of women through all manner of financial frauds called out for some corrective. In earlier periods, the dangers of speculation were usually invoked to steer women away from Wall Street. By the twentieth century, however, women's exclusion from financial activities no longer seemed tenable or even desirable. The financial exploitation of women was now cited as justification for more stringent regulation of banking and securities markets. For example, when Senator Arthur Capper of Kansas tried to outlaw commodities speculation in 1921, one of his arguments was the shocking number of women harmed by this reckless activity.[119]

The financial community was shaken by the mounting attacks directed against it, especially the government investigations and legislative schemes for regulation. Financiers fought back through a more active propaganda of their own, and through preemptive schemes for self-regulation and self-policing. Brokers positioned themselves as the defenders of women and sought to distinguish their "legitimate" activities from the "reckless" speculation of bucket shops and the criminal plots of common swindlers. While the government investigated securities and commodities exchanges, those exchanges mounted their own vigorous attacks against the bucket shops.[120]

Exchanges also sought to shift the responsibility for market volatility from themselves onto ignorant and marginal speculators outside the business community, such as women. *They* needed to be barred from commodities trading and speculative operations. It was at this time, in the early twentieth century, that some stock exchange firms refused women's speculative business, or at least made a show of doing so (see Chapter 2). In his boosterish book *The Stock Exchange from Within* (1913), the broker William Van Antwerp claimed that "it would be very difficult today for a woman to open a speculative account with any reputable firm of brokers on the major exchanges unless she were well known, peculiarly qualified for such transactions, and absolutely able to support them."[121] Banning women from certain kinds of securities trades could be represented both as protecting women from financial danger and as stabilizing securities markets.

Brokers and businessmen also created professional organizations to combat their critics. As Julia Ott has documented, in 1913 the New York Stock Exchange organized a Committee on Library to counteract the negative stereotypes of the exchange promulgated by muckraking journalists and government investigators. Initially the committee pursued a reactive strategy focusing on image control. It wrote letters to newspapers and journals refuting negative stories about Wall Street and distributed copies of pro-Exchange literature to libraries and schools around the country. By 1921 the Library

Committee had been transformed into a more proactive Publicity Committee that sponsored speaking tours and commissioned educational films.[122] During the 1920s, other newly minted organizations, like the Better Business Bureau and the Business Men's Anti Stock Swindling League, also sought to enhance public relations for corporate America. American bankers demonstrated their concern for their female depositors by establishing a National Committee for the Education of Women in Financial Matters and the Protection of Her Money. These antifraud organizations broadcast warnings about financial frauds and notified police departments about swindlers in their area. By more actively combating white-collar crime, these organizations hoped to preempt the threat of government regulation.[123]

Some female financiers argued that they were especially suited to "prevent foolish investments by women." The banker Bessie Q. Mott lamented that every year, American women lost $700 million investing in worthless securities, seduced by "a well-trained, well-groomed, high-pressure salesman." The sisterly banker could serve as a foil to the fast-talking, slick securities hustler, warning women away from "unscrupulous security sharks."[124] At least one woman stockbroker, Margaret E. McCann, advertised herself during the 1920s as a protector of "women investors against the wiles of masculine 'wolves.'" She argued that women were ill-served by male brokers and that "a friendly talk with another woman" was the most effective way to explain the intricacies of the market. Unfortunately for McCann's female clients, characterized as "women of small means who trust her implicitly," she misappropriated their funds for her personal use. Margaret McCann's brokerage business failed in December 1928, with losses of more than $400,000. She was convicted of grand larceny in March 1930 and sentenced to three years' imprisonment.[125]

Whether American women would be better protected from fraud by government oversight of the financial sector remained a moot point until 1934, when the Securities and Exchange Commission was established as part of Roosevelt's New Deal.[126] Before that date, combating financial malfeasance was uncoordinated and ineffective. During the nineteenth century, women seemed especially vulnerable to fraud, and women's financial victimization was a common theme of the popular press, economic journals, and fiction. In Victorian tales of financial danger, the usual moral was that good women should avoid the marketplace and its corrupting influence. By the twentieth century, new narratives had emerged that favored women's empowerment and financial regulation. A financial system that was too dangerous for women was increasingly hard to justify in the face of women's-rights campaigns and progressive economic reforms.

The Weaker Sex?

This chapter has documented the ease with which all manner of financial crimes could be perpetrated against the investing public in the late nineteenth and early twentieth centuries. Contemporaries assumed that women were more likely than men to be victimized by frauds and swindlers, but was this, in fact, the case? Were women really more trusting, uninformed, and incapable of managing money than men? Did frauds and hucksters target women more frequently, or did the sexist assumptions of the age distort perceptions and representations of fraud to overemphasize female victimhood?

Chapter 2 argued that women's financial ignorance and incapacity had been exaggerated in the past. As economic agents, women were not the emotional and capricious creatures found in so much popular discourse. If women were more vulnerable to fraud than men, it was, of course, on account of cultural, legal, and structural considerations rather than from some supposedly inborn feminine qualities. During the nineteenth century, women usually received inferior education and were seldom expected to earn their own living or to employ large amounts of capital.[127] Women were more likely than men to have their money managed by trustees or other financial agents. They were often excluded from the best and most profitable sources of financial information.

Many men who invested in securities were themselves businessmen whose work brought them into contact with financiers, bankers, and lawyers. These men dined and drank together in taverns, coffeehouses, and restaurants in urban business districts, and they socialized together in clubs and fraternal lodges. Clubs and coffee shops were places where business deals were cemented and information was shared and traded about all manner of investment opportunities. Judith McGaw has spoken of "mutually-made men" to describe the networks of businessmen who shared knowledge and capital to mutual advantage. Women were largely excluded from these circles and sources of information.[128] Better-informed and better-connected businessmen were probably less likely to succumb to the blandishments of fraudsters.

Of course, not all men were businessmen. Many male investors, no less than female, struggled to understand the complexities of high finance. In November 1909, Alfred C. Coxe, a judge on the U.S. Court of Appeals, sent to his broker a circular he had received from the Pennsylvania Railroad, a company in which he owned stock. Coxe admitted, "I have not read it and could not understand it if I had." The esoteric and convoluted language of many financial prospectuses and corporate reports concealed as much as it revealed. Laypersons, even those who were otherwise well educated and well informed, had few resources against such obfuscation.[129]

Women may have been excluded from certain lucrative deals, but it does not follow, as contemporaries assumed, that their outsider status inclined them toward outlandish or fraudulent schemes.[130] Indeed, as Chapter 2 has demonstrated, women were more cautious and conservative in their investment choices than men. They preferred bonds over shares and engaged in speculation less frequently than their male counterparts. An insurance company study from the 1920s, following almost $10 million of payments to widows, found that six years after receiving benefits, only 1.3% of women had lost money through speculation or swindles. The vast majority had invested their money safely and conservatively.[131] A broker from that period also praised women investors for their caution, believing that they were "less liable to get caught" by crooked schemes than men, who were more daring and reckless.[132]

Recent economic and psychological studies demonstrate a continued pattern of more cautious and conservative investment behavior on the part of women, probably linked to women's more modest economic resources and to cultural attitudes less accepting of female aggression. In surveys women report less confidence in their money-handling abilities than men and are more reluctant to take financial risks.[133] While men believe themselves to be better informed about investment and more skillful traders than women, this is not really the case. One recent study concludes that men are "overconfident" about their financial abilities. They are more likely than women to ignore their brokers' recommendations and to turn over their portfolios too frequently. This behavior results in greater net losses for men than for women.[134] One could even argue that men's overconfidence and propensity for risk-taking renders them more likely than women to invest in fraudulent get-rich-quick schemes.

Assumptions of women's greater financial victimization rest largely on anecdotal evidence and popular prejudice. In a patriarchal society, villains were presumably male and victims female. By highlighting women's vulnerability to fraud, conservative commentators could shore up the separate spheres, warning women against the dangers of the public marketplace. Progressive critics of corporate America also liked to invoke female victims of financial fraud, as images of despoiled women had tremendous cultural resonance. Women who lost money through investment were also more likely to emphasize their own victimhood in bids for sympathy and assistance, while men were expected to be stronger and more stoic.

*   *   *

The effects of financial fraud and market failure on women investors were frequently emphasized by journalists and novelists alike. Their often sensational accounts highlighted how deeply the female domestic sphere had been penetrated by involvement in securities markets and how vulnerable its welfare was to malfeasance and mismanagement by financiers. During much of the nineteenth century, discussions of fraud tended to conclude with warnings against speculative investments for women. It was better for women and other modest investors to leave the stock market to the wealthy financiers and businessmen who were more knowledgeable about its volatile operations and could better afford to take economic risks. By the twentieth century, as the number of the nation's shareholders increased and as the percentage of women investors expanded, the probity of securities markets and acceptable levels of risk came under increased scrutiny. There was less expectation that small investors could effectively navigate complex financial markets, as well as greater sympathy for women victimized by financial swindles.

4 Turning Wall Street Inside Out

Victoria Woodhull and the Feminist Debate on Finance

"We are simply turning Wall Street inside out, as we intend to do everything else."
—Elizabeth Cady Stanton in *The Revolution*, 1868

The meteoric rise and spectacular career of the women's-rights activist Victoria Woodhull during the 1870s pushed financial debates concerning women onto the front page. In her role as the nation's first female stockbroker, Woodhull seemed to open up new economic vistas for American women, and in her capacity as a crusading journalist and political activist, she subjected the stock market and the capitalist financial system to harsh criticism. Like other feminists after her, Woodhull wanted to critique financial power, but also to be part of it. The tension, however, between Woodhull's attempt to make money on Wall Street and her ruthless exposé of American finance proved too difficult to sustain. The business and political communities turned against her, denouncing her as a lewd woman who promoted "free love" and published obscenity. To Victoria Woodhull's conservative critics, the moral was clear: women were unsuited to financial careers, and entering public life caused them to abandon all moral restraints.

Subsequent generations of American women pushed against the masculine barricades surrounding Wall Street and corporate America, and in doing so they debated women's relationship to the financial sector. No single point of view about Wall Street prevailed among women's-rights advocates. Some damned the stock market as corrupt gambling, but others sought to participate more fully in market capitalism. Some argued that financial fraud and capitalist excess had plunged the nation into disarray. The domestic realm could not be isolated from the marketplace, and women's homes and families were threatened by banking crises, stock market panics, and commercial dishonesty. Men had created this mess, but women would bring their moral sensibilities to bear in cleaning things up.

The Not-So-Separate Spheres

In the financial battle of the sexes, progressives sought greater economic autonomy for women, while conservatives worked to shore up separate-spheres ideology, which they saw as divinely sanctioned. In 1854, *Hunt's Merchants' Magazine* argued that "Adam was created and placed in the Garden of Eden for business purposes," but that the temptress Eve destroyed the commercial paradise.[1] The home guarded women's purity and innocence, traditionalists maintained, but once the ladies developed a taste for moneymaking, all bets were off. As Deanna Kreisel argues in her recent study *Economic Woman*, Victorian discourse frequently associated a woman's "wise domestic management" of her household with "sexual restraint." The idealized "economic woman" was frequently contrasted with the greedy and selfish woman, whose poor economic management skills ruined her husband.[2] For example, in 1843 the conservative writer Eliza Farnham claimed that luxury-loving wives financially enslaved their husbands. This criticism was to be a long-standing trope for those who condemned the stock market and women's financial interests. Certain selfish women supposedly gambled in shares in a reckless attempt to acquire funds for jewelry and clothes, or else they drove their husbands to do so.[3]

In spite of all the moralizing, it was nearly impossible to isolate the home from the market. As Kathryn Hughes suggests, maintaining separate spheres was an "aspiration" for many middle-class Victorians, but they also realized that "actual living arrangements were far more porous."[4] Few women could avoid involvement in financial matters. As Rebecca Stern argues in *Home Economics*, the Victorian home was the site of employment, trade, and economizing and, like the wider marketplace, was vulnerable to various kinds of speculation, false dealing, and fraud. Women had to hire and fire servants, bargain with tradesmen, and evaluate the quality of foodstuffs and household merchandise.[5] Suffragists and other women's-rights advocates argued that women needed economic and political rights to effect improvements in the domestic realm and to address social problems that affected home and hearth, like the adulteration of food, unregulated utilities, and child labor.

Some advocates for women's rights saw improved financial knowledge and enhanced economic opportunities as more important for women than the vote. From the 1850s onward, women petitioned state legislatures, demanding property rights for married women. Throughout the nineteenth century, suffragists such as Susan B. Anthony and Lucy Stone advocated for women's access to credit. Financial language permeated feminist discourse, as when the socialist and women's-rights advocate Ernestine Rose demanded that men give women "our title-deed to life."[6]

American women's historians have emphasized a distinction between women's-rights advocates and feminists.[7] The nineteenth-century women's-rights movement centered on achieving legal and political rights equal to those granted men. Feminists usually pressed beyond seeking equal rights with men by mounting a broader critique of patriarchal society and its institutions. The term *feminism* was not widely used before the twentieth century, but this does not mean that no Victorian women espoused feminist ideas. Regardless of how we choose to label these women, we need to better appreciate how dedicated they were to financial literacy and economic empowerment.

Gender history, in emphasizing women's struggle for legal and political rights, especially the vote, has underplayed both the influence of capitalism on women's decision-making and their desire for enhanced economic opportunities. Many American women wanted to make money for themselves. Women who already had money were eager to invest that money and make more of it. Even the suffrage movement, far from eschewing capitalist accumulation, was shaped by commercial culture. In "The Incorporation of American Feminism," Lisa Tetrault demonstrates that in the late nineteenth century, many women's-rights advocates earned substantial sums of money on the lecture circuit and that we should view these activists as "business women, entrepreneurs who pursued profit with calculation and acumen."[8]

The Revolution, a suffrage paper edited by Susan B. Anthony and Elizabeth Cady Stanton, maintained a steadfast commitment to women's financial education and empowerment.[9] In an 1870 article from the paper, "A Business Woman," Mrs. B. C. Reede gently mocks "the female exquisite" who does nothing but "look pretty" and "wear the money which her husband bountifully provides." Were her husband to die suddenly—"and business men do die off fast"—she would be in no position to manage the estate, but would be dependent on strangers who would likely enrich themselves and cheat her. "A business woman," however, "would have taken affairs up where her husband left off . . . 'paddled her own canoe,' and carried out her husband's plans almost to the very letter." Reede concludes that every woman "needs something besides white hands, pretty teeth and a tapering waist. She needs a head, a business head."[10]

While *The Revolution* has been justly celebrated as a pioneering organ of the women's suffrage movement, historians have failed to appreciate just how much of the paper was devoted to financial matters. Published weekly between 1868 and 1870, *The Revolution* was the official voice of the National Woman Suffrage Association. The paper had a regular financial section, which published weekly gold prices and stock quotations for a number of securities, especially railway shares and government bonds. Another regular column, "Talk Among the Brokers in Wall Street," contained a compendium of financial news and gossip concerning the affairs of financiers like Daniel Drew and Cornelius Vanderbilt. This material suggests that a good many of the paper's female readers were interested in and familiar with investment matters. Insurance and railroad companies advertised in *The Revolution*, as did well-known firms of stockbrokers such as Fisk and Hatch and Jay Cooke and Company, indicating that Wall Street was also interested in securing women investors.[11]

The Revolution's editorials, however, were harshly critical of American finance as an amoral and predatory business. In an April 1868 editorial, Stanton responded to some subscribers' questions about "why we publish all that nonsense about Wall Street." She insisted that "we are simply turning Wall Street inside out, as we intend to do everything else." This was no difficult task, as the "street is nothing more or less than a grand gambling saloon on a large scale."[12] When a correspondent wrote to the paper in November 1868, praising financiers like John Jacob Astor as self-made men "who amassed wealth by hard and constant toil, indomitable perseverance, and rigid economy," Stanton would have none of it. She responded that "the foundation of Astor's wealth was the taking of valuable furs from the Indians for a mere song" and that other financiers built fortunes by means of "a hard, grinding selfishness that enabled them, by skill and cunning, to take undue advantage of their neighbors' necessities, and overreach all who had dealings with them."[13] The 1869 conspiracy by Jay Gould and Jim Fisk to corner the gold market, precipitating a financial crisis, was denounced by Stanton and Anthony as proof of men's unfitness to manage the nation's wealth.[14]

While many women saw themselves as occupying a nobler sphere than men's "bank note world," women's-rights activists like Elizabeth Cady Stanton recognized that households ran on money and that the home was often threatened by market forces over which women had little control. In order to reform the marketplace, women would need to enter it. Women's suffrage and women's employment would empower the sex to bring its moral sensibility to bear against a corrupt government and corporate economy. Stanton insisted that a financial scandal like the "Crédit Mobilier was impossible in a Congress composed partly of women." She believed that it was woman's mission to rescue the nation from capitalist excess, telling her audience at the 1869 Equal Rights Association meeting: "The need of the hour is not territory, gold mines, railroads or specie payments, but a new evangel of womanhood, to exalt power, virtue, morality, true religion, to lift man up into the higher realms of love, purity and thought."[15]

Victoria Woodhull on Wall Street

When Victoria Woodhull took New York by storm early in 1870, she might well have seemed the answer to Stanton's prayer. Indeed, she later proclaimed, "I am the evangel."[16] Woodhull first came to public attention for something more prosaic than lifting man into the higher realms. She planned to be a stockbroker. According to Woodhull, she and her sister, Tennessee Claflin, opened their brokerage house to prove "that woman, no less than man, can qualify herself for the more onerous occupations of life."[17] This venture catapulted Woodhull to fame, and within months she declared her candidacy for president, began publishing a radical newspaper, and presented a memorial on women's suffrage to the House Judiciary Committee—a number of firsts for an American woman. Woodhull's sudden rise caught the nation off guard, and for a while it struggled to come to terms with her. Some observers were dazzled, others were amused, and still others were appalled. Her passionate espousal of socialism and "free love," however, soon sealed her fate, and her fall was as precipitous as her rise.

What interests me here is Woodhull's financial activities and economic thought, which have been neglected by her biographers, who not surprisingly have been more interested in her political ambitions, sex radicalism, and unconventional personal life. In addition to her brokerage business, which challenged the male monopoly of Wall Street, Woodhull's newspaper provided extensive coverage of economic issues and pioneered a type of muckraking journalism, exposing financial scandals and corporate corruption. As a public speaker she lectured eloquently about economic matters at a time when women were not seen as authorities on such subjects. The recovery of Woodhull the financier is unfortunately hampered by a paucity of primary sources, by Woodhull's own mythmaking, and by a fuzzy historiographical trail in which undocumented and unsubstantiated stories have been passed from one work to another.

Much of our information about Victoria Woodhull, when traced back to its original sources, was actually supplied by Woodhull herself—in interviews she granted to the press, in articles she published in her own paper, and in retrospective accounts she later circulated to redeem her tarnished reputation. Biographers and scholars have drawn heavily on this material, and while they have countered some of Woodhull's more extravagant claims, they have mostly accepted her version of events, however dubious, concerning her career as a financier.

Emanie Sachs's *Terrible Siren* (1928), published in the year after Woodhull's death, dominated the public's perception of Victoria Woodhull for decades.[18] The book, very much in the debunking tradition of Lytton Strachey's *Eminent Victorians* (1918), presented Woodhull as a delusional and preposterous figure. Her brokerage firm was cast as a publicity stunt and her campaigns for women's rights and social justice treated with disdain. It took fifty years before second-wave feminism rediscovered Woodhull as an important figure. (She had been effaced from the official history of the suffrage movement written by Stanton, Anthony, and Gage in the 1890s.)[19] Not until the 1990s did a series of new biographies present a fuller and more balanced view.[20] While the new work is a welcome corrective to the distortions presented by Woodhull's hostile contemporaries and crystallized in *The Terrible Siren*, it still perpetuates a number of unsubstantiated details regarding Woodhull's Wall Street career.

When Victoria Woodhull and Tennessee Claflin opened their brokerage house, Woodhull, Claflin & Company, in January 1870, they had just recently moved to New York from the Midwest, where they had been eking out a living as clairvoyants and spiritual healers. Their father was a huckster and snake-oil salesman, and they had spent an impoverished childhood in Homer, Ohio. In 1853, at age fifteen, Victoria Claflin married Dr. Canning Woodhull, a local physician nearly twice her age. She had a son the following year and a daughter in 1861 but four years later divorced Dr. Woodhull, who was an alcoholic and drug addict. In 1866, Victoria Woodhull married Colonel James Blood, a Civil War veteran and free thinker, but she declined to take his name. In 1870 the public knew nothing of Woodhull's checkered background but still wondered how this mysterious young woman and her sister, ages thirty-two and twenty-four at the time, could operate on Wall Street. What were their qualifications? Where did they get their money?[21]

The sisters were quick to invent a splendid, and fabulous, genealogy. They were, they claimed, related to William Claflin, the industrialist and governor of Massachusetts. Their father was a lawyer and had been a wealthy man until he lost his fortune through speculation. They had studied law for six years in their father's office and had managed extensive real-estate holdings for a period. They had also been quietly dealing in oil and railroad securities for years and had recently made a fortune in the gold market. They had earned more than $700,000 on Wall Street. Vanderbilt was their close friend, they consulted him on a daily basis, and he was backing their firm.[22] Most of this was a tissue of lies, much of it is hard to believe, and none of it is verifiable.

Reporters soon uncovered Woodhull and Claflin's more humble antecedents, but to this day the sisters' biographers have accepted much of the remaining narrative, however improbable and contradictory, as true. Among the unverifiable information repeatedly cited in recent works about Woodhull is the belief that she made $100,000 as a clairvoyant, that she parlayed this money into $700,000 through gold speculation, that Cornelius Vanderbilt backed her brokerage firm and later financed her newspaper, and that her firm was a huge success.[23] In fact, $100,000 was a vast sum that, at a time when $1,000 a year was a comfortable middle-class income, lay beyond the ability of any clairvoyant to earn in a lifetime. Likewise, $700,000 was an immense fortune, and had Woodhull actually made this amount during the gold panic of September 1869, as she claimed, there would surely have been some mention of it at the time. Furthermore, with this kind of money, Woodhull would not have needed the backing of Vanderbilt, or anybody else. She could have launched her firm, published her newspaper, and lived in high style for many years, when in fact she was penniless and homeless by 1872.

Vanderbilt certainly knew Woodhull and Claflin, but the precise nature of his dealings with the sisters remains unclear. The Commodore's most recent biographer, J. T. Stiles, points out that little solid evidence exists about Vanderbilt's relationship with the two women apart from gossip and the rumors that they encouraged to boost their business. Vanderbilt had a well-known interest in spiritualism and alternative medicine, and he probably first encountered the sisters because of their reputation as magnetic healers. He may have informally advised them about investments and even assisted them in setting up their firm, but, uncomfortable with their notoriety, he soon distanced himself from them.[24]

Exaggerated claims and historiographical muddle aside, Woodhull and Claflin were the first women ever to operate as stockbrokers, and contemporaries recognized this as an extraordinary milestone. For several weeks in early 1870, the press provided extensive and extravagant coverage of the "lady brokers." The first substantial story about Woodhull and Claflin appeared in the *New York Herald* on January 22, 1870. A reporter interviewed "the Queens of Finance" and "Future Princesses of Erie" at the Hoffman House hotel on Madison Square Park, where they had their office. He immediately observed that the office looked like a "ladies' drawing room" with its piano, soft furniture, oil paintings and statuary.[25] After concluding his interview, the *Herald* reporter fantasized about "Women in Wall Street." The "speculative daughters of Eve" would surely lend charm and savoir faire to "the routine of the Stock Exchange," and "if *finesse* is woman's gift, why not finance also?"[26] The paper set the tone for most of the early press coverage. Not overtly hostile, but humorous and at times sarcastic. The lady brokers made good copy.

When the firm opened new offices at 44 Broad Street near the Stock Exchange on February 4, the streets of lower Manhattan were thronged with curious onlookers. As writer Matthew Hale Smith recalled, "All day long crowds were around the doors. Men flattened their noses against the plate glass, peeping in, and every imagined excuse was invented by parties who wanted to walk inside and look at the sights."[27] Many of the most famous financiers of Wall Street attended the opening, including Daniel Drew, Jay Cooke, and Rufus Hatch. Most of these men politely wished the women luck, but a few looked on "with skeptical faces" and "thought the ladies foolish."[28]

Not surprisingly, the press spilled much ink describing the personal appearance and wardrobes of the "Bewitching Brokers." On Valentine's Day 1870, the *New York Courier* gushed that "both have clear, decided, and excessively wide-awake blue eyes, delicately chiseled features and transparent complexions." Vicky was a sleek brunette, Tennie a buxom blonde. One day the sisters were spotted in matching purple velvet gowns; another day Tennessee's ensemble was described in loving detail. Even Susan B. Anthony, who was keen to cast the brokers as feminist role models, could not resist giving the readers of *The Revolution* a vivid description of Tennessee's stylish outfit: "a plain suit of marine blue cloth, trimmed with black astracan, astracan muff, and black velvet hat, with black feathers."[29]

Considering the depth of hostility eventually directed against Woodhull and Claflin, it is often forgotten that they initially received a fair amount of positive press, not all of it related to their appearance. The *New York Herald* saw them as "women of remarkable coolness and tact . . . capable of extraordinary endurance," while the *New York Sunday News* celebrated them as "accomplished, clever business women, full of necessary pluck and determination." *The World* noted that the sisters "talked financial matters intelligently" and "seemed thoroughly posted on all points." A Philadelphia reporter who was predisposed to mock Victoria and Tennessee was surprised to find "two ladies who are quick, active, energetic, yet womanly, moving rapidly, giving their orders decidedly but calmly, and receiving their many guests, both business and private, with perfect ease and without either confusion or hurry."[30]

Initially, the most hostile—and raciest—coverage came from *The Day's Doings*, a "sporting" paper that treated Woodhull and Claflin as fast women, little better than prostitutes. The paper printed images of them in preposterously short skirts, in languid poses, and surrounded by men with leering and lecherous expressions.[31] *The Day's Doings* provided a heady mix of sports coverage, ribald humor, and sexual scandal that appealed to the hordes of single young men who worked in New York's commercial and financial sectors, lived in boardinghouses, and congregated after hours in saloons, brothels, and casinos and at racetracks. These so-called sporting men cultivated a flashy dress and an aggressive masculinity at odds with the prescribed morality of domestic middle-class churchgoing culture.[32]

The sporting men among the young brokers and clerks of Wall Street gave Woodhull, Claflin & Company a boisterous welcome to the financial district. The *Herald* reported on "flashy young men" who caused "considerable commotion" by barging into the firm and behaving in a disruptive manner. The *Albion* noted that many visitors "proved themselves to be anything but gentlemen"—they "molested" and "insulted" the women "in their own offices." The *New York Times* provided more details about the "disgraceful" scenes enacted by the sporting men: "Insulting remarks and shameful allusions were carried to the ears of the women . . . by the throng that curiously examined everything in the offices, and who sang and whistled after the fashion of the Bowery pit." The tumultuous crowds of rude young men were intent on asserting their control over the exclusively male preserve of Wall Street.[33]

Some brokers and reporters were charmed by Woodhull and Claflin and, for a while, adopted them as "pets," while others were skeptical or openly hostile. Most onlookers, however, treated the women as an amusing diversion, not to be taken very seriously. Some suggested that Vanderbilt had set up a couple of women brokers as a joke against his male colleagues. The New York *Evening Telegram* commemorated the new firm with a front-page cartoon depicting the sisters driving a chariot pulled by bulls and bears, with the faces of Vanderbilt and Fisk, over the bodies of hapless investors.

The press was quick to note the presence of women visitors to 44 Broad Street. According to the *Herald*, "the street was surprised to observe a number of carriages with ladies roll up to the door of Mrs. Woodhull's office and enter the private room in the rear, where the divinities of finance presided." Apparently "a regular stream" of women customers arrived, representing "the highest and wealthiest in the city. They wanted to make deposits of money and to give orders for the buying and selling of shares."[34] Some men were uneasy about the female invasion of Wall Street, their discomfort expressed in facetious descriptions of Woodhull and Claflin's new customers:

Figure 8. "The Wall Street Hippodrome," *New York Evening Telegram*, February 18, 1870. (Courtesy of the New York Public Library)

> Spinsters, elderly and sedate, with a large experience of the world, but with a little larger suspicion of its monetary transactions, and with longer purses, still come to learn how they may turn their moneys, which have not practically been bearing any interest, to the best account. Blondes, fair and fresh as pippins, entered with a rich twinkle of humor in their eyes, but bewitched by curiosity, and afterwards delighted with all they saw and heard, left the premises bethinking themselves that there were other things to live for besides cosmetics, the toilet, fashion and vanity.[35]

Even as they mocked the "handsome adventuresses" and their women clients, writers acknowledged that the sisters had tapped into vast reserves of female capital.

Women's-rights activists immediately saw the advent of Woodhull, Claflin & Company as "an augury of better times to come for women—times when they shall vote the right to put food into their mouths, and money into their pockets, without asking men's leave." Since women's economic dependence had long been used to justify women's exclusion from civil society, women's-rights advocates realized that female economic achievement could pave the way to political rights. In March 1870, Susan B. Anthony published an interview with Tennessee Claflin in *The Revolution*, celebrating the "working woman." Anthony believed that "the advent of this *woman* firm in Wall street marks a new era" when women could "be at the head of a banking institution, surrounded by ledgers, high stools, and those evidences of masculine superiority that men have plumed themselves upon so long." Claflin agreed that economic independence would free women from exploitation, and being a broker was far "better than sewing drawers at ten cents a pair, or teaching music at ten dollars a quarter."[36]

Despite their initial enthusiasm, it does not appear that Woodhull and Claflin spent much time at the brokerage business. From the beginning they hired experienced workers—a manager "who will do all their buying and selling" and clerks "to attend to the office duties, the ladies exercising the general supervision over everything." After the first heady rush of business, Woodhull's husband, James Blood, oversaw the day-to-day operation of the firm.[37] The sisters had bigger fish to fry; their energies were channeled into running a newspaper, leading political campaigns, and launching careers as public speakers. Woodhull's interest in stockbroking may also have waned as her political views became more radical and even hostile to the moneyed interests represented on Wall Street. As Miriam Brody points out, there was an incompatibility in Woodhull's role as broker, where she speculated in gold, and her role as progressive journalist and speaker, where she advocated a greenback currency that would devalue gold.[38] After the collapse of the brokerage firm in 1873, Woodhull insisted that "it was never intended that we should remain permanently in Wall Street." She and Tennessee had merely apprenticed as brokers "to know the secrets of money that had heretofore been a male preserve."[39]

It is also unclear whether Woodhull, Claflin & Company was ever financially successful. Woodhull's biographers have long maintained that the firm was highly profitable and closed its doors in 1873 only when Vanderbilt, distressed by the sisters' radical views, withdrew his support.[40] There is, in fact, scant evidence to sustain this version of events. Vanderbilt probably had little to do with the firm, and even if he helped launch it, within months of its opening he publicly disavowed any business links between himself and the sisters.[41] Vanderbilt's repudiation may have dampened enthusiasm for the lady brokers. An embarrassing series of lawsuits by creditors and disgruntled women investors also undermined their reputation for wealth and business acumen.[42] The firm puttered along for a couple years, probably sustained by the lingering momentum from its spectacular opening, by Woodhull and Claflin's fame, and by a generally buoyant economy. While the famous credit-rating firm R. G. Dun & Company attributed the sisters' failure to the "peculiarity of their position, their manner of doing business and the general unfavorable opinion of them," the demise of Woodhull, Claflin & Company probably owed more to the financial downturn that culminated in the Panic of 1873.[43]

However brief, perfunctory, and ultimately unsuccessful Woodhull and Claflin's brokerage career proved to be, it remains an important watershed in women's history. Years afterward, when Woodhull had repudiated her political and sexual radicalism, she remained proud of her financial legacy: "When I first came to Wall Street not one hundred women in the whole of the United States owned stocks or dared to show independence in property ownership . . . For a woman to consider a financial question was shuddered over as a profanity."[44] While Woodhull clearly underestimated American women's stockholdings in 1870, she did not exaggerate the disgust directed at women like herself and her sister who "considered financial questions." As Susan Yohn has recently argued, Woodhull and Claflin's brokerage business was significant "because it drew a public response that highlighted the clubbishness of Wall Street, an arena where men had little interest in admitting women and where those women who did seek entrance could expect to have their reputation and morals questioned."[45]

Woodhull's Critique of High Finance

In May 1870, within four months of opening their stockbroking business, Victoria and Tennessee launched a newspaper, *Woodhull and Claflin's Weekly*, under the motto "Upward and Onward," later amended to the more radical "Progress! Free Thought! Untrammeled Lives!" The paper, initially conceived as a vehicle for promoting Woodhull's 1872 presidential bid, lasted for six years and came to espouse a number of progressive issues and causes, such as women's suffrage, spiritualism, political reform, socialism, and free love. The paper, like its women's-rights predecessor *The Revolution*, also contained a great deal of economic and financial coverage, though this aspect of its mission has been underappreciated by Woodhull's biographers and by historians of the women's-rights movement.[46]

The *Weekly* contained regular columns on "Finance" and "Labor and Capital" and was especially sensitive to the economic situation of women. The paper frequently included stories about notable business achievements by women. On July 23, 1870, for instance, it reported on a tea company and an advertising firm that were run entirely by women. Woodhull and Claflin repeatedly emphasized the importance of women being able to earn money. Economic opportunity would liberate poor women from prostitution and middle-class women from loveless marriages. A July 1870 article on "The Social Evil" argued, "Give women employment and you remove from her the need of self-destruction." Two months later the paper editorialized: "We hope all our girls and women will soon be educated up to the standard of preferring the glorious freedom of self-support . . . *She who marries for support, and not for love, is a lazy pauper, coward and prostitute*."[47]

The *Weekly*'s most profound financial achievement was the systematic exposure of corporate fraud and crooked stock exchange deals. From the summer of 1870 to the fall of 1871, a generation before the advent of muckraking journalism, the paper devoted considerable space to detailing financial fraud. Woodhull was extremely proud of this legacy, later boasting: "We exposed in our *Weekly*, one nefarious scheme after another when we realized that companies were floated to work mines that did not exist, or that, if they did exist, had nothing in them, and to make railways to nowhere in particular, and that banks and insurance societies flourished by devouring their shareholders' capital."[48] Woodhull's brief career as a broker had opened her eyes to a great deal of sharp practice.

Among the *Weekly*'s numerous stories about white-collar crime were general articles titled "The Outrages of Corporations," "How Wall Street Stocks Are Manufactured," "The Results of Watered Shares and Bonds," and "Financial Swindling—Bogus Bankers and Brokers." Other pieces detailed specific scandals, such as the over-issue of stock by the Baltimore & Ohio Railroad, the overvaluation of bonds by the Indianapolis, Bloomington & Western Railroad, and the fraudulent collapse of the Farmers' & Mechanics' Life Insurance Company. The paper frequently highlighted how women were victimized by heartless corporations. On March 4, 1871, the *Weekly* concluded that the decline in trading on Wall Street had developed because "the public has at last discovered the folly of playing against loaded dice. It has finally realized that stocks are now in the hands of cliques who manipulate them without the slightest regard to their actual value."[49]

Interestingly, given the *Weekly*'s anticapitalist bent, bankers and stockbrokers advertised heavily in the paper. A typical issue from 1872 included advertisements from the New York Savings Bank, Caldwell Bankers, and the Loaners' Bank. Prominent brokerage houses such as Fisk & Hatch, Barton & Allen, and Henry Clews & Company also advertised their services.[50] Whether or not these financiers cared for Woodhull's attacks on corporate America, they must have valued the exposure their ads received. Their patronage also suggests that bankers and brokers were eager to attract women customers.

Woodhull's economic radicalism was not confined to the pages of the *Weekly*. In the summer of 1871 she joined Section 12 of the International

Workingman's Association (IWA, Marx's First International). On August 12, the *Weekly* published an interview with Karl Marx. The paper supported the Paris Commune, and on December 17, 1871, Woodhull and Claflin paraded with the IWA in New York in honor of the martyred French Communards. On December 30, the *Weekly* published the first English-language translation of *The Communist Manifesto* in the United States. Woodhull and her supporters formed the People's Party, which championed the American proletariat—"the mechanic, the farmer and the laborer"—against a capitalist cabal of "money-lenders, land grabbers, rings and lobbies."[51]

At this time, Woodhull's public speeches also took on a more inflammatory tone. On May 8, 1871, she addressed the Labor Reform League in New York on "The Great Social Problem of Labor and Capital," denouncing the great railroad companies as corrupt monopolies.[52] On February 20, 1872, Woodhull delivered her "Impending Revolution" speech at the Academy of Music in New York, in which she condemned American finance capitalism as an immense fraud. Woodhull, who at the time still operated a brokerage business, proposed abolishing all stock gambling, "by which gigantic swindlers corner a stock and take it in at their own figures."[53] Her old friend the Commodore was singled out for criticism:

> A Vanderbilt may sit in his office and manipulate stocks, or make dividends by which, in a few years, he amasses fifty million dollars from the industries of the country, and he is one of the remarkable men of the age. But if a poor, half-starved child were to take a loaf of bread from his cupboard to prevent starvation, she would be sent first to the Tombs and thence to Blackwell's Island . . . It is a crime for a single person to steal a dollar, but a corporation may steal millions of dollars and be canonized as saints . . . Is there common justice in such a state of things?[54]

Woodhull accused her Wall Street colleagues of building immense fortunes through dishonest financial manipulations. They had "filched" the nation's wealth, which she said should be returned to the people "by legal means if possible, but it must be returned to them in any event."[55]

Victoria Woodhull's socialist rhetoric and her journalistic exposés of the sleazy workings of corporate finance alienated much of the business community and mainstream press, which had previously received her with some degree of respect, or at least tolerance. Now the gloves were off, and in the spring of 1872, Woodhull and her sister were subject to a barrage of attacks. The *New York Times*, in its review of the "Impending Revolution" speech, accused Woodhull of fomenting class warfare by "inflaming the unthinking hostility of the poor to the rich." While the paper condemned Woodhull's radicalism, it also sought to brand her as an immoral woman, cattily remarking that "Mrs.

Victoria C. Woodhull has been married rather more extensively than most American matrons, and hence it might be deemed inappropriate to style her a foolish virgin."[56] This rhetorical strategy now dominated press attacks against Woodhull. Her political and economic views were discredited not on their merits, but on account of her sexual reputation.

Some of Woodhull's detractors had always seen her as a fast woman, but this was never the prevailing view before 1872. Now the "bewitching broker" and "fascinating financier" was "a shameless prostitute." In a famous cartoon in *Harper's Weekly*, Thomas Nast depicted Woodhull as "Mrs. Satan," with horns, cloven hoof, and taloned wings, tempting women to abandon their families and follow the primrose path of free love.[57] The *Cleveland Leader* denounced Woodhull as "a brazen snaky adventuress." Her "brazen immodesty as a stock speculator on Wall Street" and as a presidential candidate clearly indicated that she was "a vain, immodest, unsexed woman."[58] When Woodhull addressed a gathering of spiritualists in Vineland, New Jersey, the *New York Herald* referred to it as "a witches' Sabbath." An Iowa minister called Woodhull a "hag from Hell."[59] The line between *bewitching* and *witch* proved especially thin.

Woodhull's divorce was cited as evidence of her immorality, as were revelations about her unorthodox household: she was living with both her current and former husbands! Victoria's first husband, Canning Woodhull, a homeless alcoholic, turned up on her doorstep, and she took him in out of pity. Her act of charity was now recast as lasciviousness and her family characterized as a polyandrous ménage.[60] Alarming rumors spread that Woodhull, Claflin & Company profited from secret information supplied them by prostitutes and mistresses of the city's leading businessmen. Allegations that Woodhull supported and practiced "free love" only confirmed presumed links between businesswomen and sexual impropriety.[61]

To its Victorian advocates, "free love" usually meant that women should be economically independent and therefore free to choose their husbands on the basis of love, respect, and compatibility, not financial necessity. Men and women should also be free to end unhappy marriages and initiate new, loving unions.[62] Conservatives, however, associated free love with sexual license and promiscuity. In a November 20, 1871, speech on "The Principles of Social Freedom," Woodhull had proclaimed: "Yes, I am a free lover. I have an inalienable, constitutional and natural right to love whom I may, to love as long or short a period as I can; to change that love every day if I please, and with that right neither you nor any law you can frame have any right to interfere."[63] The phrase "to change that love every day if I please" was later used by her enemies as evidence of Woodhull's depravity. As Lois Underhill points out, "the most intensely negative response to Woodhull's free love views appeared after her communist speech."[64] By dredging up lines from old speeches and embarrassing details about Woodhull's personal life, her foes could more easily invalidate her radical politics and her attack on high finance.

In March 1872, the *New York Times* declared Woodhull's stockbroking business a sham, which she managed to keep going only by soliciting money from male brokers in a brazen, flirtatious manner. She was never really a businesswoman, the *Times* now revealed, merely a flirt.[65] The *Times* predicted the death of Woodhull and Claflin's brokerage firm and newspaper, since reputable men would shun women who "combine flirtation with business" and "gain business favors in exchange for familiarities too freely given to be attractive."[66] As attacks on the sisters' sexual reputations mounted, their business certainly suffered. By the summer of 1872, they were broke. The *Weekly* suspended publication in June, and in July Woodhull and Claflin were homeless, unable to meet the rent on their townhouse.[67]

The sisters were the victims of a sexual double standard, but the only people upset by this were themselves and some of their friends within the women's-rights movement. *The Revolution* mocked the very idea that financiers shunned Woodhull and Claflin for alleged impropriety. "Angels and ministers of grace defend us! What wave of morality has swept over Wall Street just at this time? Would it be impossible to find a *man* in that immaculate quarter, against whom some whisper of irregular practices might have been heard?"[68] In a letter to fellow suffragist Lucretia Mott, Elizabeth Cady Stanton declared, "we have had enough women sacrificed to this sentimental, hypocritical prating about purity. This is one of man's most effective engines for our division and subjugation."[69]

Finally, her back against the wall, Woodhull sought to turn the tables on her persecutors by exposing the sexual secrets of supposedly respectable public figures—a minister and a stockbroker. She resumed publication of *Woodhull and Claflin's Weekly* on November 2, 1872, with a detailed account of an adulterous affair between the Reverend Henry Ward Beecher, one of the nation's most celebrated ministers, and Elizabeth Tilton, a member of Beecher's Brooklyn congregation and the wife of the popular journalist Theodore Tilton.[70] The story, which was certainly true and an open secret in New York society, precipitated an enormous public scandal and successfully resurrected the *Weekly*. The Beecher exposé was coupled with a lurid story by Tennessee detailing the seduction of a young woman by Luther Challis, a well-known Wall Street broker. Challis allegedly plied the woman with drink and then took her to a house of prostitution, where he raped her.[71] Woodhull sought to hold men like Beecher and Challis to the same code of behavior they used to denounce her, but this strategy proved a dismal failure and gave her enemies further ammunition to destroy her.

Most commentators condemned Woodhull and Claflin for publicizing scandalous gossip, further cementing their reputations as lewd women. Challis sued the sisters for libel. The moral-purity crusader Anthony Comstock prosecuted them for violating a new federal law against sending obscene matter through the mails, since the *Weekly* was sent to subscribers by post and the November 2 edition was deemed pornographic by many.[72] Woodhull and Claflin spent weeks in prison, trying to raise bail, and the cases against them dragged on for years. In June 1873, Woodhull and Claflin were found not guilty in the federal obscenity trial on the technical grounds that the 1872 postal law applied only to obscene books and pamphlets, not newspapers.[73]

The Challis libel case came to trial only in March 1874, and, as in the Comstock case, the prosecuting lawyer spent much of his time on questions irrelevant to the case, attempting to paint Woodhull as an immoral woman. He asked "whether she believed a woman should leave her husband and live with another man, if prompted by such a desire." His examination went into Woodhull's divorce from Canning Woodhull and her relations with Colonel Blood. The judge, clearly hostile to Woodhull and Claflin, delivered impromptu moral lectures and was apoplectic when the sisters were acquitted: "It is the most outrageous verdict ever recorded; it is shameful and infamous, and I am ashamed of the jury who rendered such a verdict."[74] However immoral the sisters may have appeared to the court, the reputation of a stockbroker like Challis was not much better, and the jury probably had little difficulty imagining him as a seducer of virgins.

Woodhull and Claflin had won their cases, but they were psychologically bruised and financially spent, with their reputations in tatters. Their brokerage house had closed in 1873. The *Weekly* dragged on for a couple of years, before shutting down in 1876.[75] Bankers and brokers had stopped advertising in the paper, though clairvoyants and magnetic healers continued to do so. Woodhull attempted to restore her finances and her good name through a series of lecture tours in western states from 1873 to 1876. In the aftermath of the 1873 financial crisis, audiences were receptive to her condemnation of Wall Street and the eastern moneyed interests.[76] In 1877, Victoria and Tennessee traveled to England in search of new audiences, settling there permanently.[77]

With the failure of Woodhull, Claflin & Company and the sisters' departure abroad, Wall Street breathed a sigh of relief. Brokers and financial writers were eager to draw conclusions about the natural incapacity of women with regard to financial matters. The broker William Worthington Fowler saw the dissolution of "the feminine firm" as "evidence how unsuited to woman's nature is such a field of enterprise."[78] Fowler's stock-exchange colleague Henry Clews agreed that the failure of Woodhull, Claflin & Company proved "that women are not qualified by nature for the speculative and financial operations in which so many men have made their mark." If someone as clever as Woodhull could not succeed in Wall Street, "where will the ordinary female be found when she essays the role of an operator?" Clews snidely remarked that Woodhull's only successful "investment" was in marrying a wealthy English banker, her third husband, John Biddulph Martin: "It is probably only in the matrimonial line that women can be successful speculators."[79] As he consigned Woodhull to financial oblivion, Clews failed to note that his firm had advertised in her newspaper for years.

The Claflin sisters not only exemplified women's financial incapacity in the eyes of conservatives, but also the association of businesswomen with sexual impropriety. In his 1875 guidebook to Wall Street, Matthew Hale Smith cemented Victoria and Tennessee's reputations as moral reprobates. The whole arrangement of their firm seemed "queer" to him. They projected "a bold, resolute and mannish air" but dressed "in the high style of Broadway promenaders" (i.e., prostitutes). An illustration in Smith's book, titled "Female Brokers Securing a Customer," underscored the link between women financiers and sexual excess.[80] The cartoon, clearly meant to depict Woodhull and Claflin, shows two women in extravagant dress, flirting with a man in their office. He sits between them; one strokes his arm, and the other leans against him, playing with his whiskers. A champagne bottle and glasses sit on a nearby table. The scene looks like something from a fancy brothel; the

Figure 9. "Female Brokers Securing a Customer," Matthew Hale Smith, *Bulls and Bears of New York* (Hartford, CT: J. B. Burr, 1875): 273. (Courtesy of the New York Historical Society)

"bewitching brokers" were little better than whores, enticing men to part with their money through the employment of feminine wiles. Only fast women, like Victoria and Tennessee, would be attracted to the life of speculation and the sordid struggle of the marketplace.

A Bastion of Male Privilege

Woodhull and Claflin had breached the exclusive fraternity of Wall Street, but not for long. During their brief sojourn on the Street, they had exposed its clubbish atmosphere and misogynist high jinks. The macho atmosphere of the stock exchange endured for decades afterward, creating a hostile environment for women. Many brokers' offices replicated the masculine ambience of saloons, with free cigars, free lunches, and paintings of naked women.[81] Brokers did not have reputations as staid businessmen, like bankers, but as "sporting gentlemen." According to Cedric Cowing, "the typical broker was pictured as pleasure-seeking and crafty, a nervous dandy with watery eyes and muddy complexion; he was not the type that made a good family man, nor the type an American mother would want her son to become."[82] One Wall Street guide from 1887 described brokers as "jolly, frisky and sportive as so many colts." Like fraternity brothers, they established aggressive hazing rituals for new members. "His $10 silk hat may be knocked off and kicked into complete collapse; his $40 coat may be torn down the back . . . he may be hoisted on a table and spun around on his sit-down until drunk with confusion."[83]

The macho atmosphere of Wall Street was receptive to neither women nor sensitive men. Woodhull and Claflin experienced the "rough music" of the Street's young brokers and clerks. In 1869, Susan B. Anthony noted the aggressive stares directed at any women, except elderly apple sellers, who ventured into the financial district. In 1887, Sophia Mattern was set upon in the street and hooted by office boys when she sued her broker for malfeasance.[84] During his 1882 lecture tour of America, the British aesthete Oscar Wilde also received a raucous welcome on Wall Street. Wilde was already notorious for his effeminate demeanor, which attracted the notice of the financial district's messenger boys. According to the *New York Times*, "Oscar looked his sweetest" with "flowing tresses" and "rainbow stockings tucked into dapper knee-breeches." The rowdy boys "crowded close around the aesthete and did him honor after a fashion which brought new horrors to his sensitive nature and affecting blushes to his cleanly cheek." Taking refuge in the nearby Stock Exchange, Wilde was immediately set upon by the brokers, who sought to send "their visitor forth to the world, hatless, coatless, and in a generally dilapidated condition." The

Times celebrated the brokers and messenger boys marking their territory by driving out the womanly man.[85]

Feminists denounced Wall Street as the embodiment of male sexual excess, and brokers and financiers seldom contradicted them. Many Wall Street men embraced the sporting lifestyle and self-image of playboy. At the turn of the century, a group of New York financiers contributed money to maintain a "house of mirth" where chorus girls and prostitutes entertained businessmen and politicians. Legendary financiers like Cornelius Vanderbilt, Jim Fisk, and August Belmont flaunted their womanizing, which was accepted by their many admirers as just another part of their oversize, aggressive personalities. According to Steve Fraser, "sexual prowess, whether real or imagined, became an enduring part of the mythos of the Wall Street titan."[86]

Little wonder that Woodhull and Claflin found their reputations in tatters after a brief spell on the Street. Given the strong association of speculation with sexual impropriety, the sisters' detractors found it fatally easy to brand them prostitutes, set up as brokers by Vanderbilt in exchange for sexual favors, or sirens, luring men to invest money through their seductive airs. For decades afterward, women investors and speculators were frequently depicted as sexual adventuresses and thrill seekers. In 1882 the *New York Times* reported on a supposedly new phenomenon of attractive young women, some of them "painted," besieging Wall Street offices and wheedling stock tips from brokers, who found it difficult "to refuse advice to a pretty woman." Apparently the opera singer Emma Abbott and the actress Sarah Bernhardt had bewitched brokers to part with secrets "which the ordinary man could not discover in a life time."[87]

The scandals that drove Victoria Woodhull out of business and out of the country cast a long shadow over other women's attempts to operate as brokers. An 1870 cartoon from *Punchinello* depicted a career in Wall Street as incompatible with a woman's domestic responsibilities. A "Lady Broker" is unable to "attend to business," as she is too busy minding her baby. The exposure of Marion Dow, the "lady broker" of Philadelphia, as a huckster in the 1880s only confirmed the chauvinist prejudice against women stockbrokers (see Chapter 3). Women who tried to earn their living selling securities risked being labeled indecent and/or fraudulent.

When Mrs. M. E. Favor opened the Uptown Stock Exchange on West Twenty-Fourth Street in 1880, established brokers and financial commentators treated her with great suspicion. Favor's newspaper advertisements and circulars, sent to "prominent ladies" inviting them to entrust their money to "a lady of standing who had a long and successful experience in stock speculation," were condemned as lures to trap unsophisticated women. One businessman feared that the ads would entice "many a woman to pledge her diamonds, or to compromise her settlements or her husband's financial standing, with the vague promise of a fortune thus held out to her." Favor responded that her circular was no different from those routinely distributed by male brokers, that her transactions "were conducted upon strictly business principles," and that she provided a valuable service to women investors who were otherwise at a disadvantage, "because their facilities for information were not equal to those of men."[88]

Another woman, Mary Gage, also opened a brokerage business for women in 1880 that was championed by the women's-rights movement. Gage, the daughter of prominent suffragist Frances Dana Gage, had previously been employed as a clerk for the Equal Rights Association and the U.S. Treasury Office in New York City. Mary Gage established her "ladies' exchange for railroad and mining stocks" at 71 Broadway in lower Manhattan because she had personally experienced "much inconvenience and annoyance in transacting her own operation" with male brokers. According to the official *History of Woman Suffrage* (1886), "after Miss Gage was fairly settled, other women who had labored under the same disadvantages, began to drop in, their numbers increasing daily." That Gage was clearly following the example and mission of Victoria Woodhull was not mentioned, as the women's-rights movement had jettisoned Woodhull as a liability.[89]

In 1894 the *New York Herald* reported on an unnamed businesswoman from Chicago who had recently opened the "Ladies' Stock Parlors" on Broadway near Thirty-First Street, the only "stock broking establishment in New York kept by a woman." Other brokers derided the business, but the proprietor defended herself by arguing that there was "no place in Wall Street where a woman could comfortably watch the market," and she had therefore merely filled a need. The *Herald* could find no evidence of impropriety but nonetheless described the business as rather shabby and pathetic: "At the ticker sits an old woman, who calls out the quotations of stocks, which are marked on the blackboard by a wan little boy, who looks like a shadow from Brownieland. Here women sit in groups, with their luncheons done up in napkins, which they fetch rather than leave the charmed spot long enough to go out for and eat a square meal." In this enchanted atmosphere the women speculators had become so mesmerized by the stock ticker that they abandoned their homes and domestic responsibilities to "sit all day and watch the quotations."[90]

Other women who tried their hand at stockbroking also received a chilly reception. Such was the case of Sophronia Twitchell, a women's-rights activist turned businesswoman. She worked as an agent for the Equitable Life Insurance Company in San Francisco and speculated heavily, and successfully, in mining shares. She moved in 1880 to New York, where at the age of fifty she opened a business on lower Broadway as a broker in mining securities. Although she ran "a genuine stock business" and sometimes made "a great deal of money," she was very unpopular with male brokers. They may have resented her success, and they certainly resented her manner, which for a "lady of uncertain age" was unusually forthright and outspoken. She was a familiar figure on Wall Street, tall and energetic, hurrying along at an "unladylike" pace and barging into brokers' offices, where she was not always welcome. Once, when a businessman ordered her out of his office, she struck him with her umbrella and was arrested for assault.[91]

Twitchell's combination of brokerage with suffrage agitation no doubt reminded some people of Victoria Woodhull. Yet, while Woodhull was depicted as a beautiful siren seducing the likes of Vanderbilt out of stock tips, Twitchell was mocked as an outlandish old crone. She was described at different times as a "crazy crank," a "nuisance," a "human curio," and "the Galloping Cow from Frisco." In 1888 the *New Haven Register* provided a lengthy and unflattering portrait: "She is a woman almost six feet tall and very masculine in build and manner. Her hair is almost white and she is well along in years, but you see her rushing around at a lively pace in Wall Street in all sorts of weather, looking for tips and watching an opportunity to play the market to her advantage."[92]

The *Harrisburg Patriot* described her as "tall, fat and fifty . . . She dresses in wretched taste, wears an old-fashioned shawl and a bonnet that would give a woman of taste the hysterics. She is loud spoken and positive, and an intrepid advocate of woman's rights."[93] Twitchell was clearly an intimidating and bewildering presence, and businessmen didn't know how to deal with her. They tried variously to freeze her out and to discredit her as an unwomanly freak.

Another eccentric, but decidedly more glamorous, broker was Marie Antoinette Nathalie Pollard, a Virginia woman who for many years combined an interest in stock speculation with public performance. She had been arrested by the Confederacy for buying federal money during the Civil War and later pieced together a living by lecturing, acting, and speculating in the stock market. Constantly on the move, she speculated in "wildcat" mining stock in California and "pestered" Cornelius Vanderbilt for stock tips in New York. She later lived in Washington, DC, where she frequently appeared onstage as an elocutionist or in the character of Princess Mui Qui, "the educated Chinese lady." Frequently described as beautiful and accomplished, Pollard clearly had a flair for the dramatic gesture, as when she shot a druggist for leading her husband to "bad habits."[94]

In 1890, Pollard, now a widow, returned to New York, where she opened an "attractively fitted up" brokerage office "for the accommodation of ladies who want to deal in stocks." She claimed to have several customers, many of whom preferred to "speculate on the quiet" since their husbands objected to this behavior. Never one to do things by halves, Pollard also announced her intention to apply for a seat on the Consolidated Stock Exchange, which would make her "the first woman in the world to become a member of a stock exchange." If the application was ever made, it was not successful. Nor was Pollard's brokerage business long-lived, as she was performing her Chinese princess act again in 1892.[95]

Press accounts of eccentric and marginal Wall Street characters like Marie Antoinette Pollard and Sophronia Twitchell reinforced conventional views of women's financial incapacity and may have discouraged other women from seeking employment as brokers. The very idea of a female stockbroker was treated with derision or as a joke. William Fowler was appalled at the prospect of women stockbrokers, since this would require the gentle sex to "change her tender heart into stone" and to "crush out her human sympathies with the unfortunate and the distressed," a sad comment on his own profession.[96] In 1898, when Tennessee Claflin (now Lady Cook, living in London and married to a baronet) announced that she was organizing England's first female brokerage business, the press treated it as a pathetic joke—history repeating itself as farce—a far cry from the furor she and her sister aroused in 1870.[97]

Feminist Financial Principles

Suffragists and feminists maintained an ambivalent relationship with Wall Street and the capitalist investment economy generally. They criticized the American financial system for its ruthless, dog-eat-dog ethos, but they realized that women could not and should not shun the marketplace, as conservative proponents of separate-spheres ideology insisted. The financial sector was an important source of employment and wealth to which women needed greater access. Hence Susan B. Anthony's initial celebration of the Claflin sisters' storming of Wall Street. Many middle-class women, barred from the professions and other lucrative means of employment, were especially dependent on investment income but had little influence over the workings of the nation's economy or the management of their own property. The government's monetary and banking policies affected prices and the availability of credit, and thus had a huge impact on household budgets and domestic economy. Women could not vote and therefore had limited ability to influence legislation that might regulate monetary policy, curtail corrupt financial practices, and end the corporate secrecy that left them especially vulnerable as passive investors. Married women also labored under legal disabilities that continued to hamper their active management of their own money. Progressive women thus pushed for greater legal equality and corporate disclosure, and they advocated distinct financial policies to reform the nation's currency and diminish the influence of big business and big banks.

At the national level, women's-rights activists in the post–Civil War era usually allied themselves with populist and agrarian parties that favored an anti-monopolist alternative to the rise of corporate capitalism. Elizabeth Cady Stanton and Victoria Woodhull spoke out against the gold standard and national banks for favoring creditors, industry, and the urban Northeast over debtors, farmers, and the West.

The popular postwar financial scheme favored by suffragists and other progressives was a government bond paying 3% interest and "interconvertible" with federally issued paper currency, or "greenbacks." It was believed that these bonds would prevent inflation and stabilize interest rates. If too much money was in circulation, then interest rates would fall below the bond rate and people would convert their greenbacks to bonds. Were interest rates to exceed 3% due to a shortage of money, people would redeem their bonds for greenbacks and more money would become available for loans. This scheme was meant to promote a decentralized and sectionally balanced economy in which the public rather than New York banks controlled interest rates and the money supply.[98] Susan B. Anthony and Elizabeth Cady Stanton supported interconvertible bonds and greenbacks in the pages of *The Revolution* and elsewhere.[99] They envisioned women as beneficiaries of a more populist financial system that promoted cheap money and easy credit.

Women's lack of access to credit was dramatized on those occasions when suffragists attempted to use financial instruments to advance their own agendas. In 1872, Victoria Woodhull issued non-interest-bearing bonds to finance her presidential campaign. The bonds, which bore Woodhull's name and an image of the goddess of liberty, were printed on high-quality banknote paper and would be redeemable when the Equal Rights Party was in power. Unsurprisingly, Woodhull's former associates on Wall Street were not enthusiastic, and the bonds did not sell.[100] In 1886 the lawyer and suffragist Belva Lockwood sought to raise money for her own political ambitions by issuing shares in the Lockwood Improvement Syndicate, also without success.[101]

Further reform of married women's property law was another financial issue widely advocated by the women's-rights movement in the years following the Civil War. Like access to credit, it was an issue that directly impinged on women's individual autonomy. The Kentuckian Mary Clay told the 1884 convention of the American Woman Suffrage Association that she recommended "to the Southern women particularly the petitioning of property rights, because pecuniary independence is one of the most potent weapons for freedom, and because that claim has less prejudice to overcome [than suffrage]."[102] Earlier laws had often reflected paternal concerns to protect daughters from profligate husbands or to preserve family property for the next generation of male heirs (see Introduction). Suffragists now sought to promote broader legislation that would allow married women to manage their own property, to keep their own wages, to engage in business without their husbands' consent, and to will their property to whom they pleased.

In 1879, Marietta Stow, a woman's-rights activist who had been cheated out of a substantial inheritance, put forth a bold plan for a federal "Equal Rights Marriage Property Act" that would have created a uniform national law of marital property, child custody, and estate management guaranteeing women half of household resources. Stow secured the support of Belva Lockwood, a pioneering female lawyer in Washington, D.C., and the first woman to plead a case before the Supreme Court. Lockwood and Stow then convinced a radical Indiana congressman and member of the Greenback Party, Gilbert De La Matyr, to sponsor their bill. No other members of the House favored federal intrusion in marriage law, hitherto the preserve of the states. Even a truncated version of the bill, which would apply only to the District of Columbia and the Territories, jurisdictions controlled by the federal government, died in committee. Lockwood and Stow continued to lobby for progressive causes, and in 1884 they ran for president and vice president on the Equal Rights Party ticket.[103]

Although by the 1880s most state legislatures had given married women control over their separate property, serious limitations remained. The new laws were not retroactive, so they applied only to property that wives acquired after their passage. Nor did they eliminate old attitudes, and many states maintained protective oversight of women. During the 1870s and 1880s, a number of states required a "privy examination" before a married woman could sell her property. In this procedure, she would be examined by a public official "to determine whether she understood the transaction and whether her husband had coerced her into it." The privy examination symbolized the state's belief that even as women "entered the world of business and commerce, they still needed special care and protection."[104]

Many women recognized that the new laws had not overturned coverture, but simply modified it. As Lelia Sawtelle pointed out in an 1891 article in the progressive journal *The Chautauquan*, "the new legislation has been in the nature of patches on the old common law garment, covering a hole here and piecing out there, improving usually by each change, but always working on the old foundation." Sawtelle employed a typically domestic metaphor in describing a bewildering patchwork of state laws.[105] She and other commentators at the century's end struggled to sort out the legal confusion. In Missouri, wives could control their personal property, but their real estate had to be held in trust. Rhode Island gave husbands the right to collect rents from their wives' property. Texas, Vermont, and Wisconsin forbade married women from carrying on businesses on their own. In Alabama and Michigan, wives could operate businesses, but only with their husbands' consent. In Idaho and Nevada, wives needed a license from a special court to run a business. In Pennsylvania and New Jersey, wives could borrow money themselves but could not stand as guarantors for other people's loans. In community-property states like Louisiana, California, and Arizona, whatever property the couple acquired after marriage was jointly owned but under the complete management of the husband. Kentucky, Tennessee, and Florida still gave husbands absolute control over wives' property, the only relief possible being a trust. In Georgia, husbands still controlled their wives' wages, and were to do so until 1943.[106] Women who worked for wages or ran small businesses remained longest under their husbands' financial supervision. Middle- and upper-class wives' ownership and control of financial securities was more secure, but their vulnerability to market volatility, financial panics, and financial fraud continued to bedevil them.

Feminist critiques of Wall Street and finance capitalism gained steam in the late nineteenth century, building on earlier attacks by the likes of Elizabeth Cady Stanton and Victoria Woodhull. As Robert McMath has explained in his history of American Populism: "Between the 1870s and the turn of the century, campaigns for temperance, woman suffrage, and economic reform were quite often blended into one righteous crusade that combined a distinctly romantic vision of womanhood with a hardheaded sense of political realities."[107] Women reformers and writers frequently questioned the achievements of corporate capitalism. In 1888, at a meeting of the International Council of Women, an umbrella organization for women's reform organizations, the temperance campaigner Zerelda Wallace exclaimed, "We hear a great deal about the growth of civilization. Dear friends, what is civilization? . . . Does it consist in your marble palaces? In your railroads; your electric lights; your telephones and telegraphs?" The material achievements of industrialism and high finance, Wallace insisted, were meaningless in a nation sunk in the vices of alcoholism, gambling, and prostitution, and where women and the poor were subject to a corrupt plutocracy of men.[108]

During the 1880s, Grace Courtland, a Wall Street investor turned public agitator, took up Victoria Woodhull's mantle as a financial insider exposing the corrupt practices of the robber barons. A colorful and eccentric character, now forgotten and about whom little evidence survives, Courtland, like Woodhull, had been a clairvoyant before becoming a stock market operator. In 1879 she was operating as a "mesmeric physician" in New York, but by 1880 she was advertising her services in the *Wall Street Daily News* as an investment advisor.[109] She audaciously dubbed herself "the Witch of Wall Street," glorying in her fearsome reputation as a troublemaker. Courtland had achieved considerable notoriety for horsewhipping a man in public for seducing her daughter, and she brought this same ferocity to bear in denouncing the monopolistic practices of Gould and Vanderbilt.[110]

In November 1881, Grace Courtland gave a speech in New York City called "The Kings of Wall Street," in which she blasted the nation's leading financiers, whose only desire was "to filch from the poor and to control the national finance for their own selfish ends." She described herself to an admiring audience as a woman who "has had the hardihood to venture among the Bulls and Bears," and she boasted "that the spirit of speculation runs through my veins." Since she had worked among the kings of Wall Street, Courtland claimed to know their secrets better than most. She warned that American democracy was at risk, as corporate monopolies were choking off free competition, and financiers escaped oversight by bribing politicians and journalists. She concluded that "corruption, financial, political and social, has fixed her deadly fangs on our national life." The speech was later published, and Courtland barnstormed the Midwest as "the mother of anti-monopoly," delivering her denunciation of Wall Street to receptive crowds.[111]

Some women contrasted an amoral, masculine world of business and finance with a moral, feminine sensibility that strived for justice and fair play. Caroline Walch's feminist novel *Doctor Sphinx* (1898), dedicated to Elizabeth Cady Stanton, exposed the sordid business practices of company promoters, as seen through the eyes of a young Wall Street stenographer, Colleen Mayner. One day, as Colleen is typing the prospectus for a company, she reads, "Capital, $3,000,000," and reacts with indignation. "What a falsehood! There is not a cent of capital in this company's treasury . . . It is bare-faced chicanery for men to send out such papers as these, to lure an innocent public into sinking more money into a bottomless pit." Men might have convinced themselves that marketing worthless securities was "a most desirable piece of business smartness . . . But Colleen, alas! was a woman . . . To her uncompromising conscience, a lying pretense was nothing more nor less than a lying pretense: no glittering possibilities could for a moment dazzle her into forgetfulness of the chicanery of such a system of financiering." The woman's perspective on business represents the interests of morality and moderation against masculine greed and intemperance.[112]

Writers espousing progressive and feminist points of view favored stronger and more independent women, but in making women the mouthpiece for moral attacks on high finance, they did not necessarily encourage women to embrace moneymaking. The case for women's economic empowerment was not made by the radical literature of the 1890s and 1900s, but by women's own dogged permeation of the workforce and by the obvious fact that many American women had money to invest. If they were to invest wisely and not foolishly, they needed to be better informed and educated regarding financial considerations.

Financial Education and Empowerment

During the late nineteenth and early twentieth centuries, greater numbers of journalists, writers, and public figures, many of them women's-rights advocates, spoke out in favor of better educating women regarding money and business. Unlike those conservative commentators who persisted in depicting women as incompetent money managers, progressives and feminists questioned whether women's financial ignorance was innate, or even desirable. They argued that a sheltered upbringing did not make women virtuous. It merely made them ignorant, weak, and vulnerable to all manner of fraud and chicanery. A practical business education and greater financial responsibility for women would in turn produce better wives, mothers, and citizens.

In 1871 the temperance reformer and women's-rights advocate Elizabeth Stuart Phelps lamented the traditional notion that women were too delicate and spiritual to be taught about economics. In an article in the progressive journal *The Independent,* she observed: "It is customary to urge the retention of women in a condition of pecuniary dependence upon men on the grounds that they are citizens of a higher country, heirs of a richer inheritance, wafted by spiritual tides above adaptation to a realm of the earth, earthy. Queens in the gardens of life, how shall they stoop to soil their fingers with filthy lucre? Used to gather lilies, how shall they handle 'greenbacks'?"[113]

Phelps dismissed the cultivation of economic ignorance among women as a dangerous "affectation," especially in a commercially developed nation like the United States. Without a proper understanding of political economy, banking, and investment, women were unable even to educate their children or advise their husbands.

Phelps further argued that women daily proved their business capacity through the vast amounts of money they raised for charity and through their ability to manage their households on tight budgets. "Does any one really think that even the wife of a country minister, who will educate a family of ten children on a salary of six hundred dollars, would be unable to keep her head straight at a broker's?" Women didn't lack "business qualities," according to Phelps, they lacked "business opportunities." Their financial dependence on men rendered them vulnerable to exploitation. The vote was certainly desirable, but what women really needed was for members of their own sex "to undertake the business of banking, of brokerage; to qualify themselves for the direction of railroads and mines." For so long as "men monopolize the conduct of trade they monopolize women."[114]

Women's-rights advocates saw economic empowerment as key to all manner of social and political reforms. Financial autonomy would lay the foundation to full citizenship. According to Ellen DuBois, activists believed that "work outside the home established women along with men as individuals whose labor contributed to the community's wealth."[115] Elizabeth Cady Stanton and Susan B. Anthony encouraged women to engage in all manner of commercial and professional occupations, arguing that as more women entered the paid workforce and enriched the nation through the payment of taxes, political rights would surely follow. In 1906, one newspaper saw the success of female financiers like Hetty Green and Ella Rawls Reader as harbingers of women's emancipation: "For, when the last word is spoken, money is power, and if women, when given the slightest opening, can make money as readily as men, her future standing—if she deliberately elects to descend from her pinnacle—is assured."[116]

While women's-rights activists like Phelps, Anthony, and Stanton welcomed women brokers and bankers, conservative commentators continued to focus on frauds and failures, like Sarah Howe in 1880, to make their case for women's financial incapacity.[117] However, a small but growing number of progressive voices now supported the arguments of women's-rights pioneers, countering the sexist assumptions of separate spheres. One observer of the Howe case, tired of the constant refrain about women's ignorance, retorted that it was "unfair and unhandsome to make such sweeping condemnations of a whole sex." If women were ignorant of basic commercial principles, it was because society had kept "them profoundly ignorant on the subject, the law not allowing them to do business on their own responsibility, and husbands usually keeping their wives from all knowledge of their money affairs." The *Woman's Journal* agreed with this position, arguing that "the fact that women could be so imposed upon is the direct result of that state of tutelage in which the great majority of men have gloried in having women held, and from which the woman's rights movement has sought to free them."[118]

An editorial from *Harper's Bazaar* in 1878, "Women and Money," condemned the prevailing view "that any degree of monetary understanding would unsex" women. The journal ridiculed men's unquestioned assumptions regarding "the dense and irremediable financial ignorance of women." Men took this supposed ignorance "as a self-evident truth, because they have always heard it so mentioned, and will continue to affirm it, for generations yet to come, for no better reason." The editor countered that "if women have no clear ideas of money, it is simply because every effort is made to preclude them from any and all intelligent acquaintance with the subject." Women's financial ignorance was entirely socially constructed and easily could be remedied with proper training. Almost any woman would "use money discreetly and profitably when she is treated like a rational being instead of like a wayward child."[119]

In 1888 the Chicago *Inter-Ocean* wrote favorably about a business school for women that was being organized in New York. The paper argued that female financial ignorance was hardly desirable and had already exposed too many women to fraud and chicanery: "In former times a woman was not expected to know the laws of wealth nor the practical rules of making and investing money; but now, after much sorrowful experience of losses caused by ignorance, a feeling is strengthening that it is not unwomanly to understand business principles, and not ungraceful to put these principles into practical use." The *Inter-Ocean* believed that all women could benefit from a better knowledge of "banking, book-keeping, and the laws of political economy." The paper still cautioned women against the stock market, for which they lacked "that peculiar kind of sharpness" necessary for speculation, but it saw much potential for women's investment in banking and real estate.[120]

The 1893 Chicago World's Fair featured a "Congress of Women" in which nationally prominent women celebrated the progress and achievements of American womanhood. A number of public lectures at the event highlighted women's accomplishments in business and finance, in particular their growing importance as investors and wage earners. Several speakers called for greater economic education and empowerment for women. Lydia Prescott, for one, warned that women's economic dependence on men would retard the moral progress of the nation, since "economic virtues" were impossible under an economic system that required "a lifelong and complete dependence of one half of the civilized world upon the other half."[121]

The late nineteenth century was a watershed moment for American women's access to higher education. In addition to the ubiquitous teacher-training programs, many colleges now offered business courses and academic study in "domestic economy." Far from being limited to cooking and sewing, home economics emphasized that the domestic household should be run like a business and conducted along scientific principles. In its emphasis on budgets, accounting, and the careful employment of resources, home economics encouraged women to think of themselves as managers and investors. In the hands of imaginative and progressive instructors, courses in domestic science could prepare women for careers in public health, nutrition, and business.[122] An emerging generation of educated women helped frame the larger discussion about women's economic independence.

Charlotte Perkins Gilman, a college graduate, feminist writer, and public intellectual, is a case in point. In her influential book *Women and Economics* (1898), Gilman insisted that women's economic liberation was necessary for the evolutionary progress of humanity.[123] Gilman's work was much indebted to Spencerian and Darwinian notions of progress and evolution, arguing that men were "thousands of years in advance of the female in economic status" and that women's financial ignorance and economic dependence "hinders and perverts the economic development of the world." Women, she wrote, have been denied "free productive expression" and kept in a "position of arrested development" through a perverted and "unnatural" educational and social regime.[124] Women's economic liberation was not only desirable, it was inevitable "under the forces of social evolution." Gilman could already see indications of a more developed social consciousness "in the increasing desire of young girls to be independent, to have a career of their own" and in "the growing objection of countless wives to the pitiful asking for money, to the beggary of their position." As more women entered the workforce and acquired "a separate bank account," the entire human race would advance.[125]

By the turn of the century, even mainstream journals were advocating women's economic education as a means of creating stronger and healthier families and of fostering general social improvement. In 1899, Frances Evans argued in the conservative *Ladies' Home Journal* that, at a time when women were entering the workforce in record numbers, it was a national disgrace that "they know as little about finance, domestic or national, as men do about nursing babies."[126] Women's magazines began featuring articles on business and investment. In March 1900, the *Woman's Home Companion* commissioned millionaire businesswoman Hetty Green to contribute an article on "The Benefits of a Business Training for Women." In 1910 the *Financial Review of Reviews* included a feature on "Women and Finance" by Louisa Creighton that outlined prudent financial strategies for female investors. In 1910, Houghton Mifflin published *Everyday Business for Women* by Mary Aronetta Wilbur, a teacher of banking and political economy at Miss Dana's School for Young Ladies in Morristown, New Jersey.[127]

Mary Wilbur wrote her guide to dispel women's economic ignorance, "which, more than their sex, is the cause of the unfortunate issue of the business affairs of so many women." Too often, Wilbur argued, young women were sheltered by their fathers, and, upon marriage, "domestic unhappiness often results," since they could not keep accounts. Husbands also failed to instruct their wives, who, when widowed, must "do business without knowing how—a most expensive way to learn." Her book featured simple instructions about banking, checking accounts, bookkeeping, mortgages, and stocks and bonds. Wilbur's own career and the popularity of her guide indicate both a growing interest among women in investment, and a declining social disapproval of women's financial activities.[128]

The increasing significance of businesswomen and female investors could no longer be denied. The number of women employed in trade, commerce, and finance had more than tripled between 1900 and 1930, rising from 297,966 to 962,680.[129] Women also owned significant amounts of the nation's bank deposits and shareholdings. During World War I, women's employment opportunities expanded dramatically, as did their ownership of financial securities in the form of war bonds.[130] Clearly, a great many American women had already proven their financial acumen.

By the 1920s, few people seriously questioned women's need for economic knowledge or their ability to handle money if properly educated.[131] Those men who still insisted on women's financial dependence now seemed cranky and antediluvian, like the writer Clarence Kelland, who joked in 1928 that all wives were "either tightwads or spendthrifts."[132] Kelland's remarks seemed left over from an earlier generation and now embroiled him in a public debate with a successful and self-confident woman, Emily Post, the author of the best-selling *Etiquette* (1922). In December 1928, the *American Magazine* published an exchange between Kelland and Post regarding women's ability to manage money.[133]

Kelland made his case in the hammy style of a vaudeville performer holding forth on the battle of the sexes. He joked that "shopping women are not astute persons—they are creatures in a frenzy" and that "women love pretty things, and men love pretty women, and women love to be the pretty women men love, and there you are." In the new era of easy credit, frivolous women were unable to restrain themselves and incapable of keeping proper accounts of their shopping binges. It just wasn't "in their nature." The result was husbands driven to distraction, their businesses crippled and their creditworthiness ruined. "A wife can go out and buy any dog-gone thing she can get, and charge it to her husband, and the poor wretch has to pay for it or go into bankruptcy. He is utterly helpless." The only relief for the poor husbands was to put women "under some sort of guardianship and protection to save them from themselves."[134]

Emily Post dismissed Kelland's article as "the plaint of an antiquated male" and characterized his suggestion that women be under guardianship as "too medieval even to answer." She reminded him "that a woman of today is a perfectly responsible, voting, and office-holding citizen. Why this fetish dragged from the Ark, that she be considered an irresponsible chattel?" Post countered Kelland's folksy anecdotes with hard facts she had attained from department stores and credit agencies. She noted that most women did not charge purchases to their husbands, but rather that "seventy to ninety percent of retail charge-account bills are paid with checks signed by women" from their own bank accounts. Post argued that the worst type of husband was "the 100 per cent he-man type" who "treats his wife as though she were a moron" rather than an equal partner fully capable of keeping the family solvent.[135]

Clarence Kelland was merely telling the same jokes about addlebrained women that men had been telling each other for decades. Now, however, this kind of humor seemed rather stale and dated. The large numbers of independent working women contradicted Kelland's sexist assumptions, and successful businesswomen were willing and able to defend themselves. Attitudes had certainly changed since the 1870s, when Victoria Woodhull tried to position herself as a financier and economic authority, only to be denounced as a sexual outlaw. By 1928, a feminist viewpoint regarding women's economic autonomy could be espoused by a respectable society matron and doyenne of etiquette like Emily Post.

*   *   *

In the early nineteenth century, when few American women worked outside the home, when women owned little property, and when they had little control over that property, it was easy to imagine business and investment as masculine phenomena. Since few Americans, male or female, owned stocks or bonds before the Civil War, Wall Street seemed remote from, even irrelevant to, most people's daily lives. By the late nineteenth century, however, profound economic and social developments had transformed the landscape. America was becoming a nation of investors, and this change included women in growing numbers. Women also swelled the ranks of wage earners, and new legislation now gave them greater control over their own property. As more women inherited wealth, entered the workforce, opened bank accounts, and bought government bonds and corporate securities, it became more difficult to endorse the conservative view that women couldn't or shouldn't invest their own money. It increasingly seemed sensible for women to be better informed about financial matters.

Women's-rights advocates pioneered campaigns for female economic autonomy and equal property rights. They realized that financial independence was key to personal freedom and could also lead to full political citizenship. Although feminists encouraged women to enter the male sphere of business, they remained deeply suspicious of American finance capitalism, which they typically saw as ruthless, predatory, and corrupt. Victoria Woodhull's career as a stockbroker and as critic of Wall Street embodied that contradiction. Woodhull and other Victorian women reformers realized that the domestic sphere was often threatened by market forces over which women had little control, but to shun the stock market was hardly an option, as this would cut them off from an important source of wealth. As women's ownership of securities increased, there was a mounting feminist critique of investment capitalism and a belief that women had to reform an economy in which they were both marginalized and deeply implicated.

5 Call Me Madam Ishmael

Hetty Green and the Female Tycoon

"If a man had lived as did Mrs. Hetty Green, devoting the greater part of his time and mind to the increasing of an inherited fortune . . . nobody would have seen him as very peculiar . . . It was the fact that Mrs. Green was a woman that made her career the subject of endless curiosity, comment, and astonishment."

—*New York Times*, 1916

The most successful and famous woman financier of the Gilded Age was Hetty Green, a whale oil heiress turned Wall Street tycoon, who became a lightning rod for debates about women and money. No one could doubt her success or financial genius, for, in the decades following the Civil War, she parlayed a modest fortune into a vast one through shrewd investments in real estate and railways. A fearless speculator, she made millions in the stock market by buying at times of financial panic. Some women cited Green as an example of women's capacity for moneymaking, if given the chance, but male commentators often marginalized her achievements as a woman, for example attributing her business success to "a powerful masculine brain." Green's detractors further demonized her as "the Witch of Wall Street"—a ruthless, miserly hag whose success was achieved at the expense of feminine charitableness and grace. Her critics constructed her life story as a cautionary tale about women's inability to handle financial success. Their warnings were issued at the very time when increasing numbers of women were entering business, albeit at more modest levels.

Green sought to counter her bad press by presenting herself as a softer, feminine alternative to the ruthless robber barons of the day. She proclaimed her opposition to monopoly and her sympathy for the common man. She argued that she *invested* in real estate and corporate bonds like any conservative matron, rather than *speculating* on Wall Street like her reckless male contemporaries Jim Fisk and Jay Gould. Few American women achieved Hetty Green's prominence as a financier, and those who did, like the pharmaceutical heiress Anne Weightman Walker or the company promoter Ella Rawls Reader, were inevitably compared to her. Like Green, these other female tycoons tried to cultivate public personas that were more conventionally feminine than prevailing stereotypes of the unsexed businesswoman.

From Princess of Whales to Queen of Wall Street

Hetty Green was the female financier par excellence of Gilded Age America. Green was the only woman of the time to amass a fortune comparable to that of her robber baron contemporaries—Carnegie, Morgan, Rockefeller. The richest woman in America at the time of her death in 1916, she left an estate of $100 million, almost all of which she had earned through her own shrewd financial decisions.[1] A national celebrity, famous for her "Midas touch" and eccentric lifestyle, miserly or frugal depending on one's point of view, Hetty Green had become an icon of popular culture by the early twentieth century. She was the subject of popular songs, like Sidney Toler's "If I Were as Rich as Hetty Green" (1905), and doggerel verse like S. E. Kiser's "Dreamers" (1901):

> If you were Pierpont Morgan
> And I were Hetty Green,
> In dismal days and sunny
> We'd just keep making money
> And stacking it between
> Our happy selves, my honey . . . [2]

In 1908 a Jersey City department store featured the Hetty Green hat, a bargain at two dollars and available in "seven different shades of green."[3]

Synonymous with female wealth, Hetty Green was the yardstick against which any rich or entrepreneurial woman was measured. In 1907, when archeologists excavated the gold-encrusted mummy of an Egyptian queen, the *Baltimore American* joked that this ancient ruler was "the Hetty Green of her times." Mary Coonie, an "Eskimo plutocrat" who had amassed a large number of mining claims in Alaska, was dubbed the "Hetty Green of the Arctic Circle" by the *Charlotte Observer* in 1909. Madame C. J. Walker, who became the first African American millionaire through her marketing of a hair straightener, was referred to by the press as the "Hetty Green of the colored race." A 1907 human-interest story about an enterprising eleven-year-old fruit seller in Naples, Italy, typically labeled the girl "a miniature Hetty Green."[4]

Hetty Green's path to celebrity and fabulous wealth was quite unconventional. She had been born into affluence, but unlike most women of her class, she did not live a life of leisure and conspicuous consumption. Nor did she allow men to manage her money for her. Born Henrietta Howland Robinson in New Bedford, Massachusetts, in 1834, she was the daughter of whale oil heiress Abby Howland and businessman Edward Mott Robinson, who managed the Howland whaling interests, among the most extensive in the nation. The Howlands and Robinsons were old Quaker families who lived comfortably but simply, in spite of their wealth. As her parents' only surviving child, Hetty had "great expectations" placed on her. When the Prince of Wales visited the United States in 1860, Hetty was introduced to him at a ball as the "Princess of Whales."[5]

Information concerning Hetty Robinson's childhood is scarce, though in later life she told many stories to explain and "normalize" her business expertise, so unusual for a woman of her generation and social class. As she told an interviewer in the early twentieth century: "My grandfather's eyesight was failing, and my father's too, and as soon as I learned to read it became my daily duty to read aloud to them the financial news of the world. In this way I came to know what stocks and bonds were, how the markets fluctuated, and the meaning of bulls and bears. By the time I was fifteen, when I went to Boston to school, I knew more about these things than many a man that makes a living out of them."[6]

She further reminisced that she was "obliged to keep a strict account of personal and household expenses" and that she even opened her own bank account at the age of eight, into which she squirreled away the nickels and dimes that other children, less thrifty, wasted on candy and toys. On another occasion she recalled that her father once gave her $1,200 to spend on clothes for the social season in New York. She spent only $200 on dress, using the rest to purchase bonds.[7]

Hetty's father died in June 1865, leaving her around $1 million in cash, and another $5 million in trust, the income to be hers, the principal to go to her children at her death. Two weeks later, her Aunt Sylvia Howland died. Hetty had expected to receive her aunt's entire estate, valued at around $2 million. She was surprised to learn that Sylvia had left $1 million to various friends and charities. The remaining million was left to Hetty in trust, the income to be hers, the principal to be divided among numerous Howland relations upon Hetty's death.[8]

Hetty Robinson contested both wills. She was convinced that her aunt had been unduly influenced to reduce her inheritance. She also could not accept that the bulk of her inheritance ($6 million) had been put into trusts, to be managed by other people. She saw the trusts as a slap in the face to her, and a public declaration that she was incapable of managing her own money. Hetty Robinson had no doubts about her own business abilities, for hadn't her family brought her up to be financially literate? Perhaps she later embellished the stories of her youthful financial apprenticeship to justify her attempts at breaking her father's and aunt's wills. If the stories were true, the trusts suggest that even Quakers, who raised daughters to be self-reliant, could not contemplate placing a lone woman in command of such a vast fortune.[9]

Hetty Robinson was unable to break the trusts but would chafe against them all her life, periodically suing the trustees for mismanagement. Her attempt at overturning her aunt's will was especially contentious, involving as it did a codicil in Hetty's handwriting, but apparently signed by Sylvia, insisting that Hetty was her sole heir and that any later wills were to be disregarded. Sylvia Howland's executors believed that Hetty had forged her aunt's signature to the codicil, and they produced distinguished authorities to prove so. Hetty's lawyers called their own experts, including Oliver Wendell Holmes, to authenticate the signature. Ultimately the judge invalidated Hetty's claim on a technicality, so she was not charged with forgery, but the suspicion hung over her in New Bedford for many years.[10]

The American public could not understand Hetty Robinson's grievances. She had $1 million in cash and $6 million in trust, which would give her an income of $300,000 a year, an immense sum in the 1860s. Wasn't this enough? The press denounced her as greedy and unwomanly. One paper referred to her as a "dried-up old maid" (at thirty-one), while another noted that "she has already got more money than a dozen persons could spend satisfactorily if they worked hard at it all the time." The writer hoped that she might become "somewhat ameliorated by marriage and motherhood."[11]

In July 1867, at age thirty-three, Hetty Robinson married Edward Green, a merchant in the China trade, thirteen years her senior. Edward Green's estimated wealth was around $1 million, so he was unlikely to be a fortune hunter. Edward Robinson's trust for Hetty had already stipulated that his daughter's profits be paid to her "without any direction, interference or control by her husband—if she should have one." In keeping with Victorian conventions, Edward Green would pay for their household expenses. For the next seven years the Greens lived in London, where Edward had interests in several banks. They had a son, Edward (Ned), and a daughter, Sylvia, during those years. Hetty led a quiet life, and the outside world seldom heard of her activities.[12]

It was probably during this period that Hetty Green became active in investing in securities. She had no control over her trust monies, which were conservatively invested by her trustees in government bonds and real estate, but she had an annual income of several hundred thousand dollars with which to play.[13] Janet Wallach cites recently uncovered correspondence from Hetty Green in London to New York brokers, for the purchase of thousands of shares in U.S. railroads, including the Reading Railroad, the Chicago & Rock Island, and the Boston & Providence.[14] One of the few press reports about Green during her London years is a story from 1870 concerning her "semi-annual raid into Wall Street," where she secured "uniformly brilliant results to her own pocket." Apparently Green had purchased around 50,000 shares of Reading Railroad stock in January at 94, which she sold in June at 105, for a profit of more than half a million dollars. As the paper humorously observed, "these little 'corners' serve to keep her in pin money."[15]

In the wake of the 1873 Financial Panic, the Greens returned to the States to better supervise their vast holdings. They settled in Bellows Falls, Vermont, Edward Green's boyhood home. During the next ten years, Hetty Green would periodically visit New York City to oversee her investments, but she was not yet well known as a Wall Street operator. To the extent that anyone outside of New England had heard of her, it was for her alleged parsimony, tales of which began to leak out of Bellows Falls. She wore old and faded clothes, haggled with local merchants over pennies, and did household repairs herself rather than hire workmen. A Vermont paper reported that Green liked "to sit down in a small grocery and make a meal off a few bits of crackers and cheese in order to save the expense of a hotel dinner."[16]

Like many wealthy Americans, Hetty and Edward Green invested heavily in railroads during the 1880s. She owned a controlling interest in the Louisville & Nashville, appointing her husband to the board, as she apparently did not approve of women directors and she herself refused to serve. Perhaps she was also trying to boost Edward's confidence at a time when his fortune, unlike hers, was in eclipse. He had lost heavily in the stock market and, unbeknownst to his wife, borrowed large sums of money in a vain attempt to recoup his losses. Lacking collateral for further loans, he pledged her securities. The financial downturn of 1884 exposed Mr. Green's dealings and propelled Mrs. Green into the national spotlight.[17]

Hetty Green burst onto the American consciousness in 1885. Rumors had reached her that the Cisco Bank on Wall Street was on the brink of insolvency following the financial panic of the previous year. Green had more than half a million dollars on deposit with the bank and now wished to transfer it to the nearby Chemical National Bank, along with some $25 million of securities left in the Cisco vaults for safekeeping. The bank refused Green's request, informing her that her husband owed the bank some $700,000 that it had lent him for a series of failed stock market speculations. He had clearly borrowed this on the strength of his wife's securities lodged at the bank.[18]

Hetty Green was shocked at the extent of her husband's losses, which he had concealed from her, and furious that the bank would confuse her money with her husband's. She insisted that she was not responsible for Edward Green's debts. She had the New York State Married Women's Property Acts on her side. The bank had centuries of tradition that a wife was economically subordinate to her husband, and it had her securities. After weeks of wrangling and threatened lawsuits, Hetty Green gave the Cisco Bank some $420,000 to settle her husband's debt. Her stocks and bonds were then released to her and moved to the Chemical National.[19]

Green never forgave her husband for his betrayal, in her eyes far worse than infidelity. From that moment, they lived apart. He was deprived of any control over her vast wealth. In October 1885, the *New York Times* noted that "the millionaire in hoopskirts" had "unceremoniously" dropped her husband from the board of the Louisville & Nashville Railroad. According to the paper, "Mr. Green being sat upon by Mrs. Green is a picture that there are stock brokers wicked enough to laugh at. Very few of them, however, presume to laugh" in her presence. Until his death in 1902, Edward Green lived a quiet life at the Union League Club in New York and in Bellows Falls. His wife now styled herself Mrs. Hetty Green rather than Mrs. Edward Green. She was fifty-one years old. For the remaining thirty years of her life, Hetty Green took care of her own money.[20]

The Midas Touch

So sudden and unlikely was Green's public entry into the financial world, that many people initially believed "that she was but a figurehead for a shrewd, unknown [male] speculator." The public, however, soon realized "that she was a new and potent factor in the banking community." In 1893 one newspaper declared Hetty Green "the personification of shrewdness when financial transactions are involved." By the turn of the century, businessmen were giving her the ultimate compliment: "no man can get the better of Hetty Green, who is a genius in the fine art of financiering."[21] Green shunned risky and volatile industrial and mining shares for safer and steadier government bonds, railway securities, and real estate. Green's investment philosophy closely mirrored the conservative advice that financial experts typically gave to American women at the turn of the century.[22]

Green herself often advised women to invest in real estate. In 1896 she spoke to a *New York World* reporter "for the benefit of women with small sums of money to invest," recommending real estate "as the safest means of investing idle money" and as "the collateral to be preferred to all others." Green advised "any woman with $500 at her command" to buy "real estate at auction on occasions when circumstances have forced the sale . . . and she will find that she can buy a parcel of land at one-third its appraised value." According to Green, real estate provided a steady income and was "less likely to depreciate in value than stocks, which are always somewhat uncertain."[23]

Hetty Green owned massive amounts of real estate and mortgages on property, especially in such rapidly growing cities as New York, Chicago, St. Louis, and San Francisco. She favored downtown business properties that paid high rents and was quick to take advantage of opportunities like the 1871 Great Fire of Chicago or the 1906 San Francisco earthquake. After the Chicago fire, Green lent several hundred thousand dollars on lots in that city at high rates of interest, and she later foreclosed on many of those properties. By the time of her death, Green's real-estate holdings in Chicago alone were worth more than $5 million, a tenfold increase over her initial investment. Altogether, she owned some eight thousand parcels of real estate across the United States.[24]

Green denounced the stock market to American investors as strongly as she praised real estate. In 1899 she told *Harper's Bazaar* that "anyone who invests his little capital" in Wall Street "is a fool. The Street is only for those with big capital." In 1900 she informed the readers of *The Ladies' Home Journal* that "I don't believe in speculation as a rule, and I don't speculate as much as people think." Green's anti-speculation rhetoric was pretty disingenuous but was probably intended to separate herself, a conservative old woman who bought real estate, from crafty Wall Street "operators" like Jim Fisk and Jay Gould, who gambled recklessly in shares.[25]

Some commentators endorsed Green's self-representation as an investor, not a speculator. According to the *Watertown Daily Times*, "she doesn't gamble. She trades in stocks" on which she has "legitimate information obtained by her through her large holdings." She also "doesn't trade on margins," but "buys the stock outright."[26] Others were quick to point out that Green's Wall Street dealings were as manipulative as any robber baron's. One Wall Street broker argued that famous stock market manipulators like Jay Gould were actually following in the footsteps of Hetty Green. "She was a master of finance before Wall Street heard of Gould and he couldn't have done better than to adopt her methods."[27]

In many of her business methods and attitudes toward money, however, Hetty Green was quite distinctive. She reinvested her profits in the various cities where it was made, a financial practice that she characterized as anti-monopolistic and that distinguished her from other financiers. Green explained her strategy to an interviewer in 1915: "Let the locality where you earn your money enjoy the business of its re-investment . . . For instance, the profits I get from Chicago holdings are always invested in Chicago. The same thing is true of my investments in Boston, New York and Texas. If every one would help build up various communities in this way, there would be less centralization of big business powers in a few financial centers."

Green's words struck a chord with "Buy-at-Home" advocates in Montgomery, Alabama, where "progressive people" were trying to make the case that local businessmen had a duty to reinvest their profits in the local community. The *Montgomery Advertiser* lauded Green as a "wonderful figure in the world of finance" whose words of wisdom would provide "untold meat for serious thought" for "the loyal residents of every community in the country."[28]

Hetty Green's legendary frugality also separated her from the big-spending plutocrats of Gilded Age America, and she grew her fortune in part because of this frugality. Green's expenses were modest, as she lived in boardinghouses or rented small apartments in middle-class neighborhoods. She spent little on entertainment, and even less on clothing. She indulged in no conspicuous consumption on mansions, yachts, jewelry, or art. She made no massive bequests to charities. She endowed no museums, libraries, or universities. Therefore, most of her immense income was ploughed back into her capital and grew yet more income. Green always maintained huge cash reserves, often as much as $20 million, with which she could buy securities or lend out to others during times of financial panic, when prices were low and money was scarce.[29]

Unlike most of her male contemporaries of comparable wealth—Vanderbilt, Carnegie, Rockefeller, Frick—she established no corporations, trusts, or foundations. She had no partners and employed few advisors or assistants. Hetty Green oversaw her own extensive financial interests and made her own investment decisions in her own peculiar ways. Before deciding on an investment, she sought out every kind of information about it.[30] When offered shares to purchase, she would sometimes "buy one share and then send out to see what it will bring. If it's a good advance, I buy the rest. If not, I don't." When buying real estate, she sought out janitors and scrubwomen, questioning them "about the number of tenants in office buildings on which loans were desired, and the state of repairs in such buildings." Some people even suggested that Green's notoriously shabby appearance enabled her to make such investigations "unknown and unnoticed."[31]

Hetty Green believed that her own careful oversight of her far-flung business interests gave her a far better sense of the nation's business conditions and market trends than professional advisers or the financial press could provide. Businessmen frequently testified to Green's uncanny knowledge of the money market and securities' values. Her son maintained that "there is no better judge of commercial paper in the United States," and Bird S. Coler, comptroller for New York City, believed that Green "had the best banking brain of anyone I ever knew." Coler was especially impressed that "she carried all her knowledge in her head and never depended upon memoranda."[32] So great was Hetty Green's reputation for financial prowess that by the 1890s, her very person was imbued with magical powers by the superstitious denizens of Wall Street. According to the *New York Mail and Express*, "the merest touch of her garments is regarded as better luck than the possession of a foot of a graveyard rabbit, killed when the moon is dark."[33]

A Disputed Legacy

While her contemporaries celebrated Hetty Green's vast wealth and financial acumen, posterity has been less kind. Since her death in 1916, she has mostly been remembered as "the Witch of Wall Street," the world's greediest and most miserly woman. Popular accounts of Wall Street figures grew harsher following the stock market crash of 1929, reviving earlier muckraking rhetoric. In December 1929 the popular magazine *The Mentor* published an article about Hetty Green by John T. Flynn. Titled "The Witch of Wall Street," Flynn's account presented Green as warped by an austere Puritan upbringing that filled her heart with an "enduring and consuming bitterness" and "which led her into all sorts of strange meannesses and in the end raised up in her mind a kind of mania of persecution."[34]

The work that cemented Green's reputation as a paranoid miser was Boyden Sparkes and Samuel Taylor Moore's 1930 biography *Hetty Green: A Woman Who Loved Money*. Reissued in 1935 as *The Witch of Wall Street*, Sparkes and Moore's unsympathetic account found an eager readership in Depression-era America, when people were happy to think of plutocrats as selfish and ruthless, though ultimately lonely and miserable, figures. For the next seventy years, *The Witch of Wall Street* set the tone for books and articles about Green.[35] In his history of Wall Street, *The Big Board* (1965), Robert Sobel referred to her as "an eccentric, a miser, and a religious fanatic." Arthur H. Lewis's melodramatic account of the Green family fortune, *The Day They Shook the Plum Tree* (1963), characterized Hetty Green as the "most detested woman in America and the mother of two children whose lives she had ruined."[36] The demonizing of Green reached its apogee in the best-selling *Guinness Book of World Records*, where Green was listed as the world's "greatest miser." She purportedly "lived off cold porridge because she was too stingy to heat it."[37]

Unlike Victoria Woodhull, her near contemporary, Green was not rediscovered and reappraised by feminist scholars in the 1960s and 1970s. As an arch-capitalist and anti-suffragist, she was hardly a congenial figure for second-wave feminism. Business historians were not much better.[38] Sympathetic versions of Hetty Green's life and career emerged only in the twenty-first century.[39] Yet even the revisionist studies of Green remain heavily indebted to the narrative framework constructed by Sparkes and Moore in the 1930s. In their worthy efforts to rehabilitate Green, the revisionists have accepted the notion that most of her contemporaries viewed her in a negative light.

In fact, during her own lifetime, Green was depicted in a number of very different ways, some critical, others admiring. In an attempt to present a more complex and nuanced image of Hetty Green, I have surveyed several thousand stories about her from a wide assortment of American newspapers over the years 1885–1916. These papers portrayed her variously as a pathetic miser, a ruthless capitalist, a brilliant investor, a virago, a devoted mother, and a folksy, old-fashioned matron. I do not want to suggest that these press accounts necessarily represent authentic information about Hetty Green. Many of these stories and "interviews" were doubtless exaggerated or even invented. The vigorous press debate over Green is important for what it says about the public's views on powerful women and women's financial autonomy.[40]

The Stingiest Woman on Earth

Hetty Green's detractors emphasized that she was unwomanly, masculine in appearance and behavior and so obsessed with moneymaking that she had abandoned her proper wifely and charitable responsibilities. *Harper's Bazaar* described her as "tall and muscular," and the *Ladies' Home Journal* noted that her face was "quite masculine in character." The *New York World* characterized Green as having "a masculine air that shows in her walk, in her gestures and in her every movement . . . when she leans back in her chair or puts her face close to yours in earnest conversation, or crosses her legs and points a finger in denunciation of an imaginary enemy—she does all these things just as a big, heavy man would do them."[41]

Almost all commentators emphasized Hetty Green's shabby appearance and disregard for fashion and personal adornment, so unusual for a woman of her social class. Her clothing was subject to intense scrutiny and criticism, emblematic of the double standard and seldom applied to famous men. In the opinion of *Harper's Bazaar*, "she dresses frightfully. There is no other word for it." The *Chicago Herald* snidely noted that "Mrs. Green dresses as comfortably as an industrious washerwoman, but no more fashionably. She wears her clothes until they are worn out, and by that time they are ready for the paper mill." Green's usual costume of faded and frayed black dress and bonnet probably contributed to the unflattering moniker "the Witch of Wall Street," which her detractors sometimes applied to her.[42]

Green's masculine and shabby appearance supposedly revealed deeper, and more transgressive, character traits. In the words of one paper, "Mrs. Green has usurped the place of men, and she does not ask the privileges of her sex." The *Cleveland Plain Dealer* joked that ruthless financier Russell Sage "was about what Mrs. Green would have been had nature followed a plain first intent and made her a man." Behind these remarks lay the assumption that Hetty Green succeeded in business because she was like a man. In the midst of a misogynist diatribe against incompetent women speculators, the broker Henry Clews conceded that Hetty Green was different. She was, however, "one among a million of her sex" and succeeded only because of "a powerful masculine brain." A money article from 1897 also concluded that Green was the "one shining exception" to female financial incapacity. Other women should not try to imitate her success, for if they did so, they too would become "unsexed."[43]

Conservative commentators emphasized Green's unconventional gender behavior. She did not keep house for her husband, nor even recognize his authority as head of the family. She kept her fortune under her own control, and when her husband infringed upon her separate holdings, she banished him from her household. In 1892, when the *New York Herald* asked Hetty Green whether her husband approved of her latest business deal, she tartly replied: "Oh, bless you, he a'n't got anything to say about such things. He does what I tell him."[44]

Hetty Green's reputed miserliness was especially cited as evidence of an unwomanly character. According to the *Indianapolis Journal*, she was "a financial amazon" who "has reduced parsimony to a fine art and let avarice curdle the milk of a woman's highest attributes. She has unsexed herself for gold, and stands a Shylock in crinoline." At the time of Green's death in 1916, several commentators argued that she was "an uninspiring example" to other women because "she used her wealth to breed wealth, as Shylock did" instead of using it for philanthropic purposes. The columnist Sam Clark maintained that "the kind of rich woman that is needed in this world is the one whose purse strings are always open to the poor, ever ready to succor the distressed and uplift the fallen." Clark contrasted Green to that paragon of true womanhood Florence Nightingale, who "gave all that was in her to relieve human suffering. Hetty Green, as far as the records show, did not contribute one jot toward the sum total of human happiness."[45]

Green was demonized and pathologized by her enemies. While successful male financiers were inevitably dubbed "wizards of Wall Street," Hetty Green was the "witch." In 1910 the press even noted that she owned a black cat named Satan.[46] All the tools of Victorian science and pseudoscience were also marshaled against Green, depicting her as abnormal and degenerate. Phrenologists noted that the contours of Hetty Green's head indicated masculine "reasoning powers and resolution" rather than feminine sentiment.[47] In 1904, Dr. George Blumer, a "noted alienist," expressed the opinion that Hetty Green was insane. Although he had never met her, he based his diagnosis on the newspaper story that she carried millions of dollars' worth of securities "in her handbag."[48]

Social conservatives agreed that Hetty Green's success had come at too high a price. She had sacrificed the normal pleasures of womanhood, and many people could not imagine that she was really fulfilled. On November 26, 1905, the *New York World* devoted an entire page of its Thanksgiving edition to the life of Hetty Green, whom the paper depicted as "friendless and alone" and oppressed with "sordid cares." Apparently her money made "no home happy" and lightened "no man's burdens."[49] Other commentators at the time imagined Green "as a tired, heartsore old woman" more to be pitied than envied. The press frequently compared her lot in life unfavorably to that of ordinary people, like "the girl stenographer who takes her dictation" and who "probably has a lighter heart under a new spring gown."[50]

The "world's richest woman" was "bankrupt in desire" because she did not understand that "the supreme happiness of womanhood" was to be a wife and mother.

At the time of Green's death, one newspaper argued that she "was not the wealthiest woman. She merely had the most money. There are a great many women who wouldn't sell their youth, or their prettiness, or the noisiest, kickingiest baby alive, or even a husband, for all that Hetty Green had." Another paper agreed that the humblest mother in America was wealthier than Hetty Green, since she preferred "the pink, tiny hand" at her breast to "all the riches in the world."[51]

A Joking, Gay Old Lady

The negative view of Green, that she was a pitiable miser who had unsexed herself in the ruthless and single-minded pursuit of wealth, did not go uncontested during her lifetime, although it did prevail in the decades following her death, crystallized in Sparkes's and Moore's withering 1930 biography. While she lived, Green had many friends and admirers who saw her in very different terms. To them she embodied the old-fashioned virtues of independence, self-reliance, and thrift. They also praised her devotion to her children, whom she protected from the dissipated lifestyle of the Gilded Age plutocracy. In 1916, the year of Green's death, the *National Cyclopaedia of American Biography* characterized her as "an extremely human person of simple tastes and kindly impulses, very shrewd, very humorous, very sociable, with a whimsical good humored disdain of the world's opinions and pretensions."[52]

Interviewers often expressed surprise that Green was not the wizened, sour-faced, mannish dowager they had been led to expect from so many press reports. In 1906, Peggy Quincy found her "a kindly, gracious, motherly old woman" with "fine skin, tinted a faint pink, and features that are small and not at all heavy and masculine or repulsively shrewd."[53] A neighbor of Green's from Hoboken also recalled a happy and contented person: "I never have known any person who appeared to get more fun out of life than Mrs. Green. I remember her as a laughing, joking, gay old lady."[54]

While Green's detractors saw her as a woman warped, corrupted, and unsexed by moneymaking, others admired her precisely because she was a successful businesswoman. In a talk called "Woman as a Financier" for the Congress of Women at the 1893 Chicago World's Fair, the writer Mary Lipscomb praised Green as "the only woman who has ever dared to venture a deal with Wall Street brokers, and in no investment has she ever been known to lose." In an 1899 work in support of women's employment, Grace Dodge boasted that Green's "fortune is the result mainly of business qualities of the first order, the possession of which any man might envy."[55] For every press report that referred to Green as "the witch of Wall Street," there were many more that labeled her "the queen of Wall Street," "the female Croesus," or simply "the richest woman in the world."[56]

Even those who ridiculed Green for her shabby clothes and penny-pinching ways conceded that she was honest. An 1886 article detailing Green's miserly behavior concluded that her "one redeeming" quality was honesty. A 1904 piece on the achievements of "the feminine sex" lauded Green for making "one of the greatest fortunes ever amassed . . . without ever having been charged with bankrupting another to get it."[57] In this line of reasoning, Hetty Green was a kind of female anti–robber baron. As Eliza Archard Conner argued in 1906: "Hetty Green never looted a bank, never bribed a legislature, never drove to bankruptcy and suicide a weaker rival or ran down by methods that should have put her in the penitentiary the stock or properties of which she wished to obtain control, as certain shiningly pious

American millionaires have done."[58] Conner was clearly comparing Green to Carnegie and Rockefeller, who, unlike Green, ran roughshod over their competitors and then sought to burnish their tarnished reputations through massive philanthropic donations.

With regard to Green's legendary parsimony, one person's miserliness was another person's thrift. While some commentators labeled her a "miser" or characterized her as "stingy," many others saw her as "frugal" and praised her for living a "simple life." In 1895, *Godey's Magazine* commended Green for her "habits of orderly economy," which she had "inherited from sturdy New England ancestors." In 1909 the *Idaho Statesman* argued that, unlike "other multimillionaires," Green did "not waste money in stupid display," but practiced a "wise and prudent" economy.[59] In a 1914 "Talk on Thrift," T. D. MacGregor believed that Green also could teach the average housewife much about "domestic economy." If all American women were as careful with their money as Green, "there would be less talk of hard times and the high cost of living."[60] For many people in rural America, Hetty Green embodied their own hostility to flashy big-city ways. In 1896 the *American Farmer* lauded her for dressing "in the cheapest and plainest fashion."[61]

While Green's critics vilified her for preferring moneymaking to motherhood, her admirers countered that she was devoted to her children and that she imparted to them the same old-fashioned values reflected in her plain dress and plain living. Green raised her son Ned to manage her business interests but expected him to work his way up the ladder. In 1892, *Harper's Weekly* noted with approval that "one of the first occupations she gave her son after he had graduated from college was to paint the front door of a carriage factory."[62] Other papers lauded Green for raising her daughter Sylvia to be "modest and retiring" and not to "go about with the airs of a Grand Duchess," in spite of her great wealth. Many admired Green for bucking the trend and refusing to "hawk her daughter through the courts of Europe" in search of a titled husband. Instead, Sylvia married an "honest gentleman," Matthew Astor Wilks, "quietly and modestly in an American made gown and hat." To Green's admirers, her old-fashioned way of bringing up her children, like her unfashionable dress, invoked nostalgia for "a time when the real foundation of American character was being laid."[63]

Hetty Green's unconventional behavior was open to a wide variety of interpretations. Depending on one's perspective, her odd dress, for example, might reflect unfeminine slovenliness, pathological miserliness, feminist disdain for fashion, or old-fashioned thrift. It might even have been a disguise, for business purposes. At the time of Green's death, a friend suggested the simplest interpretation: "She dressed that way because she wished to do so, and didn't care what anybody thought about it."[64] Green's radical independence, her insistence on living life on terms that she and she alone determined, infuriated many, but it also accounted for a great deal of her popularity. As one of Green's fans insisted, "it is a good thing to have one woman brave enough to defy world-wide comment, caustic criticism in the press every day in the year and ridicule of the most sarcastic and bitter type, and to live as she jolly well pleases."[65]

Becoming "Aunt Hetty": A Yankee Self-Fashioning

It should hardly surprise us that Hetty Green was such a divisive figure. She was a successful businesswoman at a time when Americans were bitterly divided over both the costs and benefits of industrial capitalism and the appropriate roles for women. People projected on her their hopes and fears regarding the nation's economic and social order. In the popular imagination she was, at different times and to different people, a ruthless, selfish financier and a populist champion of the people; an unsexed virago and an old-fashioned, doting mother; a powerful New York plutocrat and a retiring New England Quaker. Green's eccentric behavior sometimes brought to mind a Dickensian character, but people again disagreed about which one she most resembled. To some she was a "female Gradgrind," after the heartless materialist of *Hard Times*, while to others she was the very image of Betsy Trotwood, David Copperfield's strong-willed but kindly aunt—"an amazon who had a heart," in the words of a Hetty Green admirer.[66] Green herself was aware of these contradictory interpretations, and, whenever possible, she tried to manipulate her public image more favorably.

Despite her protestations to the contrary, Green did seem to care what people thought about her. In 1895 she admitted to a reporter that "she read every line written about her in the newspapers," and in 1908 she hired a clipping bureau to send her "all newspaper references to Mrs. Hetty Green."[67] For the most part, she did not like what she saw. As she told the *New York Times*, "I have been more abused and misrepresented than any woman alive." On another occasion, she complained that "my life is written for me down in Wall Street by people who, I assume, do not care to know one iota of the real Hetty Green. I am in earnest; therefore they picture me as heartless. I go my own way, take no partners, risk nobody else's fortune, therefore I am Madam Ishmael, set against every man."[68]

In her efforts to counter bad press, Green liked to present herself as a plainspoken, no-nonsense Yankee matron. She emphasized her frugal Quaker upbringing and maintained her preference for the old-fashioned values of work, religion, and family life over the "highfalutin" temptations of fashion and society. Green's populist self-fashioning may well have been influenced by the earlier career of another financier, Daniel Drew, who had constructed his own folksy alter ego. Drew took Wall Street by storm in the 1850s and was associated with some of the most duplicitous stock operations of the era. He countered his ruthless robber-baron image as "Uncle Dan'l," an unpretentious backwoods huckster, plain of speech and plain of dress. In the words of Steve Fraser, Uncle Dan'l "appeared a Jacksonian democrat come to Wall Street without airs, whose self-presentation mocked precisely those aristocratic inflations of dress and rhetoric that were so alien to the American sensibility."[69] Decades later, stockbroker Rufus Hatch aimed for the same homespun approach when he published *The Sayings of Uncle Rufus* (1881), a collection of financial anecdotes and yarns told in a folksy manner.[70] By the 1890s, many Americans now referred fondly to "Aunt Hetty," a cantankerous old lady who made millions in Wall Street but looked like a farmer's wife come to town.[71]

Although born in affluence and educated at an exclusive finishing school, Green played the role of "Aunt Hetty" to the hilt, peppering her speech with folksy aphorisms and railing against the foolishness and "folderol" of modern life: "I always have said that if there was less foolish talk there'd be more sensible work and not so much tea-party nonsense." She asserted a preference for life in a simple flat in Hoboken to the bright lights of New York and dismissed the temptations of the big city in her characteristically salty style: "I never had time to eat lobsters or watch ladies in pink tights with Wall Street brokers."[72] In a nation still in the midst of urbanization, Green probably reminded many Americans of their own country grandmothers, frugal, hardworking, and plainspoken. She railed against modern contraptions like automobiles and airplanes and newfangled fashions for women like makeup and sleeveless dresses. She also preferred home remedies like mustard plasters to modern medicine, boasting that she had outlived six doctors. "Why, away back in '65 the doctors told me I hadn't another year to live, but I could do a skirt dance in the moonlight now if I wanted to entertain you."[73]

Knowing she was good copy, reporters dogged Hetty Green around the financial district, often lying in wait for her outside the Chemical Bank, where she kept a desk. She seemed to enjoy parrying with them, relishing her role as the unpretentious businesswoman. On her seventieth birthday, she came to the bank as usual, dismissing a reporter's birthday greetings as so much foolishness: "No one's caring how an old woman spends her birthday . . . If you'd had as many of 'em as I have had, young man, you'd attend to your business, too. I've got a lot of things to attend to, and I'm coming right down here to see to it."[74] Green, like Ben Franklin, was always ready with a pithy aphorism about the virtues of thrift and hard work. She urged young people to "take care of your money; it isn't half as hard to earn it as to take care of it."[75]

Green frequently employed religious language in justifying her behavior and outlook on life. Indeed, much of her folksy persona was grounded in a supposed fondness for "old-time religion." She often maintained that she was merely a pious old Quaker endeavoring to live simply and righteously. As she told a reporter in 1909, "I am a Quaker, and am trying to live up to the tenets of that faith. That is why I dress plainly and live quietly. No other kind of life would please me."[76] On other occasions she referred to herself as "a God-fearing woman" who relied upon the Lord for guidance in all her business dealings.[77] Green even couched her lawsuits against business rivals in religious terms. "It is a sin to allow anyone to rob you! That is why I fight."[78]

Charity, however, had no place in Hetty Green's religious outlook. Like other Victorian liberals, she believed that merely giving money to the poor demoralized them and undermined their self-reliance. As she told the *New York World* in 1911, "I have got no use for the beggars and I never give them a cent, but I do like to help people to help themselves." She argued that it was far better to assist the needy by providing employment, and she advised her son to "never give a penny to a well man . . . When a man is willing to work, give him a steady job if you can." She once boasted that you'll never see "my name on a charity list . . . but I built whole blocks of buildings in Chicago when the workingmen there had to have employment."[79]

Green had little patience for the "so-called philanthropy" of Carnegie and Rockefeller, which she believed was "inspired simply by vanity." In 1913, Green told an interviewer: "One way is to give money and to make a big show. That is not my way of doing. I am of the Quaker belief, and although the Quakers are about all dead, I still follow their example. An ordinary gift to be bragged about is not a gift in the eyes of the Lord." Green refused to make a show of philanthropy, even though she realized that this contributed to her reputation as a miser. "Because I do not have a secretary to announce every kind act that I perform, I am called close and mean and stingy."[80]

Aunt Hetty vs. the Plutocracy

Hetty Green saw through the robber barons' efforts to redeem their soiled reputations through charitable giving, and she often contrasted her own "sound business methods" with the "crooked business methods" of men like Jay Gould and C. P. Huntington. Following the Financial Panic of 1907, she lamented that "business is not conducted in the same way today that it was 40 years ago. Then a man's word was his bond. Today you should have good glasses when you inspect his bond." When Green heard that Jay Gould was to be included in the Hall of Fame, she retorted: "Why, they couldn't do that if they try. The people whom Jay Gould has fleeced would tear it down."[81]

Green claimed to be "a friend of the laboring men" and an implacable foe of trusts and monopolies. In 1895 she told the *Boston Herald*:

> I am sure that all the poor man wants is a chance to earn a decent living for himself and his family. But he has no chance to do that in many parts of this country. Why? Because the railroads absorb what should go to the farmer. That is, they make extortionate charges for freight . . . Out West there are whole states that do nothing but work hard day and night to provide dividends for the railroads.[82]

Green's diatribe was worthy of Frank Norris, and her favorite target was railroad magnate C. P. Huntington, with whom she had once struggled for control of certain Texas railroad lines. When the government threatened to send troops against striking railroad workers in 1895, Green suggested that it arrest Huntington instead, since "he and his railroads and the men about him have been grinding wealth out of the poor for years and defying the authorities." She argued that "the poor have no chance in this country. No wonder anarchists and socialists are so numerous."[83]

Green liked to represent herself as a champion of the common man against the moneyed interests. She defended her many lawsuits (which her enemies characterized as signs of paranoia and pettiness) as righteous battles against the corrupt forces of big business. "The poor can't sue," she reasoned, "and if the rich won't, who is to bring rogues to justice?" Once, when Green won a lawsuit against an insurance company, she was cheered by "a lot of poor people who had been cheated out of money by that company." She spoke to them from the steps of the courthouse, promising "that if the company ever tried to rob a poor woman again . . . I would come, no matter where I was, and fight for them."[84]

Green's detractors scoffed at the idea that this millionaire capitalist was a tribune of the people. They pointed out that she went to extraordinary lengths to avoid paying taxes and that she was a slum landlady on an epic scale. In 1896, William Jennings Bryan singled out Green as the nation's worst tax evader.[85] Green also owned extensive real-estate holdings, which she often failed to maintain or improve. In 1906, New York's *Daily People* reported that health inspectors in Chicago raided the "House of Blazes," a "firetrap" tenement owned by Green, and were shocked by its "filth and unsanitary conditions."[86] In spite of such contradictions, Aunt Hetty's frequent attacks on monopolies and corrupt business practices proved an effective rhetorical strategy, distancing her in the minds of many from the robber barons.

Hetty Green's indictment of Wall Street operators extended to the plutocracy in general and the materialistic and sinful ways of "society," which she characterized as "living in a worse manner than the people of Sodom and Gomorrah." She didn't like the robber barons' business methods, and she didn't like their wives' and daughters' way of living: "Society doesn't have enough to do to keep it out of mischief. Those so-called fashionable women spend all their time these days smoking cigarettes and drinking pale tea and strong whiskey."[87] Green's jeremiads against the hedonistic ways of wealthy Americans bolstered her image as an old-fashioned, plain-living Quaker.

Aunt Hetty on Women and Money

Aunt Hetty's stand for old-fashioned values included traditional views about woman's proper sphere: "A woman's place is in her own home taking care of her husband and children. I took care of my husband and his stomach and he lived to be 83 years old." Green did not favor women's suffrage and spoke slightingly of the "new woman." She lamented that too many modern women "never learn to keep house. They get married and their sole ambition is to wear fine clothes, bleach their hair, wear gay ribbons and fine laces. Home is the last place they ever think of." Women's vanity and thrill seeking were pushing the entire nation into insolvency, Green argued in the wake of the 1907 Financial Panic. "The women of America have helped to make hard times. All they live for—all they care about is clothes—the latest shapes in hats, the newest fangled skirts." Green urged women to follow her prudent example, spending less and saving more.[88]

Green did not, however, encourage women to imitate her entrepreneurial bent. She insisted that "Wall Street is no place for the unsophisticated woman, and I doubt whether it is a good place for any woman." She acknowledged the growing body of businesswomen—bookkeepers, stenographers, and typists—but remained ambivalent about women working for wages outside the home.[89] Green usually presented herself as a special case or exception to a woman's lot in life, ironically confirming the conservative assessment that she was an oddity, not a role model. On many occasions she claimed that she was forced by necessity into a life of business. As she told a reporter in 1905, she did not choose to be a financier. "A fortune was left me by my father," she said, "and I had to look after it." Over time she found that she "could handle affairs as well as any man . . . It became a habit." This life, however, was not one that she recommended to other women, and she had no intention of burdening her own daughter with such cares: "My daughter hasn't been reared to be a business woman. She knows a great deal about business, and she'll be able to take care of what she may have, but I wouldn't want her to follow in my footsteps."[90]

Hetty Green also endorsed the conservative view that most women were financially incompetent. In 1901 she told the *New York Times* that "women don't get rich" because they "spend so much." Their preoccupation with personal adornment led them to "spend every cent they make . . . As long as women won't save, we're not likely to have many women millionaires in this country." In March 1900, Green penned an article for *Harper's Bazaar* on "Why Women Are Not Money Makers," in which she rehearsed many of the usual clichés. Women were too impulsive, impatient, and emotional to succeed in financial investments. "The fluctuations of the stock market will send her to the seventh-heaven of delight, or the lowest depth of despair." A shrewd businessman, in contrast, kept his eye on long-term market trends, waiting coolly and patiently for developments to turn in his favor.[91]

Unlike most conservative commentators, however, Green was not an essentialist. She attributed women's financial incapacity to the "conventional sort of schooling" that taught girls only "how to read, write, sing, cook and sew," rather than to "any design on the part of creation." Green argued that "with the same environment . . . woman is quite as capable as man in conducting business affairs . . . Mentally, I do not believe woman to be inferior to man, save as she has become so by a mistaken course of training." With proper instruction, almost all women could become effective money managers.[92]

On more than one occasion, Green advocated greater financial literacy and financial responsibility for American women. Most famously, in February 1900 she wrote an article titled "The Benefits of a Business Training for Women" for the *Woman's Home Companion*. Given the nature of this publication, and given Green's conservative pronouncements on woman's proper sphere, it should come as no surprise that she did not advocate for preparing women to "go out to work." Rather, she had in mind a business training to make women better housekeepers, to enable them to better manage their own private affairs, and to better advise and assist their fathers, brothers, husbands, and sons. Women needed to understand about banking, insurance, mortgages, compound interest, and stocks and bonds. Even housewives might safely invest money, and they should be prepared to wind up their husbands' estates and to protect their children's inheritance.[93]

Benefits of a Business Training for Women

Is the title of an article written by Mrs. Hetty Green for the February number of the WOMAN'S HOME COMPANION.

Mrs. Hetty Green is the wealthiest woman in the world. Her remarkable business ability has been demonstrated in the accumulation and management of a vast fortune. She writes with the authority of the successful man of business and with the intimate knowledge of her sex that a woman only can have.

Figure 10. "Benefits of a Business Training for Women." Advertisement in the *Boston Journal*, January 26, 1900. (Courtesy of the Boston Public Library)

Parents should not spoil and shelter their daughters, Green advised, but teach them the hard facts of political economy. "Every child," she said, "should be taught from the beginning that a piece of money is something that is hard to obtain, and that it ought to be taken care of accordingly." Rather than indulging a girl's every whim, parents would do better to require her to earn a little money by doing additional chores. The girl should also be given an account book, into which she could record any money she earns, as well as any expenditures she made, and she should be encouraged to save some part of her money. The *Woman's Home Companion* piece was widely advertised and excerpted in American papers, cementing Green's reputation as a respected financial authority.[94]

Although Green discouraged women from business careers, she believed that with proper training they could succeed as well as men. As she once pithily asserted, "A woman's head is as good as a man's any day if she plays the game the way he does and forgets the frills." Too many women were afraid to "venture into the regions where man reigns supreme" and, as a result, lost out on lucrative investment opportunities. This attitude, Green insisted, was "foolish timidity, for a woman can get along as well as a man in any office if she only conducts herself properly and looks out for herself."

A good businesswoman even possessed certain qualities that gave her an advantage over men: "She seems to have an intuitive perception which man lacks, and the diplomacy to shape affairs to her will."[95]

Green dismissed as "poppycock" and "sheer nonsense" the widespread notion that business dealings and financial savvy would unsex a woman and "crush all the poetry out of her life." A woman with a knowledge of business appreciated art as much as anyone else, Green insisted, and she had greater opportunities to gratify her tastes: "She can get more tickets to concerts and art-galleries, she will have more money to become the possessor of more beautiful things than a woman without business training, and a woman with a sure income before her feels a great deal more like studying poetry than a woman who is compelled to worry about her future bread and butter."[96]

Green maintained that "a woman need not lose her femininity because she has a good business head on her shoulders." Financial literacy was simply another accomplishment necessary for modern women and in no way made them less womanly.[97]

Hetty Green's ideas about women's rights and duties were complicated, as one might expect from a woman whose own life and career were subject to intense scrutiny and bitter debate. She endorsed separate-spheres ideology, but she imagined a domestic realm where women had checkbooks and savings accounts and managed their own property. So long as a wife balanced the household accounts and kept her husband well-fed, there was no reason why she should not invest in real estate and securities. Better for women to buy government bonds than the latest silly fashions that would soon be out of style. Of course, Green herself spent little time keeping house and could on occasion be facetious about domestic bliss, as when she told a reporter in 1907: "The happiest woman is the one who sits by the fireside and says, 'Yes, dear,' to every stupid remark her husband makes." Green opposed women's suffrage but could not resist getting her digs in at male superiority, sarcastically asking a journalist in 1905, "What can I know about business when I don't know enough to vote?"[98]

While Green was "willing to leave politics to the men," she was keenly aware of women's financial exploitation and economic disabilities. She realized that most women's wages were atrocious, remarking bitterly: "A girl has a hard time being decent on $6 a week." Green also knew that "a woman hasn't as many chances for making money as men have," as she lacked connections and good information about new investment opportunities. Businessmen refused to take women seriously; they "think that women are fools and treat them that way. They try to take advantage of a woman in many ways that they wouldn't of a man and they try to appeal to a woman's emotions." In 1904,

Green admitted to an interviewer that she wished "women had more rights in business and elsewhere than they now have . . . I could have succeeded much easier in my career had I been a man."[99]

Despite her phenomenal success, Hetty Green could never overcome sexist prejudices against businesswomen. However much she courted popular approval by denouncing monopoly and the idle rich, and however successful she was as presenting herself as an old-fashioned, plain-living Quaker matron, the fact remained that Hetty Green was a woman who devoted her life to the accumulation of wealth above all else. There were some wealthy men who, like Green, aggressively amassed riches and lived abstemious and reclusive lives. In these respects, Russell Sage was a comparable figure and was sometimes linked with Green in press accounts of "eccentric" millionaires, but he never received a fraction of her bad press.[100] As the *New York Times* noted after Green's death: "If a man had lived as Mrs. Hetty Green, devoting the greater part of his time and mind to the increasing of an inherited fortune . . . nobody would have seen him as very peculiar . . . It was the fact that Mrs. Green was a woman that made her career the subject of endless curiosity, comment, and astonishment."[101]

Hetty Green behaved like an industrious businessman (wrapped up in investments, contracts, and lawsuits), not like a wealthy society woman (preoccupied with fashion, display, and good works), and it was this transgression of her expected gender role that received the harshest criticism. Or, as Green herself once poignantly observed: "If I were a man, people might believe me. But because I'm a woman, they say I'm crazy."[102]

Hetty Green's Rivals

Most people agreed that Hetty Green was in a class by herself, but during the early twentieth century, as more women entered business, female capitalists seemed less unusual than during the Victorian era. As the *Daily People* observed in 1908: "In these days of Suffragettes and emancipated females generally, one is not surprised to find women boldly entering the arena of finance." *Everybody's Magazine* argued that "action and achievement are not exclusively masculine prerogatives in the modern business world" and that "many a woman capitalist is running her own affairs with a sagacity that quite takes her out of the category of the 'unprotected.'" In 1909 the *Boston Herald* agreed that "evidences are everywhere apparent that more and more women are thoroughly understanding business and the necessity for systematic work." Heiresses who once gave themselves over entirely to pleasure were now managing their own wealth. Helen Gould, for one, "has her time completely engaged in her duties."[103]

The press competed to find new examples of women financiers, such as Miss Mollie O'Bryan and Miss Katherine Giles. O'Bryan was a successful organizer of mining companies in Colorado, where "she is regarded as one of the best judges of gold ore in the district." According to the Biloxi *Daily Herald*, she "has a charming personality, which is in quite refreshing contrast to the prosaic surroundings of a grim mining camp." Giles, "the cotton queen," was a statistician specializing in cotton shares. Her predictions were taken as "gospel" on Wall Street, where her reports largely determined cotton prices. Both women were described as pretty and feminine, though reporters invariably registered surprise that such attractive women would be engaged in business. "Strangest of all," one reporter wrote of Giles, "this woman of Wall Street is young and extremely good looking. She has reddish-golden hair, a tea-rose complexion and a trim, natty figure."[104]

Only two women, however, came close to generating excitement in the financial world comparable to Hetty Green: the pharmaceutical heiress Anne Weightman Walker and the company promoter Ella Rawls Reader. For a brief moment in the early twentieth century, Green's reign as the nation's most celebrated female tycoon was threatened by these two "rivals." While neither Walker nor Reader pitted themselves against Green, the press inevitably compared them to her, emphasizing how both women were more conventional and "womanly" than Green in appearance, deportment, and style of life. The women themselves also went to great lengths to project more acceptable, less threatening public personas than "the witch of Wall Street." As Susan Yohn has pointed out, successful businesswomen often employed "veiling strategies" to downplay their achievements and make themselves less threatening to men.[105]

Like Hetty Green, Anne Weightman Walker achieved her celebrity late in life. In 1904, at age sixty, she inherited the massive Philadelphia-based Weightman pharmaceutical empire, the world's leading producer of quinine and morphine. Dubbed "the quinine queen," Walker was now worth around $60 million, giving Hetty Green a run for her money as the richest woman in America. To the surprise of the business community, Walker took over the management of the company. She was already familiar with its operations, since, following the deaths of her brothers and husband, she had assisted her father, the company founder, in running the business.[106] William Weightman recognized his daughter's good business sense. Past ninety when he died, he had "lived long enough to find out that no man can excel a woman in business acumen when she sets her head to it."[107]

Walker's talent for business and the vast extent of her fortune led to frequent comparisons with Hetty Green. In 1904, when Walker inherited her father's company, one paper argued that "the immense interests which she now controls give her national prominence as ranking with Hetty Green, the foremost business woman of America." Others pointed out that the two women shared "an intense love for business life and amazing skill in high finance." Some people even wondered whether Walker's devotion to business had warped her feminine sensibilities, as they assumed to be the case with Green. For example, when Walker sold her family home in 1906, permitting "no sentimental feeling toward the house to stand in the way of a profitable use of the property," the *Philadelphia Inquirer* accused her of following the "example of Hetty Green."[108]

Walker's admirers were quick to point out that she shared only Green's love of business, not her eccentric lifestyle. An extended comparison of the "Two Women Financiers" in the *Springfield Republican* set Green's miserly habits against Walker's luxurious lifestyle. According to the paper, Hetty Green lived in "a shabby flat" in Hoboken for which she paid $300 a year. Anne Weightman Walker's lavish apartment at the Hotel Renaissance cost her $15,000 annually. Green allowed herself "just one personal servant," while Walker employed a dozen servants, including a French chef with a yearly salary of $2,500. "Totally unlike Mrs. Green, Mrs. Walker loves beautiful horses, French frocks, diamonds and the like. She likes to surround herself with interesting persons, and positively abhors eccentricity in any form."[109]

Above all else, Walker was celebrated as a "womanly woman" who, despite her business responsibilities, never forgot her duty to her family, to those less fortunate than herself, and to the gentle refinements of civilization. Unlike Hetty Green, Walker acknowledged that "wealth has its responsibilities," and she maintained a "charity bureau" that annually gave large sums of money to the poor of Philadelphia and to benevolent organizations like the Society for the Prevention of Cruelty to Children. Even Walker's hobby—collecting lace—was seen as reflecting a feminine sensibility. She hung lace all over her home, so that the delicate "bits of filmy white relieved the severity of the rooms."[110]

The press depicted Anne Weightman Walker as a gentler and more refined alternative to Hetty Green, but her moment of triumph was short-lived. Managing the Weightman drug empire proved too much for Walker, and within a year of inheriting the business she merged the company with another pharmaceutical giant, Rosengarten & Sons, creating a quinine and morphine trust in which she would no longer play an active role. According to press reports, she had encountered employee opposition to her leadership, and "her health began to give way." Having retired from the business, she would now have more time "for the laces that fill bureaus and cabinets at her home." Three years later, Walker married the writer and diplomat Frederic Courtland Penfield, devoting the remainder of her life to his career in the foreign service. At the time of her death in 1932, she was remembered as the widow of Congressman Walker and Ambassador Penfield. Her brief moment as the nation's most important businesswoman was not mentioned in her obituary.[111]

Shortly after Walker's retirement, another woman, Ella Rawls Reader, also took shape as "the financial rival of Hetty Green." On March 16, 1905, Mrs. Reader, a thirty-two-year-old businesswoman from Alabama, was thrust into the national spotlight. During Senate debates over a treaty with Santo Domingo (as the Dominican Republic was then known) empowering the U.S. government to manage the island nation's finances, Democratic senator John T. Morgan of Alabama made sensational charges against the Roosevelt administration. Citing Mrs. Reader as his source, Senator Morgan claimed that she and her husband had been on the verge of concluding their own "treaty" with President Morales of Santo Domingo to make her the nation's financial agent, and that Roosevelt, fearful of losing influence in the region, sent a naval gunboat to the island and pressured Morales into abandoning his financial agreement with the Readers in favor of a treaty with the United States.[112]

This tale of "petticoat diplomacy" riveted the nation, and journalists hastened to provide biographical details for the hitherto unknown Ella Rawls Reader.[113] The most detailed history of her early career remains the profile in *Everybody's Magazine*, published in four installments from September to December 1905. Penned by the popular novelist Juliet Wilbor Tompkins, the piece was extremely complimentary, proclaiming Reader "the greatest business woman in the world." Tompkins appears to have done little original research, basing her account almost entirely on material supplied by Reader. Employing a florid and melodramatic style, she constructed Reader's life as a classic rags-to-riches story.[114]

Born Ella Rawls in Marion, Alabama, her middle-class family became impoverished due to her father's investment in a failed railroad scheme. Vowing to recoup the family fortune, in 1891 an eighteen-year-old Ella traveled to New York, where "she was a friendless southern girl alone in that great Yankee stronghold!" After weeks in the city, having pawned her clothes and jewelry, and starving from lack of food, she finally secured a modest position addressing envelopes for the *Evening Post*. Scrimping and saving, she trained to be a typist and was soon earning more money. She organized her own stenographic firm in 1893, and within four years she supposedly had forty women in her employ and was earning $50,000 annually.[115]

With her newfound wealth she moved to London, where she secured a position as financial agent to the engineering firm J. G. White & Company. A much sought-after dinner guest, Rawls soon befriended the highest in the land. Little wonder she secured for White and Company lucrative government contracts for improving the London Underground Railway and for building a new railroad line in Johore, a British protectorate in Malaysia. The latter feat required Rawls to win over the Sultan of Johore, a hard-nosed, "coffee-colored" "oriental" potentate. Where other more devious financial agents failed, "this straightforward young American" succeeded, persuading the sultan with her "clear, businesslike exposition."[116]

In 1901, while in London, Rawls married Athole B. Reader, a New Zealand businessman who was then involved in developing South American copper mines, and she joined him in this endeavor. Mrs. Reader's business abilities apparently spread throughout the continent, and she was approached by Carlos Felipe Morales, president of Santo Domingo, who begged her to serve as the island's financial agent. But before Reader could finalize her agreement with Morales, Theodore Roosevelt sent his own agent to the island in 1905 onboard the U.S. gunboat *Castine*, demanding that the Dominicans deal directly with him. Cheated of her prize, Reader appealed to her old friend and fellow Alabaman, Senator Morgan, who, by denouncing Roosevelt's use of "the Big Stick," transformed Reader into an instant celebrity.[117]

Separating fact from fiction in *Everybody's Magazine*'s partisan biography is no easy task. Much of this fabulous account of Reader's early career is unverifiable and frankly preposterous. Surviving archival records and modern historical research do not confirm this version of events.[118] During Reader's lifetime, however, most subsequent stories about her accepted the biography from *Everybody's Magazine* as essentially accurate, often shamelessly cribbing from it for background information. Even writers hostile to Reader seldom challenged the events depicted in *Everybody's*, although they might well have subjected them to different interpretations. For example, some commentators doubted Ella Rawls Reader's financial acumen, suggesting that any influence she may have had over Latin American presidents and Malaysian sultans was entirely of a sexual nature.[119]

As Reader's contemporaries debated her achievements, they evaluated her in terms long familiar to discussions of women financiers. First and foremost, observers scrutinized her physical appearance. Everyone agreed that she was beautiful. According to the *Belleville News Democrat*, "her complexion is a wonder; her figure is girlish." Another paper described her as "a finely built woman" with "merry blue eyes." Writers expressed surprise that one so lovely would be involved in business, often comparing Reader to Hetty Green. The

Figure 11. "Mrs. Ella Rawls Reader, The Greatest Business Woman in the World," *Everybody's Magazine* (September 1905): 610. (Collection of the author)

Boston Herald pointed out that both women knew how "to make financial coups," but that only Reader knew "how to wear gowns." According to the *Herald*, "Mrs. Green is shrewd looking, careless of her dress and unattractive. Mrs. Reader is another individual. She does not resemble at all the usual conception of the business woman . . . She is fair, with a suggestion of faint pink coloring, and blue-eyed. She wears wonderful gowns."[120] If Hetty Green was the witch of Wall Street, then Ella Rawls Reader was its fairy queen. To underscore Reader's contrast to other businesswomen, *Everybody's Magazine* published a glamorous photograph of her, posing like a debutante in white gloves and a trailing gown of white lace.

Reader's admirers held that her lovely appearance was matched by an equally attractive demeanor. She was "a charming, womanly woman" with "a very pretty Southern manner, gracious and unaffected." If Hetty Green was impersonating a plainspoken Yankee matron, then Reader was playing the part of a southern belle. She moved languidly and spoke softly. Her femininity permeated her business interactions, which she carried out in an unhurried, relaxed manner. According to *Everybody's Magazine*, "she deals with large operations, with politics and intrigues, as composedly as the average housekeeper deals with the grocer and the laundress. . . . Most feminine of all," *Everybody's* applauded, "she frequently acts because of 'a feeling.'"[121]

Reader's reputation for beauty and charm was a mixed blessing. It brought her admiration as a lovely and gracious "womanly woman"—so unlike the brusque Hetty Green—but it also undermined people's willingness to take her seriously as a business figure. To some she was too pretty to be clever, while to others she merely used her feminine charms to twist foolish men around her little finger. Writers acknowledged "her peculiar power to bend men to her own ends." The *Boston Herald* maintained that "being beautiful and agreeable, men made way for her and let her do things." The London press saw her as a charming "hostess," rather than a skilled financier. Apparently her success in South America relied on the "tropical gallantry" of Latin men, who were "peculiarly open to feminine influence."[122]

Reader herself was keenly aware of the double standard whereby men sought to brand successful women as immoral for their breaching of the separate spheres. As she asked a reporter in 1907, "Did you ever notice that the moment a woman has anything to do with affairs of importance, jealous persons strive to taint her reputation? They speak of her as 'the woman in the case,' and seem to desire to make her out improper."[123] Reader and her admirers sought to counter claims that she traded on her feminine charms by emphasizing her masculine business sense.

Reader insisted that she never sought special treatment on account of her sex and that she conducted business like a man, a view endorsed by the *Boston Herald*: "She desires to be treated in business precisely as a man is treated. She asks people who talk business with her to forget that she is a woman, to put the talk on the plane they would adopt if they were talking to a man."[124] Reader's admirers especially commended her emotional equanimity. Unlike most women investors, she took "her chances like a sportsman," never losing her cool when the market went against her. As Reader admonished other women, "if an undertaking fails, take your medicine like a man."[125]

Like other women financiers before her, Ella Rawls Reader was faced with an impossible dilemma. How could she operate like a businessman without becoming "unsexed" and appearing too masculine? On the one hand, she insisted that "the young girl who decides to enter upon a business career must not think that it is necessary to become masculine in her manner," and that in her own dealings with men, "I never permitted them to think that I wanted to be regarded as 'one of the boys.'" On the other hand, Reader admitted that "the idea of one sphere for man and another for woman was always repulsive to me." Her motto, "if you want a thing, go get it," seemed too aggressive for a "womanly woman." Ultimately, these contradictions proved Reader's undoing.[126]

Reader's initial good press was probably grounded in the public's admiration for her as a feminine alternative to the usual Wall Street operator. She appeared gracious, charming, and kindly, rather than vulgar, selfish, and dishonest. Reader certainly tried to cultivate this positive impression. She maintained that unlike other promoters, she risked only her own money, and that "in all her varied undertakings, she has never caused anybody the loss of a cent." As a woman, she was primarily interested in assisting those in need, believing that "if I miss a chance to help anyone who needs my help, then my luck will go wrong."[127]

For a brief moment, the public saw Ella Rawls Reader as "the queen of promoters," presiding serenely and benignly over all she surveyed. This idealized image was unsustainable, especially for a woman engaged in financial promotion. Anne Weightman Walker could pose as the motherly protector of her family's business, and even Hetty Green could position herself as a conservative investor, opposed to speculation and monopoly. Reader, however, operated in the freebooting world of company promotion, where the ethical standards were notoriously low. As the public learned more about her business deals and as she became embroiled in nasty financial disputes, Reader seemed increasingly like one of the boys.

Following the "Santo Domingo treaty tangle," Reader and her husband focused their energies on copper promotions, but without much success. They floated a mining company with a nominal capital of $6 million, though Ella kept $5 million of the stock for her services. The American "copper king" J. B. Haggin denounced the Readers, circulating a letter in Wall Street against the company they were promoting: "It has no property and no mines, and is a fraud on those who have been induced to buy its stock. It is a fake concern, its officers are frauds, blackmailers and liars." The Readers sued Haggin for libel, demanding $1 million in damages.[128]

The Readers lost their court case and lost their reputations in the process. Athole Reader's testimony was so contradictory that a New York grand jury indicted him for perjury. The Readers were further embarrassed when a letter Athole had written to a business associate was read out in court. In it, he claimed that "Ella knows everything and everybody," that a dozen wealthy men, including Sir Thomas Lipton and an Indian prince, had proposed to her, and that she was planning to make him "a millionaire and Prime Minister of England." Many people now saw Mrs. Reader as an unscrupulous adventuress and Mr. Reader as her naive minion.[129] In 1909 the *New York Times* referred to Ella Rawls Reader as little better than a swindler, noting that "as an anti-climax to her fight for millions, she was sued by various creditors, from butchers to landlords, for sundry insignificant bills."[130]

At the height of her fame, she was known as the "lightning financier" and the "queen of promoters."[131] Unlike Walker, who managed a large corporation, or Green, who invested in other people's businesses, Reader was that rarest of beings—a female company promoter. She put together business deals and raised capital for new commercial schemes. These activities required skills for publicity and salesmanship that, in the popular imagination, veered dangerously close to hucksterism and confidence games. That a woman would choose such disreputable work was especially troubling, and Reader, despite her celebrity, was never able to overcome the stigma attached to financial promotion.

Ella Rawls Reader's sudden rise to fame and precipitous fall from grace recall the earlier short-lived financial career of Victoria Woodhull. Reader, like Woodhull, initially impressed her contemporaries as an attractive young woman with unique and unusual financial abilities. The public's infatuation for both women faded fast when they were knocked off their pedestals. Reader's financial achievements were certainly overhyped—by herself and by a novelty-seeking press—but her business dealings were probably no more egregious than those of many other company promoters of her time. Like Woodhull, Reader was brought down by the double standard. People expected more from her than they did from male financiers. Her shameless self-promotion, bravado, acquisitiveness, and questionable accounting were all bad enough when practiced by men but were intolerable in a woman.

*　*　*

A handful of women financiers rose above the ranks of ordinary businesswomen to achieve national prominence. They were subject to especially intense scrutiny, much of it centering on the question of whether women could succeed in the male world of finance without losing their womanly nature. So few women operated at the upper levels of American business that they all could be dismissed as "odd women"—exceptions to the rule that only men were capable of making the big deals and looking after the big money. It was generally assumed that wealthy, successful, and high-profile businesswomen like Hetty Green, Anne Weightman Walker, and Ella Rawls Reader were somehow different from normal women—more intellectual, less emotional—in ways that facilitated their financial activities. Businesswomen frequently adopted such views themselves, endorsing their own special status and confirming other women's economic incapacity. They also represented their financial responsibilities as a burden, insisting that they did not choose this work but that it was thrust upon them through necessity or circumstances beyond their control. Refusing to act as role models, they discouraged other women from following in their footsteps.

Whether businesswomen were admired or derided depended a great deal on their self-presentation. The soft-spoken Anne Weightman Walker received more favorable coverage than the assertive Hetty Green. Literary depictions of businesswomen followed a similar pattern, as exemplified by two popular novels: Margaret Deland's *The Iron Woman* (1911) and Charles John Cutcliffe Hyne's *Kate Meredith, Financier* (1906). Deland, a community activist and supporter of women's rights, portrayed her mill-owner protagonist, Sarah Maitland, as a hard-hearted capitalist. A mannish woman, unable to appreciate beauty or art, Sarah neglects her only child for her business. In the end she dies horribly, in an explosion of molten iron ore at her factory.[132] Cutcliffe Hyne, best known as the author of adventure stories, imagined a very different sort of businesswoman. Kate Meredith, a successful merchant, is also a beautiful and tender-hearted young woman. Her struggle to reconcile a life in business with a womanly nature mirrors many of the contemporary debates this chapter has examined about women's capacity for business and the effects of financial occupations on women's personalities and private lives.

Kate Meredith inherits her uncle's palm oil company and, to the amazement of her family, decides to manage the business herself. When her aunt tells her, "I don't believe in business women . . . I'd rather see a womanly woman," Kate replies, "You will see the two combined in me presently." Kate corners the palm oil market, and she subdues a recalcitrant African chief who stands in her way, but she never loses her sense of femininity. At one point she leads an expedition into the African jungle dressed in a green silk dress with matching hat and parasol. Kate's "natural craving for a home" expresses itself in the "rose-pink brocade, dainty carpets, and graceful flower bowls" with which she redecorates her uncle's old office. But an office is not a home, and her aunt asks her, "Do you ever bring up into mind that there is something more in life than mere financial success?" Kate realizes that her business triumphs are not enough, and she experiences true happiness only when the man she loves proposes to her.[133]

Businesswomen, in fiction and in fact, struggled against sexist assumptions that painted them as eccentric, aggressive, coarse, and mannish. Their very femininity was suspect, and they therefore felt compelled to demonstrate or enact typical womanly qualities to counteract the masculine taint of their occupations. The fictional Kate Meredith did so by redecorating her office. Real-life financiers Ella Rawls Reader and Anne Weightman Walker did so through fashionable dress and ladylike deportment, Hetty Green through professions of old-fashioned piety, and all three through expressions of maternal or familial devotion. For women, business success was almost something to be ashamed of. It could not be enjoyed or accepted without reservations but needed to be explained, excused, or papered over in pink brocade.

Epilogue and Conclusion

In the decades since the 1920s, American women have made notable progress as both investors and financial-sector employees, but in many areas of high finance, gender parity remains a distant dream. On Wall Street, women still hold few positions in upper management. The "old boys' network" in investment firms has long resisted female encroachment on what they believe is a masculine preserve, in spite of equal-employment legislation and class-action lawsuits. Popular media, in the guise of films like *Wall Street* (1987) and *The Wolf of Wall Street* (2013), continue to depict stockbroking as an aggressive and hypermasculine profession, not unlike its representation in Progressive Era novels from a century ago. Victorian attitudes about gender and finance can be seen in other areas, as well. Businesswomen are still subject to evaluations of their physical appearance in ways that male bankers and brokers are not. Different investment patterns by men and women are still characterized as emblematic of an essential, even biological, difference between the sexes.

Although the stock market crash of 1929 depressed overall levels of personal investment, it did not diminish women's position in Wall Street in proportion to men's, despite the prediction by the *New York Times* that women traders were "going back to bridge games."[1] In fact, during the Great Depression, women constituted 40% of the shareholders of America's big corporations. By the 1950s, women were half the nation's shareholders, a position they have held to this day.[2]

Despite women's growth as shareholders, Victorian stereotypes of women's financial incapacity had incredible staying power in the popular imagination. The trope of the silly woman who can't balance her checkbook or manage the household budget remained common well into the twentieth century, finding its last flowering on television sitcoms of the 1950s such as *I Love Lucy* or *My Little Margie*. In a 1952 episode of *Margie*, the vivacious and impulsive heroine, a twenty-something who still lives at home and doesn't work, vexes her banker father with her unrealistic attitude toward investment. In response to Margie's query "What's hot on the ticker tape?" her father suggests that she use her $400 capital to purchase stock in a reliable company, paying dividends of 4%. A $16 annual profit doesn't satisfy Margie, who wants to "triple her money fast!" and buy a new car. Vowing to change her father's pessimistic "opinion of a woman's ability to handle money," Margie inevitably falls into the clutches of a con artist.[3]

Like their Victorian predecessors, twentieth-century stockbrokers welcomed women's capital, even as they made fun of women customers. In 1962 the New York Stock Exchange produced a short film, *The Lady and the Stock Exchange*, designed to encourage female investment. The lady of the title is a suburban housewife who consults a broker about investing $4,500 for her son's college fund. She explores different possibilities recommended by the broker and sensibly prevails over her husband, who wants to follow a "hot tip" supplied by a friend. The heroine is absolutely clueless about investment but levelheaded enough to understand the need for professional advice from financial intermediaries, all of whom are men.[4]

Recent studies of investment behavior continue to assert that women are more risk-averse than men and that they are less comfortable managing money. In a 2004 study by Northwestern Mutual, only 30% of women believed that they were knowledgeable about money, compared to 50% of men.[5] Like their Victorian foremothers, women investors today are also more likely than men to buy and hold securities than to speculate on a quick return.[6] Such continuity can probably be explained by women's more modest financial resources, then as now, as well as social conditioning that still favors more cautious behavior from women than men. However, gendered analyses of financial behavior continue to emphasize essential differences between men and women. During the Victorian period, women were seen as too emotional to deal with a volatile financial system. They needed the steadying influence of men to counterbalance their natural impulsiveness. Today, much popular discourse still invokes biology to explain different financial behavior between the sexes.

A 1997 Smith Barney advertisement aimed at women investors proclaimed: "A woman's intuition is a powerful tool. Use it." The ad went on to maintain that, for women, "an investment has to feel right to be right." Nonetheless, a woman's "instinct" becomes "even more powerful when it's connected to knowledge." In other words, a woman's "intuitive decisions" needed to be combined with "the insight and analysis" of a (presumably male) "financial consultant."[7] A Citibank ad from 2002 argued that women were "natural investors," since they invested "time, energy and love" in the people around them.[8] In her best-selling guidebook *Women and Money* (2007), Suze Orman also insists that women are naturally nurturing and that this quality can be harnessed to teach them how to nurture their money.[9] Into the twenty-first century, attitudes toward women investors remain problematic, even as the number of women shareholders grows in significance.

The simultaneous growth of women workers within the financial sector has been far less dramatic and has been met with far greater hostility. In 1936, out of thousands of American stockbrokers, only seventy-two women were partners at brokerage houses that had seats on the New York Stock Exchange.[10] Of course, none of these women were themselves members of the nation's premier exchange. During World War II, a few women were employed on the floor of the New York Stock Exchange as quotation clerks and pages, but returning veterans replaced them at the war's end. Even in the midst of wartime manpower shortages, less than 1% of executive and managerial positions in American banks were held by women.[11]

The few women financiers who achieved positions of prominence struggled for respect in a male-dominated field. Isabel H. Benham became a leading analyst of railroad securities during the 1950s but signed her correspondence I. Hamilton Benham, fearing that businessmen might not respond if they knew she was a woman.[12] Mary Roebling, chairman of the board of the Trenton Trust Company, was referred to as a "Banker in High Heels."[13] Even women financial journalists, like Elizabeth Fowler at the *New York Times*, wrote about women on Wall Street in a different manner than they employed for men. In a 1957 profile of stockbroker Elizabeth E. Kennedy, Fowler noted that the "lady broker" was "the mother of two children and the owner of 150 hats."[14]

In the absence of male acceptance, women in finance assisted one another. In 1956 a group of eight female security analysts, excluded from professional organizations, founded the Financial Women's Association. In 1964 a group of women brokers formed the Women's Stockbrokers' Association for similar reasons. By the 1970s, these organizations had more than a hundred members, who assisted one another in career advancement.[15] A few milestones were passed during the 1960s: In 1965 Phyllis Peterson and Julia Montgomery Walsh became the first women brokers admitted to membership of the American Stock Exchange, and in 1967 Muriel Siebert became the first woman to purchase a seat on the New York Stock Exchange.[16]

Siebert had struggled to gain her seat. Although she had the purchase price, she was turned down by nine prospective sponsors before finding the requisite two. Upon her admission to the exchange in 1967, the press coverage included such sexist headlines as "Skirt Invades Exchange" and "Powder Puff on Wall Street." The *New York Times* described her as a thirty-nine-year-old blonde whose "black alligator shoes with fashionably thick two-inch heels" clicked across the trading floor. In fact, Siebert phoned in her orders for years, avoiding the trading floor out of fear that her presence there would elicit wolf whistles and other boorish behavior on the part of male colleagues.[17]

Deregulation of the securities industry in the 1970s, and the consequent expansion, led to new opportunities for women, especially in research and sales. Elaine Garzarelli emerged as one of Wall Street's most successful quantitative analysts during the 1980s, as did Abby Joseph Cohen during the 1990s.[18] In the thirty years since Muriel Siebert broke the barrier, fifty more women had become members of the New York Stock Exchange by 1999, though this represented only about 4% of the exchange's 1,366 members. Siebert herself sounded a cautionary note: "Firms are doing what they have to do, legally . . . women are coming into Wall Street in large numbers—and they are still not making partner and are not getting into the positions that lead to the executive suites. There's still an old-boy network."[19] In 2011, women constituted 55.4% of financial services employees, but only 16.6% of executives.[20]

The Equal Employment Opportunity Commission brought several sex-discrimination lawsuits against Wall Street firms starting in the 1970s.[21] Brokerage houses began promoting more women, though not necessarily treating them well. Susan Antilla's *Tales from the Boom-Boom Room: Women vs. Wall Street* (2002) documented a pattern of sexual harassment and discrimination in the financial industry during the 1980s and 1990s. Women on Wall Street were paid less than men for the same positions and frequently demoted after maternity leaves. In 1994, male sales assistants at Smith Barney were eight times more likely to become brokers than their female counterparts.[22] Women employees at brokerage houses were also subject to a constant barrage of sexist behavior: male colleagues called them bitches and "Playboy bunnies," threatened to rape them, and displayed pornographic images in shared office space. Unfortunately, it was next to impossible for women to get legal redress for such behavior, as Wall Street firms required their employees to waive the right to sue and instead to submit to an industry-sponsored arbitration. The procedure was secret and designed to avoid scandal but afforded complainants little in the way of due process.[23]

In 1996 a group of women at Smith Barney were able to circumvent mandatory arbitration by instituting a class-action lawsuit. Another gender-based class-action suit was filed in 1997 by female employees at Merrill Lynch, and in 1998 the New York state attorney general began public hearings on gender discrimination in the securities industry. Negative press coverage generated by the lawsuits and hearings encouraged Smith Barney to settle out of court, for an undisclosed amount. The unwanted publicity also caused the brokerage firm to mount an advertising campaign aimed at protecting its image.[24] In the aftermath of other discrimination lawsuits, the securities industry's trade group promised to issue regular "diversity studies" on the hiring of women by financial firms, but they dropped the practice after the 2007 report showed that little progress had been made.[25]

Women's foothold in Wall Street is far from secure, and in the aftermath of the 2008 financial crash, many of the industry's top female executives lost their jobs. Ina Drew was removed as chief investment officer at JPMorgan Chase. Sallie Krawcheck was ousted as chief executive officer at Citigroup and Zoe Cruz as co-president of Morgan Stanley. Cruz's hard-hitting style had earned her the nickname "Cruz missile," as well as the enmity of many male executives at the firm. Her friends suspected that "her status as a demanding woman in a male-dominated industry" did her in.[26] In 2012, women constituted only 19% of board members on Fortune 500 finance companies and 16% of banking executives in the United States.[27]

Popular representations of Wall Street have changed little in tone during the past century, although they have become more sexually explicit. They still perpetuate the notion that the world of high finance is presided over by greedy and priapic brokers. The Victorian incarnation swilled champagne, while his modern counterpart prefers cocaine. Female financiers in both eras have been the subjects of sexual parody.

The hyperaggressive, macho environment of American finance was personified during the 1980s by Gordon Gekko, the antihero of Oliver Stone's film *Wall Street* (1987). Two years later *Playboy* published its "Women of Wall Street" issue, which featured nude pictures of nine women office managers and sales assistants from Wall Street firms. The photo spread was bizarrely juxtaposed alongside a text by financial journalist Louis Rukeyser celebrating the achievements of women brokers like Muriel Siebert and chiding "the old fogeys of the exchange" for opposing women's advancement.[28] An even more demeaning scenario was envisioned by *Wanda Whips Wall Street*, an X-rated film from 1982. Wanda Brandt, "executive coordinator of human services" at a Wall Street investment firm, takes control of the business by seducing the key shareholders and sexually blackmailing them into supporting her takeover bid. The poster advertising the film depicted a buxom and scantily clad Wanda tearing through a giant stock certificate astride a charging bull.[29]

A century after Victoria Woodhull established her brokerage business in New York, some people continued to imagine that a woman could succeed on Wall Street only through the use of sexual wiles.

Businesswomen are still scrutinized in popular media in ways that male executives are not. For example, during Martha Stewart's 2004 trial for an illegal stock trade, the press devoted an inordinate amount of time to descriptions of her clothing, shoes, and handbags. In a 2005 profile of financial reporter Maria Bartiromo, James Brady referred to her as a "gorgeous journalist" whose nickname was "Money Honey."[30] In a recent story about former JPMorgan executive Ina Drew, Susan Dominus described her as "tall, with expensive blond hair," also noting her preference for "classic Chanel suits and Manolo Blahnik shoes, as well as a blinding emerald-cut diamond ring."[31]

Perhaps the oddest recent juxtaposition of women, finance, and sex involved Debrahlee Lorenzana, a thirty-three-year-old banking officer from Citigroup, who sued the bank in 2010 for sex discrimination, claiming that she was fired for being "too hot." She said that her bosses demanded that she alter her attire, since her voluptuous body was too distracting to her male coworkers, who could not concentrate on their work if she was nearby.[32] The story provides an update to a 1916 incident in Newark, where a stenographer at an insurance company was sent home because her hemline was too high and her blouse too transparent. She too had been distracting the men in the office.[33]

Only recently have representations of Wall Street women begun to reflect a female point of view. Maureen Sherry's comic novel *Opening Belle* (2016) depicts a savvy woman broker, Isabelle, who triumphs over the sexist taunts of coworkers. Sarah Megan Thomas and Alysia Reiner's suspense film *Equity* (2016) centers on the struggles of Naomi Bishop, an ambitious and talented investment banker. Both projects counter prevailing images of women in books and movies about Wall Street as "background players, hookers, strippers," and both draw upon the personal experience of their creators. Maureen Sherry was a former managing director at Bear Stearns. The funds to produce *Equity* were largely raised by twenty-five female financiers, "who also shared their own war stories of working in a male-dominated industry."[34]

Recent discussions of Wall Street's culture of machismo have invoked biological explanations that echo Victorian assumptions about sexual difference. In a *New York Times* article from 2000, the conservative writer Andrew Sullivan suggested that women were less successful in financial undertakings than men because they lacked testosterone, rendering them less aggressive and less open to risk-taking.[35] CNBC reported in 2012 that the latest trend among stockbrokers was testosterone shots to give them an extra push on the trading floor.[36]

In the aftermath of the financial crash of 2008, some commentators countered that too much testosterone was the problem and that more women brokers and financial analysts were needed to stabilize the market. In a 2009 editorial from the *New York Times*, Nicholas Kristof suggested that the current financial crisis might not have transpired "if Lehman Brothers had been Lehman Sisters." Kristof went on to cite scientific studies that linked male stock traders' testosterone levels with risk-taking. In the worst-case scenario, high testosterone levels could "shift risk preferences and even affect a trader's ability to engage in rational choice."[37] In contrasting a reckless masculine financial behavior with a more cautious feminine approach, Kristof and other commentators echo Victorian feminists' critique of Wall Street. Likewise, in its hormonal explanation of distinct male and female financial styles, the new "science" of "neuroeconomics" sounds remarkably similar to Victorian invocations of separate spheres.[38]

*   *   *

The continuation of sexist attitudes and practices on Wall Street should not blind us to the new economic avenues opened to women since the Financial Revolution. Much recent scholarship has shown that as early as the eighteenth century, propertied women were quick to take advantage of new investment opportunities supplied by banks and joint stock companies. Industrialism greatly expanded the choice of securities available to women, especially the stocks and bonds of railroad companies. As the middle classes grew in size and affluence, bourgeois women joined their wealthy and aristocratic sisters across the western world as shareholders and annuitants. This study has documented American women's affinity for the stock market during the Gilded Age and early twentieth century.

American women's shareholdings were facilitated and promoted by wealthy and middle-class families who recognized the convenience of financial securities in providing dowries, trusts, and legacies for their female relations. The propertied classes also championed legal reforms to protect women's marriage portions and inheritances from husbands and husbands' creditors, thus granting women greater financial agency. Fathers and trustees usually envisioned women submitting to the guidance of male financial advisors. While many women did so, others acted with remarkable independence. Even those women subject to trusts were free to reinvest the profits from the trusts as they saw fit. Some did so with greater success than their male trustees.

Women's financial achievements flew in the face of patriarchal assumptions and censorious public commentary that characterized capital accumulation as more suitable for men. This tension between practice and representation is one of the themes of this book. Indeed, literary condemnations of women investors became so pronounced in the nineteenth century that they have overshadowed and obscured the actual experiences and achievements of real women. Prescription does not equal practice, however, and separate-spheres rhetoric was most intense during the very period when women were vigorously contesting their legal, political, and economic subordination.

Representations of women investors tended to emphasize their financial vulnerability and incapacity. This was especially true of depictions by novelists and mainstream journalists, who were generally distrustful of Wall Street and stock "gambling." Such viewpoints reflected the prejudices of a professional middle class that upheld ideals of service and social responsibility against the supposedly selfish, moneygrubbing ways of capitalists. Progressive Era novels and journalistic exposés of high finance also drew upon Victorian melodramatic conventions that emphasized female victimhood.

The Wall Street novels of Upton Sinclair, Frank Norris, and Edith Wharton and the muckraking journalism of Louis Brandeis and Louis Guenther are better remembered today than capitalist apologies by their conservative contemporaries. Literary attacks on a culture of getting and spending still resonate with modern-day academics, for whom the professional worldview is more congenial than the entrepreneurial. Thus the past century's depictions of hapless women investors preyed upon by the wolves of Wall Street have crowded out other, contradictory representations.

Nineteenth-century financial journalists, in contrast, upheld the ideals of the commercial middle class. They defended the stock market as essential for financing the nation's economic growth and development. Investment guides and money articles offered their advice to women as well as men. Far from warning women away from Wall Street, as most novelists did, financial writers recognized female investors as a fact of life and sought to guide women's capital into certain safe and useful channels. Only recently have historians and literary scholars studied financial writings with the same respect they once paid to Victorian novels and muckraking journalism. As more varied sources are examined, more complicated depictions emerge of women as financial agents. While some writers emphasized women's financial incapacity and sought to shore up separate spheres, others championed greater economic opportunities and better financial education for women.

Women commentators have also expressed a wide array of opinions about women investors, colored by political, religious, and ideological differences.

Women were not a monolithic group, and even women's-rights advocates disagreed about Wall Street. Some were harshly critical of high finance, others eager to reap the benefits of capitalist accumulation. Many, like Victoria Woodhull, vacillated between these positions. All could agree that women needed to know more about how the family money was earned and invested. By the twentieth century, feminist critiques of women's financial subordination had become more accepted, even among people not normally thought of as advocates for women's rights.

An important corrective to literary and ideological debates about women and Wall Street is an examination of actual investment practices. Perhaps the most important contribution of this study is the recovery of American women's investment behavior, based on their stock portfolios and their correspondence with financial agents and advisors. While women as a whole were more cautious and conservative in their investment behavior than men, they were far removed from the literary stereotypes of the day that emphasized feminine indecision and incompetence. Some women were passive investors, dependent on the advice of their brokers and holding securities for steady income. Others were more active, even aggressive stewards of their own capital, seeking profits in the stock market no differently than businessmen. Nowhere in the historical records do we find the fussbudget, hysterical women shareholders that were so common in the novels, magazine articles, and films of a century ago.

It is also doubtful whether women as a whole were more victimized by financial fraud than men. Some white-collar criminals certainly preyed upon women, and many American women were ill-equipped to deal with the complexities of the share market, but then so were many men. That some fraudsters were themselves women further complicates the picture. These "petticoated sharks" were ingenious and unscrupulous enough to exploit an unregulated and opaque financial system to their own benefit. Their victims included men as well as women. Generalizations about female victimhood are highly problematic. Some women were crippled by the patriarchal structure of big business and high finance, but their stories have received a disproportionate share of attention as they conformed to prevailing gender stereotypes and could also serve to warn other women away from a lucrative male enclave. Women as a whole were not all equally vulnerable to financial exploitation.

Women investors, like their male counterparts, differed from one another in many respects. A crucial element that this study has emphasized is social class. Women shareholders were a minority of their sex and wealthier than the average American woman. But even within this rather privileged group, significant variations of wealth and status affected investment outcomes. Those women who were members of the Gilded Age plutocracy, like their male counterparts, were most likely to have access to privileged financial information. Their fortunes enabled them to take greater risks and offered them greater protection against the vicissitudes of the market. Some of these women embraced speculation with gusto and would have heaped scorn on the notion that they were too delicate or emotionally unstable to deal with stock market volatility.

Further down the social scale were middle-class widows living off the interest from government bonds, mortgages, and railroad securities, or schoolteachers with their small earnings squirreled away in savings banks. These more modest women investors were less cushioned against sudden downturns in the market and may have been tempted by dubious get-rich-quick schemes like the Boston Ladies' Depository. These were the "poor widows and spinsters" beloved of Victorian melodrama, but they were far from representative of the average female investor, nor were they necessarily helpless.

Hetty Green, "the female Croesus," has long been considered the antithesis of the average woman, but she was not nearly as exceptional as imagined. As this book has demonstrated, many other American women proved themselves extremely competent at managing their own money. These women investors and financiers were often subjected to discrimination and derision, but this was not always the case, nor did it prevent them from pursuing their economic self-interest. Like Hetty Green, they had admirers as well as detractors.

Unfortunately, characterizations of Hetty Green as "the witch of Wall Street" and women investors as "lambs to be fleeced" have been remembered better than the actual lives and experiences of the women themselves. Historians, cultural commentators, and popular writers of the mid–twentieth century celebrated the supposed progress, liberation, and modernity of their own era by imagining a nineteenth-century epitomized by extreme gender segregation, sexual repression, and patriarchal tyranny. While we should not discount the very real cultural, legal, and economic constraints on Victorian women's ambitions, they should not blind us to other possibilities. The "angel in the house" was also the "lady of the stock ticker." She could read the financial pages as well as the fashion pages, balance her own checkbook, and claim the profits from her stock portfolio on dividend day.

Notes

Introduction

1. Some notable examples of this work include Wendy Gamber, *The Female Economy: The Millinery and Dressmaking Trades, 1860–1930* (Urbana: University of Illinois Press, 1997); Mary A. Yaeger, ed., *Women in Business* (Cheltenham: Edward Elgar, 1999), 3 vols.; Erika Rappaport, *Shopping for Pleasure: Women and the Making of London's West End* (Princeton, NJ: Princeton University Press, 2000); Tammy Whitlock, *Crime, Gender and Consumer Culture in Nineteenth-Century England* (Aldershot: Ashgate, 2005); Ellen Hartigan-O'Connor, *The Ties That Buy: Women and Commerce in Revolutionary America* (Philadelphia: University of Pennsylvania Press, 2009); Alison C. Kay, *The Foundations of Female Entrepreneurship: Enterprise, Home and Household in London, c.1800–1870* (London: Routledge, 2009); and Laurence, Maltby, and Rutterford, eds., *Women and Their Money*.

2. Davidoff and Hall, *Family Fortunes*, 277.

3. Robertson and Yohn, "Women and Money," 221.

4. Barbara Hanawalt, *The Wealth of Wives: Women, Law, and Economy in Late Medieval London* (Oxford: Oxford University Press, 2007), 6–11, 65, 96; O'Day, *Women's Agency in Early Modern Britain*.

5. P. G. M. Dickson, *The Financial Revolution in England: A Study in the Development of Public Credit, 1688–1756* (New York: St. Martin's Press, 1967).

6. Carlos and Neal, "Women Investors in Early Capital Markets," 200–201; Anne Laurence, "Women and Finance in Eighteenth-Century England," in Laurence et al., *Women and Their Money*, 30–31. See also Peter Earle, *The Making of the English Middle Class: Business, Society and Family Life in London, 1660–1730* (Berkeley: University of California Press, 1989), 173.

7. Laurence, "Women, Banks and the Securities Market," 47; Furman, Pearson, and Taylor, "Between Madam Bubble and Kitty Lorimer," 95.

8. O'Day, "Matchmaking and Moneymaking," 273–96.

9. Froide, "The Business of Investing." See also Amy Froide's book *Silent Partners: Women as Public Investors during Britain's Financial Revolution, 1690–1750* (Oxford: Oxford University Press, 2016).

10. Carlos and Neal, "Women Investors in Early Capital Markets," 205–17, 223; Carlos, Maguire, and Neal, "Women in the City," 219–43. See also Laurence, "Women Investors, 'That Nasty South Sea Affair,'" 245–64, and Laurence, "Women, Banks and the Securities Market," 46–58.

11. Ingrassia, "The Pleasure of Business," 192. See also book by Ingrassia, *Authorship, Commerce, and Gender.*

12. Quoted in Staves, "Investments, Votes and 'Bribes,'" 269–70.

13. Kwolek-Folland, *Incorporating Women*, 9–24; Cleary, "'She Will Be in the Shop," 181–202; Elaine Crane, *Ebb Tide in New England: Women, Seaports and Social Change, 1630–1800* (Boston: Northeastern University Press, 1998); Cleary, *Elizabeth Murray*; Hartigan-O'Connor, *Ties That Buy*, 101–28.

14. Wright, *Hamilton Unbound*, 182–84; Wright, *The Wealth of Nations Rediscovered*, 70. See also Wright, "Women and Finance in the Early National U.S."

15. Holton, *Abigail Adams*, 189–90, 212–13, 238, 249, 273.

16. Wright, "Women and Finance," 5; Cleary, *Elizabeth Murray*, 96.

17. Staves, *Married Women's Separate Property*; Bailey, "Favoured or Oppressed?" 351–72.

18. Conger, *The Widow's Might.*

19. Some people have attributed the authorship of *The Hardships of the English Laws in Relation to Wives* to Sarah Chapone, the wife of a Gloucestershire clergyman. See Thomas Keymer, "Sarah Kirkham Chapone," *Oxford Dictionary of National Biography* (Oxford: Oxford University Press, 2004). For the significance of *feme sole* status, see Amy Froide, *Never Married*, 15, 144–51.

20. O'Day, *Women's Agency*, 264; Carlos and Neal, "Women Investors in Early Capital Markets," 201.

21. Phillips, *Women in Business*, 33; Wright, *Hamilton Unbound*, 180.

22. O'Day, *Women's Agency*, 263–94, 478–80. See also Lloyd Bonfield, *Marriage Settlements, 1601–1740: The Adoption of Strict Settlement* (Cambridge: Cambridge University Press, 1983).

23. Cleary, *Elizabeth Murray*, 86, 159.

24. *The Hardships of the English Laws in Relation to Wives* (London, 1735), 33.

25. Basch, *In the Eyes of the Law*, 109. For comparable information about English women, see Berg, "Women's Property and the Industrial Revolution," 238, 248.

26. Marylynn Salmon, "Equality or Submission?," 110; O'Day, *Women's Agency*, 267, 273–74.

27. Kerber, "Separate Spheres, Female Worlds," 22; Lebsock, "Radical Reconstruction and the Property Rights," 201.

28. Salmon, "Republican Sentiment," 452–54.

29. Basch, *In the Eyes of the Law*, 137.

30. Ibid., 115.

31. Quoted in Beach Laurence, "The Marriage Laws of Various Countries," 287.

32. Basch, *In the Eyes of the Law*, 159.

33. Shammas, "Re-Assessing the Married Women's Property Acts," 160.

34. Lebsock, "Radical Reconstruction and the Property Rights," 186–87.

35. Chused, "Late Nineteenth-Century Married Women's Property Law," 18–22; Warren, *Women, Money, and the Law*, 48–51.

36. Lebsock, "Radical Reconstruction and the Property Rights," 52.

37. Basch, *In the Eyes of the Law*, 213.

38. David Stewart, "Married Women Traders," 355–62.

39. Chused, "Late Nineteenth-Century Married Women's Property Law," 28.

40. Shammas, "Re-Assessing the Married Women's Property Acts," 21.

41. For broad historiographical discussions of the separate-spheres debate, see Kerber, "Separate Spheres, Female Worlds," 11–26, and Jan deVries, *The Industrious Revolution: Consumer Behavior and the Household Economy, 1650 to the Present* (Cambridge: Cambridge University Press, 2008), 102–3, 205–37.

42. Gerda Lerner, "The Lady and the Mill Girl: Changes in the Status of Women in the Age of Jackson," *Midcontinent American Studies Journal* 10 (Spring 1969): 5–15; Neil McKendrick, "Home Demand and Economic Growth: A New View of the Role of Women and Children in the Industrial Revolution," in *Historical Perspectives: Studies in English Thought and Society in Honour of J. H. Plumb*, edited by Neil McKendrick (London: Europa, 1974), 152–210; Heidi Hartmann, "Capitalism, Patriarchy and Job Segregation by Sex," *Signs* 1 (1976): 137–69; Nancy F. Cott, *The Bonds of Womanhood: "Woman's Sphere" in New England, 1780–1835* (New Haven, CT: Yale University Press, 1977); Sonya Rose, "Gender Antagonism and Class Conflict: Exclusionary Strategies of Male Trade Unionists in Nineteenth-Century Britain," *Social History* 13 (1988): 191–208; Louise A. Tilly, "Women, Women's History, and the Industrial Revolution," *Social Research* 61 (1994): 115–37; Mary P. Ryan, *Cradle of the Middle Class: The Family in Oneida County, New York, 1790–1865* (Cambridge: Cambridge University Press, 1981); Davidoff and Hall, *Family Fortunes* (1987).

43. Kerber, "Separate Spheres, Female Worlds," 11–19; Vickery, "Golden Age to Separate Spheres?" 391, 383–414; Hunt, *The Middling Sort*, 125–26.

44. M. Jeanne Peterson, "No Angels in the House: The Victorian Myth and the Paget Women," *American Historical Review* 89 (1984): 677–708; Stephen P. Walker, "Philanthropic Women and Accounting: Octavia Hill and the Exercise of 'Quiet Power and Sympathy,'" *Accounting, Business and Financial History* 16 (July 2006): 163–94.

45. Goldin, "The Economic Status of Women in the Early Republic," 375–404.

46. Wendy Gamber, *The Female Economy: The Millinery and Dressmaking Trades, 1860–1930* (Urbana: University of Illinois Press, 1997); Hannah Barker, *The Business of Women: Female Enterprise and Urban Development in Northern England, 1760–1830* (Oxford: Oxford University Press, 2006); Nicola Phillips, *Women in Business, 1700–1850* (Woodbridge, UK: Boydell Press, 2006). See also Lucy Eldersveld Murphy,

"Business Ladies: Midwestern Women and Enterprise, 1850–1880, *Journal of Women's History* 3 (Spring 1991): 65–89; Susan Ingalls Lewis, "Female Entrepreneurs in Albany, 1840–1885," *Business and Economic History* 21 (1992): 65–73; and Joyce Burnette, "Businesswomen in Industrial Revolution Britain: Evidence from Commercial Directories," *Essays in Economic and Business History* 14 (1996): 387–408.

47. Rutterford and Maltby, "'The Widow, the Clergyman and the Reckless,'" 111–38; Maltby and Rutterford, "'She Possessed Her Own Fortune,'" 220–53; Henry, "'Ladies Do It?'" 111–32. See also Freeman, Pearson, and Taylor, "'A Doe in the City,'" 265–91, and Robb, "Ladies of the Ticker," 120–40. For Canadian women's investments, see Peter Baskerville, *A Silent Revolution? Gender and Wealth in English Canada, 1860–1930* (Montreal: McGill-Queen's University Press, 2008).

48. Robb, *White-Collar Crime in Modern England*, 29–30, 92, 184–85, and Robb, "Women and White-Collar Crime," 1,058–72.

49. Yohn, "Crippled Capitalists," 85.

Chapter 1. *The Vortex of Speculation*

1. For recent histories of the Progressive Movement, see Michael McGerr, *A Fierce Discontent: The Rise and Fall of the Progressive Movement in America, 1870–1920* (New York: Free Press, 2003), and Shelton Stromquist, *Re-Inventing "The People": The Progressive Movement, the Class Problem, and the Origins of Modern Liberalism* (Urbana: University of Illinois Press, 2006).

2. Mark Twain and Charles Dudley Warner, *The Gilded Age: A Tale of Today* (New York: Harper and Brothers, 1873).

3. For discussion of Thoreau's economic thought, see Christian Becker, "Thoreau's Economic Philosophy," *European Journal of the History of Economic Thought* 15 (June 2008): 211–46, and Leonard Neufeldt, *The Economist: Henry Thoreau and Enterprise* (New York: Oxford University Press, 1989). Thomas Carlyle coined the term *cash nexus* in an 1839 essay, "Chartism," which lamented the dissolution of meaningful relationships between masters and men, replaced by impersonal cash payment. Carlyle elaborated on his social critique in *Past and Present* (1843). Matthew Arnold later criticized the materialism of middle-class "Philistines" in *Culture and Anarchy* (1869). John Ruskin's views of a "social economy" were expounded in *Unto This Last* (1862).

4. Perkin, *Origins of Modern English Society*, chapter 7.

5. For a history of the Social Gospel Movement, see Donald K. Gorrell, *The Age of Social Responsibility: The Social Gospel in the Progressive Era, 1900–1920* (Macon, GA: Mercer University Press, 1988). For related studies of religious attitudes toward capitalism in Victorian Britain, see Boyd Hilton, *The Age of Atonement: The Influence of Evangelicalism on Social and Economic Thought* (Oxford: Clarendon Press, 1988), and G. R. Searle, *Morality and the Market in Victorian Britain* (Oxford: Clarendon Press, 1998).

6. For a classic statement on the nineteenth-century cult of womanhood, see Nancy F. Cott, *The Bonds of Womanhood: "Woman's Sphere" in New England, 1780–1835* (New Haven, CT: Yale University Press, 1977).

7. Smith, *Bulls and Bears*; Smith, *Plain Truths*.

8. Smith, *Bulls and Bears*, 150.

9. Smith, *Plain Truths*, 27.

10. Ibid., 20.

11. Penny, *The Employments of Women*, 8–9.

12. Day, *Life with Father*, 5.

13. Smith, *Plain Truths*, 136–37; Smith, *Bulls and Bears*, 277.

14. Smith, *Plain Truths*, 138.

15. Fraser, *Every Man a Speculator*, 253.

16. Bok, "The Return of the Business Woman," 16.

17. For examples of investment advice from women's magazines, see Walker, "Hints to Women on the Care of Property," 250, and Barrett, "Investment in Stocks and Bonds," 10.

18. Anderson, "Women in Wall Street," 22–25.

19. "Women Gamblers in Wall Street," 104, 106, and 108.

20. Raskob, "Everybody Ought to Be Rich," 9.

21. For examples of articles favorable to speculation, see Smith, "Speculation and Investment," 524–47, and Atwood, "Secret of Riches," 31.

22. A few surviving Populists, such as Robert La Follette and William Borah, continued to criticize high finance. Most of the press had thrown in its lot with Wall Street, with an occasional objection raised by *Harper's* or *Christian Century*. See, for example, Merz, "The Bull Market," 640–46, and "Playing the Stock Market," 255.

23. Barnard, "Ladies of the Ticker," 406, 410.

24. Poovey, *Genres of the Credit Economy*, 247; see also Poovey's chapter 4 on financial journalism.

25. Thompson, "Early Books on Investing," 83–110.

26. Poovey, "Writing about Finance in Victorian England," 41.

27. Parsons, *The Power of the Financial Press*, 49.

28. Itzkowitz, "Fair Enterprise or Extravagant Speculation," 98–119.

29. Creighton, "Women and Finance," 20.

30. Banker's Daughter, *Guide to the Unprotected*.

31. Ibid., 1881 edition, vii.

32. Banker's Daughter, *Guide to the Unprotected*, 13, 14.

33. Nichols, *Safe Methods of Business*, 146–47.

34. Banker's Daughter, *Guide to the Unprotected*, 9, 10–12.

35. Cromwell, *American Business Woman*, vi–vii, 96–99.

36. Ibid., 389–90.

37. Itzkowitz, "Fair Enterprise or Extravagant Speculation," 111.

38. Poovey, "Writing about Finance," 41. Poovey is referring to entertaining narratives of Britain's financial culture, but her characterization is equally applicable to writings about Wall Street. For some British examples comparable to the American works I discuss, see John Francis, *Chronicles and Characters of the Stock Exchange* (London: Willoughby, 1849), David Morier Evans, *Facts, Failures and Frauds* (London:

Groombridge and Sons, 1859), and H. R. Fox Bourne, *Romance of Trade* (London: Cassell, Petter and Galpin, 1871).

39. Percy, *Our Cashier's Scrap-Book*, 111–12.

40. See, for example, Powell, "The Views of Viola," 4.

41. See, for example, the poem by Edgar Guest, "Ma and Her Checkbook," *A Heap o' Livin'* (Chicago: Reill and Lee, 1916), 100.

42. Day, *Life with Father*, 98–99.

43. *Sayings of Uncle Rufus*, 14–17.

44. Lefevre, "A Woman and Her Bonds," 21–30.

45. Fowler, *Twenty Years of Inside Life in Wall Street*, 242, 449–50.

46. Clews, *Twenty-Eight Years in Wall Street*, 437, 444. For more information on Clews's career, see "Henry Clews" in *Encyclopedia of American Business History: Banking and Finance to 1913*, edited by Larry Schweikart (New York: Facts on File, 1990), 120–22.

47. Westbrook, *Wall Street in the American Novel*, 9.

48. Walch, *Doctor Sphinx*, 339.

49. French, *The Lion's Share*, 309.

50. Among the extensive scholarship on Victorian literature's engagement with commercial and financial themes, see Elsie B. Michie, *The Vulgar Question of Money: Heiresses, Materialism, and the Novel of Manners from Jane Austen to Henry James* (Baltimore: Johns Hopkins University Press, 2011); Wagner, *Financial Speculation in Victorian Fiction*; Henry and Schmitt, eds., *Victorian Investments*; Ranald Michie, *Guilty Money: The City of London in Victorian and Edwardian Culture* (London: Pickering and Chatto, 2009); O'Gorman, ed., *Victorian Literature and Finance*; Paul Delany, *Literature, Money and the Market: From Trollope to Amis* (Basingstoke: Palgrave, 2002); Martha Woodmansee and Mark Osteen, eds., *The New Economic Criticism: Studies at the Intersection of Literature and Economics* (New York: Routledge, 1999); Russell, *The Novelist and Mammon*; John Vernon, *Money and Fiction: Literary Realism in the Nineteenth and Early Twentieth Centuries* (Ithaca, NY: Cornell University Press, 1984); and Reed, "A Friend to Mammon," 179–202.

51. Westbrook, *Wall Street in the American Novel*, 129.

52. Theodore Dreiser, *The Financier* (1912), *The Titan* (1914), and *The Stoic* (1947); Upton Sinclair, *A Captain of Industry* (1906), *The Moneychangers* (1908), and *The Metropolis* (1908); David Graham Phillips, *The Master-Rogue* (1903), *The Cost* (1904), and *The Deluge* (1905). Frank Norris wrote *The Octopus* (1901) and *The Pit* (1902); a planned third volume, *The Wolf*, was never written.

53. Very little scholarship has addressed the role of women in American financial novels. There is, however, an abundance of recent scholarship about women and finance in British novels of the Victorian period. See note 50, above. This work has proved useful in my reading of the American literature.

54. Hawley Smith, *The Promoters*.

55. Norris, *The Pit*, 40.

56. For a perceptive analysis of women and money in Wharton's work, see Westbrook, *Wall Street in the American Novel*, 130–41.

57. Wharton, *The Buccaneers*, 23.

58. Walch, *Doctor Sphinx*, 346.

59. For a discussion of financial melodramas, see Jane Moody, "The Drama of Capital: Risk, Belief, and Liability on the Victorian Stage," in O'Gorman, *Victorian Literature and Finance*, 91–109.

60. Dreiser, *The Financier*, 104. In the later volumes of the Cowperwood trilogy, the protagonist's sexual promiscuity came to dominate the novels and embroiled Dreiser in frequent censorship battles.

61. Sinclair, *The Moneychangers*, 69.

62. Wharton, *The House of Mirth*, 89–90.

63. Ibid., 123, 153–54.

64. In a later novel, *The Custom of the Country* (1913), Wharton details the social ascent of Undine Spragg, bankrolled by her father's shady financial dealings.

65. Kirk, *Queen Money*, 16, 333.

66. Walch, *Doctor Sphinx*, 346–47. See also Herrick, *The Gospel of Freedom*.

67. Boyesen, *A Daughter of the Philistines*, 35, 71.

68. Kirk, *Queen Money*, 483.

69. Flagg, *Wall Street and the Woods*, 92, 100, 102, 103, 104. Flagg's novel embodies the populist, agrarian hostility to the urban financial centers of the Northeast that controlled the nation's cash and credit. Midwesterners and southerners especially felt themselves at the mercy of Wall Street tycoons and eastern bankers who manipulated railroad rates and grain prices and controlled farm mortgages.

70. Campbell, *Mrs. Herndon's Income*, 530. Campbell had a strong interest in women's economic condition and was best known for her sociological studies of women workers, such as *Women Wage-Earners* (1893) and *Prisoners of Poverty* (1900). She was for many years professor of home economics at the University of Wisconsin, where she wrote cookbooks and books on household management. For another Christian fable about women and money, see Margaret Deland, "The House of Rimmon," in *The Wisdom of Fools*, 116–28.

71. Field, "A Woman's Romance in Wall Street," 151, 152, 158.

72. Clews, *Fortuna: A Story of Wall Street*, 4–5.

73. Ibid., 67, 68.

74. Ibid., 72–73.

75. Margaret Mayo and Edgar Selwyn, *The Wall Street Girl* (1912).

76. Frederick Orin Bartlett, *The Wall Street Girl* (New York: Houghton Mifflin, 1916).

77. See, for example, two Wall Street novels by Edwin Lefevre: *The Reminiscences of a Stock Operator* (1923) and *The Making of a Stockbroker* (1924).

78. Cather, "The Novel Démeublé," 46.

79. For the early history of American film, see George C. Pratt, *Spellbound in Darkness: A History of the Silent Film* (Greenwich, CT: New York Graphic Society, 1966).

80. M. Keith Booker, *Film and the American Left: A Research Guide* (Westport, CT: Greenwood Press, 1999).

81. The film has not survived, but a detailed description of the story is given in the Edison Company's *Kinetogram* (1914), 12.

82. "Women in Wall Street," *New York Times*, 12 December 1909.

83. For discussions of *The Cheat*, see Janet Staiger, *Bad Women: Regulating Sexuality in Early American Cinema* (Minneapolis: University of Minnesota Press, 1995), 166–76, and Sumiko Higashi, *Cecil B. DeMille and American Culture: The Silent Era* (Berkeley: University of California Press, 1994), 100–112.

84. Hofer, *The Games We Played*, 78–91; Fraser, *Every Man a Speculator*, 247.

85. Quoted in "Dear Alibel," *Times Literary Supplement* (11 February 2005): 5.

Chapter 2. Engendering Finance

1. Cowing, *Populists, Plungers, and Progressives*; Geisst, *Wall Street*; Fraser, *Every Man a Speculator*.

2. Quoted in "Speculating Women," *New York Times*, 17 January 1875.

3. Fowler, *Twenty Years of Inside Life in Wall Street*, 449.

4. "Women Seeking 'Points,'" *New York Times*, 24 September 1882.

5. Geisst, *Wall Street*, 101; Fraser, *Every Man a Speculator*, 90; Sobel, *The Big Board*, 103.

6. Michie, *London and New York Stock Exchanges*, 196–99.

7. Sobel, *The Curbstone Brokers*, 62–63; Michie, *London and New York Stock Exchanges*, 212. For a discussion of regional stock exchanges, see Mary O'Sullivan, "The Expansion of the U.S. Stock Market," 511–17.

8. Sobel, *The Big Board*, 87. The significance of the stock ticker can be gauged in David Hochfelder, "'Where the Common People Could Speculate,'" 338–40.

9. "Women Seeking 'Points,'" *New York Times*, 24 September 1882.

10. New York Historical Society, G. V. Fox Papers, series 10, volume 4, Property Book.

11. Davidoff and Hall, *Family Fortunes*, 277–79.

12. New York Historical Society, G. V. Fox Papers, Property Book.

13. Ibid.

14. New York Historical Society, Morton, Bliss & Company, Stockbrokers, Letter Book (March 1880–January 1881), 13 November 1880.

15. New York Historical Society, Morton, Bliss & Company, Stockbrokers, Ledgers, 6 volumes (1884–99), and Letter Books of George Bliss, 12 volumes (1876–91); George P. Butler & Brother, Stockbrokers, Ledgers, 4 volumes (1905–10), and Letter Books, 3 volumes (1906–10).

16. "George Bliss," *Dictionary of American Biography*, edited by Allen Johnson (New York: Charles Scribner's Sons, 1964), 1:372–73, and "Levi P. Morton," ibid., 7:258–59. See also "Levi P. Morton" *Encyclopedia of American Business History and Biography: Banking and Finance to 1913*, edited by Larry Schweikart (New York: Facts on File, 1990), 365–72.

17. Data in this paragraph and in those that follow, concerning Morton, Bliss investment accounts for 1886–87, are derived from New York Historical Society, Morton, Bliss & Company, Ledger 7 (1884–88).

18. In examining investment income for Morton, Bliss clients, detailed information is available for twenty-one of the firm's twenty-four women's accounts for 1886–87.

A sample of twenty men's accounts from the same period (out of thirty-nine total) was used for comparison.

19. To contextualize this investment income, average annual salaries for the 1880s might range from $200 for a farm laborer, to $400 for a factory worker, to $1,000 for a skilled worker, to $3,000 for a middle-class professional. See Stuart M. Blumin, *The Emergence of the Middle Class: Social Experience in the American City, 1760–1900* (Cambridge: Cambridge University Press, 1989), 272–74, and Susan B. Carter et al., eds., *Historical Statistics of the United States* (New York: Cambridge University Press, 2006), 2:271.

20. Rutterford and Maltby, "'The Widow, the Clergyman and the Reckless,'" 111–38; Maltby and Rutterford, "'She Possessed Her Own Fortune,'" 220–53.

21. For a discussion of trusts, see Hendrick Hartog, *Man and Wife in America: A History* (Cambridge, MA: Harvard University Press, 2000), 169–74; Davidoff and Hall, *Family Fortunes*, 208–10; Chantal Stebbings, *The Private Trustee in Victorian England* (Cambridge: Cambridge University Press, 2002).

22. Morton, Bliss & Company, Ledger 7, 289.

23. Ibid., 411.

24. Ibid., 456.

25. Ibid., 328–29, 413.

26. Ibid., 407, 536.

27. Ibid., 467.

28. Ibid., 440–41, 548, 578, 586, 598.

29. O'Sullivan, "The Expansion of the U.S. Stock Market," 495.

30. Morton, Bliss & Company, Ledger 7, 210.

31. Ibid., 601.

32. Ibid., 243–44. Bliss frequently advised women to diversify their holdings. See Morton, Bliss & Company, Letter Book (May 1884–October 1885); 17 July 1884; 28 January 1885; 22 May 1885.

33. Morton, Bliss & Company, Ledger 7, 78–79, 272–73. See also case of Mahlon Sands, 319, 321.

34. Morton, Bliss & Company, Letter Book (April 1879–March 1880); 3 October 1879; and 9 October 1879.

35. Ibid., Letter Book (December 1877–May 1879); 24 December 1878; and Letter Book (April 1879–March 1880), 14 July 1879.

36. Ibid., Letter Book (January 1881–January 1882), 17 May 1881.

37. Ibid., Letter Book (January 1882–March 1883), 5 April 1882.

38. Pinto, *Ye Outside Fools!*, 45.

39. Morton, Bliss & Company, Letter Book (December 1877–May 1879), 9 February 1879.

40. Ibid., 15 March 1878; 15 May 1878; and 5 June 1878.

41. Ibid., 17 May 1878. Josephine Price was another married woman of the era who enhanced her family's standing through successful stock-market investments. Laura Claridge, *Emily Post* (New York: Random House, 2008), 17–18.

42. Morton, Bliss & Company, Letter Book (April 1879–March 1880), 17 May 1879; 14 July 1879; 15 July 1879; 25 July 1879.

43. Freeman, Pearson, and Taylor, "'A Doe in the City,'" 281. For a general discussion of the financial press, see Parsons, *The Power of the Financial Press.*

44. Morton, Bliss & Company, Letter Book (June 1887–January 1889), 9 December 1887.

45. Ibid., (March 1890–May 1891), 4 June 1890.

46. Ibid., (March 1883–May 1884), 3 October 1883.

47. Ibid., (April 1879–March 1880), 10 January 1880.

48. Ibid., (October 1885–June 1887), 6 December 1886. See also Bliss's advice to Mrs. W. F. Fogg, 7 December 1886 and 10 December 1886.

49. Ibid., (October 1885–June 1887), 26 June 1886; (June 1887–January 1889), 9 November 1887.

50. Michie, *London and New York Stock Exchanges,* 169, 177.

51. O'Sullivan, "Expansion of the U.S. Stock Market," 495–99, 503.

52. Means, "The Diffusion of Stock Ownership," 565.

53. Steve Fraser, for instance, conflated Means's figures for book stockholders with individual investors. *Every Man a Speculator,* 250.

54. Cowing, *Populists, Plungers, and Progressives,* 95.

55. "Women Squeal," *Cleveland Plain Dealer,* 13 May 1894; "Woman Saves Girls Who Made Bad Investments," *Colorado Springs Gazette,* 27 December 1911; "In Quest of Great Fortune," *Omaha World Herald,* 8 January 1895.

56. Hudson, *The Making of "Mammy Pleasant,"* 8–9, 32, 34.

57. W. C. Van Antwerp noted that in 1912, the nation's 247 largest corporations had some 1 million shareholders. *Current Opinion* cited 1913 data from 252 major corporations in which the number of women shareholders was 310,000. Assuming considerable overlap between the samples, women would account for 31% of the nation's shareholders. A 1909 Report for the National Banks had revealed that 31% of bank shareholders were women. This percentage should probably be adjusted downward, as women were more likely to own bank stock and the shares of major corporations, and less likely to own shares in smaller companies unrepresented in Van Antwerp's and *Current Opinion*'s samples. Hence my "guesstimate" that 20–25% of the nation's shareholders were women circa 1910. Van Antwerp, *The Stock Exchange from Within,* 15, and "Women's Ownership of Corporations," 304.

58. *New York Times,* 12 December 1909.

59. "Women's Ownership of Corporations," 306.

60. "Excluding Women from Brokers' Offices," *New York Times,* 13 July 1902.

61. For the growing importance of the telephone among women investors, see "Wall Street Connected with Many Camps and Cottages," *New York Times,* 12 August 1903.

62. "Confessions of a Stockbroker," 1,469.

63. Cowing, *Populists, Plungers, and Progressives,* 115.

64. *New York Times,* 12 December 1909.

65. "A Woman's Adventure in Investments," *The World's Work,* 144.

66. For the early history of bucket shops in America, as well as possible derivations of the name, see Fabian, *Card Sharps, Dream Books, and Bucket Shops*, 188–200.

67. Hochfelder, "Where the Common People Could Speculate," 340–45. For discussion of British bucket shops, see Itzkowitz, "Fair Enterprise or Extravagant Speculation," 113–118.

68. Michie, *London and New York Stock Exchanges*, 196–99; Hochfelder, "Where the Common People Could Speculate," 343–44; Fabian, *Card Sharps, Dream Books, and Bucket Shops*, 191–92.

69. Lefevre, *Reminiscences of a Stock Operator*, 34.

70. "Female Bucket-Shops," 4; "Wall St. Shys at Women," *Watertown (NY) Daily Times*, 18 September 1897.

71. Field, "A Woman's Romance in Wall Street," 157.

72. Anderson, "Women in Wall Street," 24.

73. Field, "Woman's Romance in Wall Street," 158; Anderson, "Women in Wall Street," 25.

74. Hochfelder, "Where the Common People Could Speculate," 350–58. For the New York Stock Exchange's hostility to bucket shops, see Van Antwerp, *Stock Exchange from Within*, 144.

75. Obituary for Arthur W. Butler, *New York Times*, 22 November 1949.

76. Shareholder data for George P. Butler & Brother are based on information from Ledger 6 (1908–99). Ranald Michie has estimated that the average shareholding for an American investor in 1912 was $25,700. *London and New York Stock Exchanges*, 228.

77. Specific investment information for Butler Brothers in 1908–9 is based on an analysis of the stock portfolios of twenty women clients (out of twenty-five) and a sample of thirty men (out of sixty-five). The dominance of bonds is typical. Before 1927, bonds accounted for about 75% of all new securities coming onto the market. Sales of corporate and government bonds on the New York Stock Exchange also typically outnumbered sales of shares by a factor of ten. Geisst, *Wall Street*, 159.

78. In 1910, industrial shares represented 46% of stocks traded on the New York Stock Exchange. O'Sullivan, "Expansion of the U.S. Stock Market," 499. Male clients at Butler Brothers had 37% of their capital invested in industrial securities.

79. George P. Butler & Brother, Ledger 6, 557.

80. Ibid., 359.

81. George P. Butler & Brother, Letter Book, 3 December 1909. Emphasis in original.

82. Margaret Munn was married to the painter George Frederick Munn, who died in 1907. Her play, *Will Shakespeare of Stratford and London*, was published in 1910. It was later staged on Broadway in 1932 as *The Passionate Pilgrim*. *The Art World* 2 (April 1917): 69.

83. George P. Butler & Brother, Letter Book, 6 December 1909.

84. Dickinson, *A Paying Investment*.

85. George P. Butler & Brother, Letter Book, 10 July 1909; 23 August 1910.

86. Ibid., 1 May 1909; 5 May 1909.

87. Ibid., 29 July 1909.

88. Ibid., undated.

89. Ibid., 13 August 1909.

90. Ibid., 16 July 1909.

91. Ibid., 25 October 1909.

92. Ibid., 11 February 1909.

93. Ibid., 28 June 1909.

94. Morton, Bliss & Company, Ledger 7, 259. See also case of Mrs. E. S. Billings, ibid., 250.

95. Means, "Diffusion of Stock Ownership," 595. Although there was a huge broadening of the number of shareholders, most people's investments were not extensive. As late as the 1920s, probably about 75% of the total value of U.S. securities was held by no more than half a million people. At the time of the market crash in 1929, only 1.5 million Americans (out of 120 million) had brokerage accounts. Fraser, *Every Man a Speculator*, 391; Galbraith, *The Great Crash*, 78.

96. Hochfelder, "Where the Common People Could Speculate," 357.

97. Julia C. Ott, *When Wall Street Met Main Street*, 151–63; Marchand, *Creating the Corporate Soul*, 80; Means, "Diffusion of Stock Ownership," 569.

98. Marchand, *Creating the Corporate Soul*, 74–77.

99. "Our Stockholders," *National Geographic* (May 1919).

100. Geisst, *Wall Street*, 157–58; Means, "Diffusion of Stock Ownership," 587–91.

101. Eleanor Roosevelt Papers, Box 2078, 1918 Income Tax Return, 1919 List of Personal Investments, Franklin D. Roosevelt Library, Hyde Park, NY. Eleanor received an additional $3,800 in income from three family trust funds, of which almost 40% was derived from government securities.

102. Fraser, *Every Man a Speculator*, 347; Geisst, *Wall Street*.

103. Geisst, *Wall Street*, 149–50; Fraser, *Every Man a Speculator*, 350; Lefevre, *Making of a Stockbroker*, 308.

104. Ott, *When Wall Street Met Main Street*, 55–74; Fraser, *Every Man a Speculator*, 351; Whitfield, *Pickford*, 178–80.

105. Mary Carolyn Waldrop, ed., *60 Great Patriotic Posters* (Mineola, NY: Dover, 2010), 16.

106. Caplan, *Petticoats and Pinstripes*, 80.

107. Ginzburg, "Wall Street Under the New Deal," 70.

108. Greig and Gibson, "Women and Investment," 174–82, quoted in Maltby et al., "The Evidence for 'Democritization' of Share Ownership in Great Britain in the Early Twentieth Century," in *Men, Women, and Money: Perspectives on Gender, Wealth, and Investment, 1850–1930*, edited by David R. Green, Alastair Owens, Josephine Maltby, and Janette Rutterford (Oxford: Oxford University Press, 2011), 198.

109. "Women Gamblers in Wall Street," *Forum* (January 1918): 101, 103–4.

110. Ibid., 102–3, 107.

111. Strom, *Beyond the Typewriter*, 93; Ott, *When Wall Street Met Main Street*, 187.

112. Eva Vom Bauer, "Accounting," Lecture 23, part 2, 11 April 1916, 35, and Elizabeth E. Cook, "Finance," Lecture 23, part 1, April 11, 1916, 16, Bureau of Vocational Information Archives, Schlesinger Library, Harvard University. For information on pioneering women brokers, see "Women Who Earn $10,000 a Year," *Evening Star* (Washington, DC), 27 June 1915; "Radcliffe Girl Is Bond Salesman," *Boston Herald*, 11 July 1915; "Woman Manages Bond Department for Women, *Boston Herald*, 23 April 1916; "Women Who Manage Your Affairs," *Boston Herald*, 10 January 1916; "Mrs. Jacob Riis," *Riverside Independent Enterprise*, 22 February 1921.

113. Gildersleeve, *Women in Banking*, 7–13; Mott, *An American Woman and Her Bank*, 129–30.

114. Census Bureau, Sixteenth Census of the United States, 1940, *Comparative Occupation Statistics*, 69, 171; Hill, *Women in Gainful Occupation*, 178–79. The 1910 census had found four black women stockbrokers.

115. "Women's Investment Invasion," *Barron's* 7 (15 August 1927); 4, 18; Listing of Stockholders as of January 31, 1925, Insurance Company of North America, ACE Archives, Philadelphia.

116. Ott, *When Wall Street Met Main Street,* 284; Barnard, "Ladies of the Ticker," 406; Janice Traflet, "'Everybody Ought to Be Rich,'" 23.

117. "Women Now Investing Millions: Housewives Big Stock Buyers," *New York Times*, 16 February 1927.

118. "Women and Wall Street," *North American Review* 229 (January 1930): 121.

119. Wendt, *Classification and Financial Experience of the Customers*, 50; Barnard, "Ladies of the Ticker," 408.

120. White, "Women's Savings Club Earns $80 per Share," 942–43.

121. Barnard, "Ladies of the Ticker," 405–6; "100,000 Women Play the Market Here," *New York Sun*, 7 November 1929.

122. "The Business Woman's Investments," 1199, 1246.

123. Barnard, "Ladies of the Ticker," 409.

124. "Women Stockholders Rapidly Increase," 116.

125. Barnard, "Ladies of the Ticker," 408; "Women's Investment Invasion," 18.

126. Frazer, "Did You Lose Your Shirt in the Market?" 15; "100,000 Women Here Play the Market," 35; Barnard, "Ladies of the Ticker," 405.

127. Ott, *When Wall Street Met Main Street,* 186–88; Barnard, "Ladies of the Ticker," 407.

128. "Baird and Warner Plan," 970.

129. "Wall Street Bids for the Woman Speculator," 86; "100,000 Women Here Play the Market," 35.

130. Barnard, "Ladies of the Ticker," 405–6, 410.

131. Eleanor Roosevelt Papers, Box 2082, Correspondence with Banks, Franklin D. Roosevelt Library, Hyde Park, NY.

132. Klein, *Rainbow's End*, 148; Barnard, "Women in Wall Street Wielding a New Power," 23 June 1929.

133. "30 Billions in Bonds Handled by Woman," *New York Times*, 6 April 1927; "Working Girls Buying Wall Street Securities," *New York Times*, 5 January 1928.

134. Census Bureau, 1940, *Comparative Occupation Statistics*, 69; Census Bureau, *A Social-Economic Grouping*, 138.

135. "Woman Seeks a Seat on the Stock Exchange," *New York Times*, 14 January 1927; New York Stock Exchange Archives, Minute Books of Admissions Committee, vol. 12 (1924–29).

136. Robison, "Women Learn How to Invest on Big Scale," *New York Times*, 25 July 1926.

137. Ibid., 409.

138. Frazer, "Did You Lose Your Shirt?" 122.

139. "Wall Street Bids for the Woman Speculator," 86; Frazer, "Did You Lose Your Shirt?" 124.

140. "100,000 Women Here Play the Market," 35.

141. Barnard, "Ladies of the Ticker," 409.

142. Vickery, "Golden Age to Separate Spheres?" 400.

Chapter 3. Lambs to be Fleeced and Petticoated Sharks

1. Henry Norman, "The Feminine Failure in Business," *Forum* (April–May 1920): 457.

2. See, for example, Yohn, "'Men Seem to Take a Delight in Cheating Women,'" 226–42. For a comparative British/American study, see Robb, "Women and White-Collar Crime," 1,058–72.

3. For criminological studies of women and fraud, see Elizabeth Szockyj and James G. Fox, eds., *Corporate Victimization of Women* (Boston: Northeastern University Press, 1996); J. Gerber and S. L. Weeks, "Women as Victims of Corporate Crime: A Call for Research on a Neglected Topic," *Deviant Behavior* 13 (1992): 325–47; K. Daly, "Gender and Varieties of White-Collar Crime," *Criminology* 27 (1989): 769–94.

4. Perkin, *Origins of Modern English Society*, 442.

5. For a general discussion of how the corporate form and new financial instruments were vulnerable to fraud, see Robb, *White-Collar Crime in Modern England*, 11–30.

6. The lack of corporate accountability is detailed in Hawkins, "Development of Modern Financial Reporting Practices," 135–68. See also Hawkins, *Corporate Financial Disclosure*.

7. Smith, *Bulls and Bears of New York*, 140.

8. Warwick, "Wall Street Wrecks," 221. See also Nichols, *Safe Methods of Business*, 226, 289–95.

9. Smith, *Plain Truths*, 27.

10. Starkweather, "Woman as an Investor," 63–64. Starkweather was head of the Woman's Department of the Mutual Life Insurance Company in New York.

11. Cromwell, *The American Business Woman*, v–vi.

12. "Women Gamblers in Wall Street," 101.

13. "Just a Few Thousand Dollars," 22.

14. Green, "Financial Fools and Their Money," *Daily Illinois State Journal*, 11 December 1899.

15. *Harper's Weekly* (January 30,1909), 33.

16. *Woodhull and Claflin's Weekly*, 18 March 1871 and 27 May 1871.

17. "Charged with Running a Bucket Shop," *New York Times*, 5 April 1893.

18. "Excluding Women from Brokers' Offices," *New York Times*, 13 July 1902.

19. "A Broker's Commissions," *New York Times*, 7 April 1880. See also the case of Sophia Mattern: "Miss Mattern's Ventures," *New York Times*, 20 March 1887, and "Miss Mattern's Suit," *New York Times*, 6 May 1887.

20. For a discussion of trusts, see Hendrick Hartog, *Man and Wife in America: A History* (Cambridge, MA: Harvard University Press, 2000), 169–74.

21. "A Faithless Trustee," *New York Times*, 24 November 1877.

22. "A Capitalist Charged with Fraud," *New York Times*, 22 November 1884. See also "A Trustee Charged with Fraud," *New York Times*, 16 January 1879; "Faithless Trustees," *New York Times*, 23 April 1877.

23. For cases of women being defrauded by their own relatives, see "An Orphan Girl's Estate," *New York Times*, 3 February 1878; "Young Woodruff's Crime," *New York Times*, 22 July 1887; "Pepperday Called to Account," *New York Times*, 26 February 1893.

24. Starkweather, "Woman as an Investor," 64.

25. "Denounced in Court," *New York Times*, 17 September 1897.

26. "Wanted to Be a Second Hetty Green," *St. Louis Republic*, 24 June 1900; "Sue Broker for $30,000," *New York Times*, 10 March 1905; "Widows Duped by Land Sharks," *Duluth (MN) News-Tribune*, 24 March 1906; "Charge Big Fraud," *Grand Rapids (MI) Press*, 29 October 1906.

27. "Hold 'Yogi' Garnett for Duping Women," *New York Times*, 19 October 1909.

28. Denison, "Fleecing the Public of Its Liberty Bonds," 91; Guenther, "Pirates of Promotion," 29–33.

29. *Buffalo (NY) Commercial*, 2 December 1922. See also Frazer, *A Woman and Her Money*, 164, 166–80.

30. Alborn, "A License to Bet," 13–14.

31. "Mrs. Chadwick Guilty," *New York Times*, 12 March 1905.

32. "She 'Squealed,' Says Vahey of Mrs. Briggs," *Boston Herald*, 3 April 1907; "Finance and Frills: Is It Possible for Women to Understand Business?" *Boston Herald*, 7 April 1907.

33. "Miss Mattern's Ventures," *New York Times*, 20 March 1887.

34. "Money Poured into Fraud Stock Office," *New York Times*, 23 November 1910.

35. Denison, *An Iron Crown*, 341.

36. For a discussion of commercial frauds perpetrated by Victorian women, see Tammy Whitlock, *Crime, Gender and Consumer Culture in Nineteenth-Century England* (Aldershot, UK: Ashgate, 2005). A contemporary criminological perspective can be found in Dorothy Zietz, *Women Who Embezzle or Defraud: A Study of Convicted Felons* (New York: Praeger, 1981).

37. Ponzi schemes are named after a 1920s Boston swindler, Charles Ponzi, but this type of fraud was quite common in the nineteenth century. In a classic Ponzi scheme, investors make payments to a business that then distributes returns to these investors from their own money or money paid by subsequent investors, rather than from any actual profits earned by the business. Ponzi schemes are doomed to failure since they work only by bringing in new investors to pay off old ones. For the dynamics of Ponzi schemes, see Catherine Rampell, "A Scheme with No Off Button," *New York Times*, 21 October 2008.

38. "A Mysterious Bank," *Boston Daily Advertiser*, 25 September 1880. For a more detailed discussion of the case, see George Robb, "Depicting a Female Fraud: Sarah Howe and the Boston Women's Bank," *Nineteenth-Century Contexts* 34 (2012): 445–59.

39. "The Deposit Company," *Boston Daily Advertiser*, 4 October 1880.

40. "Ladies' Deposit Banking—How It Is Supposed to Work," *Boston Daily Advertiser*, 4 October 1880.

41. "The Ladies' Deposit," *Boston Daily Advertiser*, 29 October 1880.

42. "Guilty on Four Counts," *The Boston Globe*, 26 April 1881; "The Boston Woman's Bank," *New York Times*, 23 April 1881.

43. "The Woman's Bank of Boston," *Banker's Magazine* 35 (November 1880): 351–52.

44. "The Broken Bank," *Boston Daily Advertiser*, 18 October 1880.

45. "The Right View of It," *Boston Daily Advertiser*, 8 October 1880; "The Ladies' Deposit," *Boston Daily Advertiser*, 20 October 1880.

46. "Mrs. Howe's 'Bank' Again," *New York Times*, 16 April 1887.

47. "The Woman's Bank of Boston," *Banker's Magazine* 35 (November 1880): 351.

48. "The Woman's 'Bank,'" *Boston Daily Advertiser*, 5 October 1880.

49. "A Mysterious Bank," *Boston Daily Advertiser*, 25 September 1880; "The Defunct Bank," *Boston Daily Advertiser*, 19 October 1880.

50. "The Woman's 'Bank,'" *Boston Daily Advertiser*, 5 October 1880.

51. For Victorian criminological debates about women, see Lucia Zedner, *Women, Crime and Custody in Victorian England* (Oxford: Clarendon Press, 1991), and Carol Smart, *Women, Crime and Criminology* (London: Routledge, 1977).

52. "The Woman's Bank of Boston," *Banker's Magazine* 35 (November 1880): 352.

53. "A Pen Picture of the Remarkable Head of the Establishment," *Boston Herald*, 15 October 1880.

54. "The Woman's Bank of Boston," 352.

55. "Mrs. Howe's Unsavory Record," *Boston Herald*, 15 October 1880.

56. For Cesare Lombroso's influential theory of criminal atavism, especially as it applied to women, see Mary Gibson, *Born to Crime: Cesare Lombroso and the Origins of Biological Criminology* (Westport, CT: Praeger, 2002), chapter 2.

57. For a discussion of degeneration theory applied to women, see Ruth Harris, *Murders and Madness: Medicine, Law and Society in the fin-de-siècle* (Oxford: Clarendon Press, 1989), chapters 2 and 3.

58. Gail Hamilton was the pen name of Mary Abigail Dodge, an influential writer and advocate of women's rights and political reform. See "Mary Abigail Dodge,"

in *Dictionary of American Biography*, edited by Allen Johnson (New York: Charles Scribner's Sons, 1964), 2:350.

59. "Gail Hamilton's Defense of the Ladies' Deposit," *Boston Daily Advertiser*, 5 October 1880; "Gail Hamilton's Letter," *Boston Daily Advertiser*, 7 October 1880; "The Right View of It," *Boston Daily Advertiser*, 8 October 1880.

60. "The Ladies' Deposit," *Boston Herald*, 17 October 1880; "The Deposit Company," *Boston Daily Advertiser*, 4 October 1880.

61. "Another Coil Taken," *Boston Daily Advertiser*, 22 October 1880.

62. "At Her Old Tricks Again," *New York Times*, 4 December 1884; "Mrs. Howe and Her Bank," *New York Times*, 7 December 1884.

63. Mrs. Howe a Fugitive," *New York Times*, 15 April 1887; "Many Women Defrauded," *Hartford (CT) Daily Courant*, 15 April 1887.

64. "Another Woman's Bank," *New York Herald*, 14 November 1887; "Still Working the Women," *Boston Herald*, 9 December 1888; "Mrs. Sarah E. Howe at Liberty," *Boston Journal*, 28 March 1889; "Death of Mrs. Howe," *New York Times*, 21 January 1892.

65. "Mrs. Howe of Woman's Bank Fame Again," *Boston Daily Advertiser*, 15 April 1887; "Mrs. Howe's 'Bank' Again," *New York Times*, 16 April 1887; "The Confidence Woman," *New York Times*, 20 January 1888; "A Noted Female Swindler," *New York Times*, 9 December 1888.

66. For Victorian debates about free trade and financial regulation, see Robb, *White-Collar Crime*, 147–55.

67. For example, see "The Woman's Deposit at Munich," *Boston Daily Advertiser*, 12 October 1880; "The Story of Adele Spitzeder, Mrs. Howe's Model," *Boston Daily Advertiser*, 18 October 1880.

68. "Local Business Troubles," *New York Times*, 13 November 1880.

69. Unidentified newspaper article, 12 November 1880, from James Mitchell Scrapbook, vol. 1 (1878–80), New York Stock Exchange Archives.

70. "A Female Broker Arrested," *New York Times*, 21 December 1881; "The Arrested Female Broker," *New York Times*, 22 December 1881; "Asking About Mrs. Dow," *New York Times*, 11 January 1882. See also "The Female Broker," *Philadelphia Inquirer*, 22 December 1881; "A Female Stock Broker Under Surveillance," *Philadelphia Public Ledger*, 23 December 1881.

71. "A Commonplace Swindler," *New York Times*, 9 December 1887.

72. "A Woman's Poor Speculation," *New York Times*, 18 October 1882.

73. "Losing Her Money in the Street," *New York Times*, 1 April 1884; "Mrs. Carrie Morse's Victims," *New York Times*, 6 April 1884; "The Female Stock Broker," *New York Times*, 8 April 1884; "Convicting a Female Stock Broker," *New York Times*, 12 June 1884.

74. "A Female Broker Arrested," *New York Times*, 8 December 1887; "A Commonplace Swindler," *New York Times*, 9 December 1887; "How the Trick Is Done," *New York Times*, 10 December 1887; "City and Suburban News," *New York Times*, 15 February 1888. See also "Swindled Society Ladies," *Elkhart (IN) Daily Review*, 8 December 1887; "A Female Ferdinand Ward," *Columbus (GA) Daily Enquirer*, 25 December 1887; "Marie Latouche Goes Free," *New York Herald*, 15 February 1888.

75. "A Notorious Woman's Suit," *New York Times*, 31 January 1883.

76. "A Female Broker Arrested," *New York Times*, 21 December 1881.

77. "Using Her Eyes on the Jury," *New York Times*, 17 May 1884; "A Female Broker Arrested," *New York Times*, 8 December 1887.

78. "A Female Broker Arrested," *New York Times*, 21 December 1881; "Using Her Eyes on the Jury," *New York Times*, 17 May 1884.

79. "Using Her Eyes on the Jury," *New York Times*, 17 May 1884.

80. "A Female Broker Arrested," *New York Times*, 8 December 1887.

81. "Mrs. Carrie Morse's Victims," *New York Times*, 6 April 1884.

82. On the problems of criminal identification, see Simon A. Cole, *Suspect Identities: A History of Fingerprinting and Criminal Identification* (Cambridge, MA: Harvard University Press, 2001), 6–31.

83. Byrnes, *Professional Criminals of America*, 200–201.

84. Ibid., 375.

85. "Says Woman Aided Swindle," *New York Times*, 19 December 1914.

86. "Broker Hatch," *Wheeling (WV) Register*, 9 May 1888; "The Hatch Inquest," *New Haven (CT) Register*, 15 May 1888.

87. "Victim of Blackmailers," *Daily Inter-Ocean* (Chicago), 16 May 1888; "Wily Women," *Cleveland Plain Dealer*, 20 May 1888.

88. "The Woman in the Case," *Canton (OH) Repository*, 11 May 1888.

89. Oscar Willoughby Riggs, "Petticoated Sharks," *Harrisburg (PA) Patriot*, 5 July 1888.

90. Riggs, "Petticoated Sharks," 4.

91. For Lillian Scofield's later career, see "Afraid of Broker Hatch's Ghost," *Trenton (NJ) Evening News*, 24 May 1888; "Mrs. Lillian Scofield Again," *New Haven (CT) Register*, 1 February 1889; "Lillian Scofield Smiles," *New York Herald*, 1 March 1890; "Lillian Scofield Held for Theft," *New York Herald*, 15 October 1890; "'Lady Lansmere' Played Possum," *New York Herald*, 4 March 1893; "Lillian Scofield Again," *New York Herald*, 26 April 1895; "Actress's Estate Valued at $80,193," *New York Times*, 18 July 1916.

92. Norman, "Feminine Failure in Business," 457.

93. "American Woman Is Accused of Forgery," *New York Times*, 3 September 1901.

94. "Miss Eastwick Subject to Hallucinations," *New York Times*, 4 September 1901; "Miss Eastwick Committed," *New York Times*, 2 October 1901; "Miss Eastwick Sentenced," *New York Times*, 19 November 1901; "Miss Eastwick to Be Released Today," *New York Times*, 18 April 1902.

95. "Mrs. Chadwick Got Millions on Securities," *New York Times*, 30 November 1904; "Cassie Chadwick Dies in Prison," *New York Times*, 11 October 1907.

96. "Ohioans at Dinner Cheer for Fairbanks," *New York Times*, 19 March 1905; "New and Old South Sea Bubbles," 31–33. The Chadwick case was later the subject of a lurid pulp novel: David Loth, *Gold Brick Cassie* (New York: Gold Medal Books, 1954).

97. "Chadwick Furnishings Under the Hammer," *New York Times*, 27 April 1905.

98. "Imbecile Finance," *New York Times*, 2 December 1904; "Reynolds Tells Story of How He Was Duped," *New York Times*, 12 December 1904; "Cassie Chadwick Dies in Prison," *New York Times*, 11 October 1907.

99. "Imbecile Finance," *New York Times*, 2 December 1904.

100. "Hetty Green Takes Mrs. Chadwick's Part," *Fort-Worth Star Telegram*, 15 December 1904; "Two Adventuresses," 475. For the story of a copycat crime inspired by Chadwick, see "Second Mrs. Chadwick Works Several Rich Pittsburg Men," *Aberdeen (SD) Daily News*, 17 February 1908.

101. "Woman Brains of Syndicate," *New York Times*, 27 March 1905; "Off with Million: Sweet-Faced Sophia Beck Managed a Fake Concern," *Oregonian* (Portland, OR), 27 March 1905.

102. "Think Confidence Queen Is Caught," *Cleveland Plain Dealer*, 26 September 1909.

103. "Off with Million," *Oregonian* (Portland, OR); "Woman Has Million of Storey Cash," *Philadelphia Inquirer*, 26 March 1905; "Sophie Beck Fined $500," *New York Times*, 10 July 1910.

104. "Woman a Leader as a Promoter," *Grand Rapids (MI) Press*, 19 May 1908; "Finance Queen's Chum Held on Fraud Charge," *Columbus (GA) Daily Enquirer*, 29 May 1908; "Seven Children Lost," *Kalamazoo (MI) Gazette*, 22 May 1908; "Woman Broker Still Sought," *Wilkes-Barre (PA) Times-Leader*, 1 June 1908.

105. *Salt Lake Herald-Republican* (Salt Lake City, UT), 24 October 1909.

106. "Present Day Sampson Discovers His Delilah," *Grand Forks (ND) Herald*, 22 May 1908; "Women Make Best Assistants in Get-Rich-Quick Games," *Boston Herald*, 17 December 1911. For another example of an investment scam perpetrated by a woman, see the case of Mrs. Ray Hyman: "Accuse Woman of Swindle," *New York Times*, 13 June 1917; "Mrs. Hyman Admits She Has No Funds," *New York Times*, 16 June 1917; "Mrs. Hyman Confesses a $300,000 Swindle," *New York Times*, 20 June 1917; "Mrs. Hyman, 'Financier,' Indicted," *New York Times*, 21 June 1917.

107. Quoted in Hawkins, "Development of Modern Financial Reporting Practices," 141.

108. Ibid., 136–37, 143–44.

109. See, for example, Lawson, "Frenzied Finance," *Everybody's Magazine* 12 (January 1905): 40–53 and (February 1905): 173–86. See also Thomas Lawson, *Frenzied Finance: The Crime of Amalgamated* (1905), reprint (New York: Greenwood, 1968), viii.

110. Ott, *When Wall Street Met Main Street*, 30–31.

111. Cowing, *Populists, Plungers, and Progressives*, 67–68.

112. Fraser, *Every Man a Speculator*, 294–302.

113. Brandeis, *Other People's Money*.

114. Guenther, "Pirates of Promotion," 29; Denison, "Fleecing Public of Liberty Bonds," 93.

115. Guenther, "Pirates of Promotion," 509.

116. Burns, "Male Vampires," 183–85.

117. Witten, "Pretty Girls and Handsome Men," 174.

118. Frazer, "Widow's Mite," 94, 96.

119. Cowing, *Populists, Plungers, and Progressives*, 90–91.

120. See, for example, "Digest of the Special Committee on 'Bucket-Shop' Organizations" (1913), New York Stock Exchange Archives. For the securities exchanges' war against bucket shops, see Hochfelder, "'Where the Common People Could Speculate,'" 335–58.

121. Antwerp, *Stock Exchange from Within*, 56.

122. Ott, *When Main Street Met Wall Street*, 40–44.

123. Ibid., 117–18; Mott, *An American Woman and Her Bank*, 13, 211.

124. Mott, *An American Woman and Her Bank*, 211; and Seward, *The Women's Department*, 76, 78–80.

125. Dorman, "A Woman Broker in Wall Street!" *The Canton (OH) Sunday Repository*, 13 January 1924; "Wall Street Splurge May Lead Ex-Stenog to Prison," *Charlotte (NC) Sunday Observer*, 9 December 1928; "Women Broker Given Sentence," *Greensboro (NC) Daily News*, 20 March 1930.

126. Hawkins, "Development of Modern Financial Reporting Practices," 162–65.

127. For women's education, see John L. Rury, *Education and Women's Work: Female Schooling and the Division of Labor in Urban America, 1870–1930* (Albany: SUNY Press, 1991); Joan Burstyn, *Victorian Education and the Ideal of Womanhood* (London: Croom Helm, 1980), 48–69.

128. Laird, *Pull: Networking and Success*, 81–91; Rotundo, *American Manhood*, 194–221.

129. George P. Butler & Brother, Letter Book, 22 November 1909, New York Historical Society.

130. Women were frequently linked with professionals, especially clergymen, as lacking in business sense. See Rutterford and Maltby, "'The Widow, the Clergyman and the Reckless,'" 111–21.

131. Barnard, "Ladies of the Ticker," 409.

132. Ibid., 410.

133. Prince, "Women, Men and Money Styles," 176; Bajtelsmit and Bernasek, "Why Do Women Invest Differently," 5–7.

134. Barber and Odean, "Boys Will Be Boys," 262, 275, 281.

Chapter 4. Turning Wall Street Inside Out

1. Quoted in Basch, *In the Eyes of the Law*, 142.

2. Kreisel, *Economic Woman*, 8–9, 14.

3. Basch, *In the Eyes of the Law*, 143. For later examples of women's speculation linked to unbridled consumption, see Chapters 1 and 3.

4. Ibid., 104; Hughes, "Respectable Punch," 4–5.

5. Stern, *Home Economics*, 1–18. For economic concerns of the women's-rights movement, see Barbara J. Berg, *The Remembered Gate: Origins of American Feminism* (New York: Oxford University Press, 1978), 145–71; and Basch, *In the Eyes of the Law*, 164, 172–75.

6. Kwolek-Folland, *Incorporating Women*, 53; Basch, *In the Eyes of the Law*, 169.

7. See the debate in *Signs* over the definition and historical meaning(s) of feminism: Karen Offen, "Defining Feminism: A Comparative Historical Approach," *Signs* 14 (1988): 119–57; Ellen Carol DuBois, "Comment on Karen Offen's 'Defining Feminism,'" *Signs* 15 (1989): 195–97; Karen Offen, "Reply to DuBois," *Signs* 15 (1989): 198–202; Nancy F. Cott, "Comment on Karen Offen's 'Defining Feminism,'" *Signs* 15 (1989): 203–5; Karen Offen, "Reply to Cott," *Signs* 15 (1989): 206–9.

8. Tetrault, "The Incorporation of American Feminism," 1,027–56.

9. Gabriel, *Notorious Victoria*, 41.

10. Reede, "A Business Woman," 100–101.

11. See for example, "Talk Among the Brokers in Wall Street," *The Revolution*, 5 February 1868, 77.

12. Stanton, "Wall Street," 225–26.

13. Stanton, "Finance for the People," 330.

14. Ackerman, *The Gold Ring*, 271.

15. Quoted in Woodhull, *The Human Body*, 541, and Goldsmith, *Other Powers*, 214.

16. "I am the evangel—I am the saviour if you would but see it. But I, too, come not to bring peace but a sword." Victoria Woodhull in *Woodhull and Claflin's Weekly*, 2 November 1872, 12.

17. Quoted in Clews, *Twenty-Eight Years in Wall Street*, 442.

18. Sachs, *The Terrible Siren*.

19. Several popular works from the 1960s still bore the firm imprint of Sachs: Ishbel Ross, *Charmers and Cranks: Twelve Famous American Women Who Defied the Conventions* (New York: Harper and Row, 1965); Johanna Johnston, *Mrs. Satan: The Incredible Saga of Victoria C. Woodhull* (New York: Popular Library, 1967); and M. M. Marberry, *Vicky: A Biography of Victoria C. Woodhull* (New York: Funk and Wagnalls, 1967). One of the first biographies to present a more positive, and feminist, view of Woodhull is Marion Meade, *Free Woman: The Life and Times of Victoria Woodhull* (New York: Alfred A. Knopf, 1976), targeted at young readers. The first work to take Woodhull seriously as a financial figure was Madeleine B. Stern, *We the Women: Career Firsts of Nineteenth-Century America* (Lincoln: University of Nebraska Press, 1962), 251–72. Stern later edited a collection of Woodhull's writings: *The Victoria Woodhull Reader*.

20. For the most important biographies of Woodhull, see Underhill, *The Woman Who Ran for President*; Gabriel, *Notorious Victoria*; and Goldsmith, *Other Powers*. For an insightful review essay on these works, and the historiographical tradition related to Woodhull, see Helen Lefkowitz Horowitz, "A Victoria Woodhull for the 1990s," *Reviews in American History* 27 (March 1999): 87–97. More recent studies of Woodhull include Horowitz, "Victoria Woodhull, Anthony Comstock, and the Conflict over Sex," 403–34; and Frisken, *Victoria Woodhull's Sexual Revolution*. A recent short but effective biography is Brody's *Victoria Woodhull: Free Spirit for Women's Rights*. The latest treatment of Woodhull and Claflin, Myra MacPherson's *The Scarlet Sisters: Sex, Suffrage, and Scandal in the Gilded Age* (New York: Twelve, 2014), offers little in the way of fresh perspectives.

21. For accounts of Woodhull and Claflin's early years, see Brody, *Victoria Woodhull*, 8–33, and Underhill, *The Woman Who Ran for President*, 11–39.

22. For Woodhull and Claflin's inventive accounts of their business experience, see "The Queens of Finance," *New York Herald*, 22 January 1870; "The Queens of Finance," *New York Herald*, 5 February 1870; and Anthony, "The Working Woman," 154–55.

23. Among the undocumented "facts" about Woodhull cited in recent works, are (1) that she made $100,000 as a clairvoyant (Brody 43); (2) that she made a fortune on Black Friday, 1869 (Brody 43, Gabriel 41, Goldsmith 190, Underhill 57); (3) that Vanderbilt backed the firm (Brody 44, Goldsmith 190–92, Horowitz 411, Underhill 61–62); (4) that Vanderbilt financed Woodhull's newspaper (Brody 56, Horowitz 413); and (5) that Woodhull's brokerage business was a great success (Goldsmith 191, Horowitz 411).

24. Stiles, *The First Tycoon*, 484–85, 501–5.

25. "The Queens of Finance," *New York Herald*, 22 January 1870.

26. Ibid.

27. Smith, *Bulls and Bears of New York*, 273.

28. "The Queens of Finance," *New York Herald*, 5 February 1870; "Woodhull, Claflin and Co.," *The Sun* (New York), 7 February 1870; "The Broad Street Novelty in Brokerage," *The World* (New York), 8 February 1870.

29. "The Women Brokers of Broad Street," *New York Courier*, 14 February 1870; Brody, *Victoria Woodhull*, 48; Gabriel, *Notorious Victoria*, 52; Anthony, "The Working Woman," 155.

30. "The Bewitching Brokers," *New York Herald*, 13 February 1870; "The Broad Street Novelty in Brokerage," *The World* (New York), 8 February 1870; "Woman's Progress—The Female Operators of Wall Street," *New York Sunday News*, 30 January 1870; *The Philadelphia Press*, 7 April 1870.

31. *The Days' Doings* (New York), 26 February 1870. Amanda Frisken is the first scholar to discover widespread reportage in the sporting press about Woodhull and Claflin. Frisken, *Victoria Woodhull's Sexual Revolution*, 2–6, 15–17.

32. For discussion of the "sporting man" phenomenon, see Timothy Gilfoyle, *City of Eros: New York City, Prostitution, and the Commercialization of Sex, 1790–1920* (New York: W. W. Norton, 1992), 92–116; and Patricia Cline Cohen, *The Murder of Helen Jewett: The Life and Death of a Prostitute in Nineteenth-Century New York* (New York: Vintage Books, 1999), 230–47, 301–29.

33. "The Bewitching Brokers," *New York Herald*, 13 February 1870; *The Albion*, 12 February 1870; "Wall Street Aroused," *New York Times*, 6 February 1870.

34. "The Bewitching Brokers," *New York Herald*, 10 February 1870.

35. "The Queens of Finance," *New York Herald*, 6 February 1870.

36. Anthony, "The Working Woman," 155.

37. "The Broad Street Novelty in Brokerage,"; Underhill, *Woman Who Ran for President*, 72–74.

38. Brody, *Victoria Woodhull*, 98.

39. Gabriel, *Notorious Victoria*, 41; Underhill, *Woman Who Ran for President*, 69.

40. Goldsmith, *Other Powers*, 329; Gabriel, *Notorious Victoria*, 165.

41. Stiles, *The First Tycoon*, 504–5. Within a month of Woodhull, Claflin & Company's opening, Vanderbilt publicly denied any connection to the firm. See "The Petticoat Financiers in Another Flutter," *New York Sun*, 26 March 1870.

42. "Woodhull and Claflin in Court," *New York Daily Tribune*, 22 February 1871; "Woman's Right to Speculate," *New York Times*, 22 February 1871.

43. R. G. Dun & Company rating quoted in Yohn, "Crippled Capitalists," 86. See also Underhill, *Woman Who Ran for President*, 215.

44. "Woman's Investment Invasion," *Wall Street Journal*, 11 August 1927.

45. Yohn, "Crippled Capitalists," 89.

46. For discussion of the *Weekly* by Woodhull's biographers, see Underhill, *Woman Who Ran for President*, 86–93; Gabriel, *Notorious Victoria*, 58–67; and Goldsmith, *Other Powers*, 212–14. For questions of authorship of articles in *The Weekly* and of Woodhull's intellectual influences, see Horowitz, "Victoria Woodhull, Anthony Comstock and the Conflict over Sex," 412–13; and Frisken, *Victoria Woodhull's Sexual Revolution*, 9–12.

47. "The Social Evil," *Woodhull and Claflin's Weekly*," 23 July 1870; "Woman's Ability to Earn Money," *Woodhull and Claflin's Weekly*, 17 September 1870.

48. Quoted in Clews, *Twenty-Eight Years in Wall Street*, 442.

49. The following articles from the *Weekly* demonstrate the paper's extensive financial coverage: "The Outrages of Corporations," 17 December 1870; "How Wall Street Stocks Are Manufactured," 31 December 1870; "The Results of Watered Shares and Bonds," 2 March 1871; "Financial Swindling—Bogus Bankers and Brokers," 27 May 1871. See also issues for 4 March 1871 and 18 March 1871.

50. See front page of the *Weekly*, 2 March 1872.

51. Underhill, *Woman Who Ran for President*, 196–97; *Weekly*, 6 April 1872.

52. Woodhull, *The Great Social Problem of Labor and Capital*, 10–11.

53. Woodhull, *The Impending Revolution*, 18. The speech had been given earlier, on 1 February 1872, in Boston.

54. Ibid., 12, 14.

55. Ibid., 16.

56. *New York Times*, 22 February 1872.

57. *Harper's Weekly*, 17 February 1872.

58. Quoted in Frisken, *Victoria Woodhull's Sexual Revolution*, 31.

59. *New York Herald*, 10 August 1873; Frisken, *Victoria Woodhull's Sexual Revolution*, 128.

60. Frisken, *Victoria Woodhull's Sexual Revolution*, 30–32.

61. Goldsmith, *Other Powers*, 159–62. Goldsmith accepted the gossip of the day that Woodhull consorted with prostitutes.

62. For discussions of Victorian ideas about "free love," see Hall D. Sears, *The Sex Radicals: Free Love in High Victorian America* (Lawrence: Regents Press of Kansas, 1977); and Taylor Stoehr, *Free Love in America: A Documentary History* (New York: AMS Press, 1979).

63. Woodhull, *The Principles of Social Freedom*, 23, 35.

64. Underhill, *Woman Who Ran for President*, 201.

65. "Women in Wall Street," *New York Times*, 31 March 1872. Similarly, in Harriet Beecher Stowe's novel *My Wife and I*, a character based on Victoria Woodhull, Audacia Dangyereyes, wheedles money out of investors using her sexual wiles. Stowe, *My Wife and I* (New York: J. B. Ford, 1871), 269.

66. "Women in Wall Street," *New York Times*, 31 March 1872.

67. Underhill, *Woman Who Ran for President*, 215–18.

68. "Wall Street Aroused," *The Revolution*, 24 February 1870.

69. Quoted in Gabriel, *Notorious Victoria*, 92.

70. Tilton had earlier written a fulsome biography of Woodhull. Theodore Tilton, *Victoria C. Woodhull: A Biographical Sketch* (New York: McDivitt, Campbell, 1871).

71. *Weekly*, 2 November 1872.

72. For a discussion of the scandal provoked by the *Weekly*'s exposé of Beecher and Challis, see Horowitz, "Victoria Woodhull, Anthony Comstock, and the Conflict over Sex." One line in particular from the 2 November 1872 issue was especially cited as obscene: "And this scoundrel Challis, to prove that he had seduced a maiden, carried for days on his finger, exhibiting in triumph, the red trophy of her virginity."

73. Frisken, *Victoria Woodhull's Sexual Revolution*, 94–112.

74. Sachs, *Terrible Siren*, 226–27.

75. Underhill, *Woman Who Ran for President*, 268–71.

76. Frisken, *Victoria Woodhull's Sexual Revolution*, 115–45; Woodhull, *The Human Body*, 483.

77. For a history of the sisters' later years, see Gabriel, *Notorious Victoria*, 245–301.

78. Fowler, *Twenty Years of Inside Life in Wall Street*, 456.

79. Clews, *Twenty-Eight Years in Wall Street*, 439, 443, 444.

80. Smith, *Bulls and Bears of New York*, 273, 274.

81. Ann Fabian, *Card Sharps, Dream Books, and Bucket Shops*, 192.

82. Cowing, *Populists, Plungers, and Progressives*, 35.

83. Smith, *Plain Truths*, 17–18.

84. Anthony, "The Working Woman," and "Miss Mattern's Suit," *New York Times*, 6 May 1887.

85. "Oscar in Wall Street," *New York Times*, 20 September 1882.

86. Fraser, *Every Man a Speculator*, 99, 216, 225–26.

87. "Women Seeking 'Points,'" *New York Times*, 24 September 1882.

88. "Ladies as Stock Speculators," *New York Times*, 3 February 1880, 8. See also advertisement for "Uptown Stock Exchange," *New York Herald*, 1 October 1880.

89. Stanton, Anthony, and Gage, *History of Woman Suffrage*, vol. 3, 402. See also Ann D. Gordon, ed., *The Selected Papers of Elizabeth Cady Stanton and Susan B. Anthony, vol. 2: Against an Aristocracy of Sex, 1866–1873* (New Brunswick, NJ: Rutgers University Press, 2000), 87.

90. "Women Who Speculate," *New York Herald*, November 11, 1894, section 6, 2.

91. "Mrs. Sophronia Twitchell Dead," *New York Herald*, 4 August 1893. See also "A Female Broker," *Daily Inter-Ocean* (Chicago), 3 December 1887; "Judgment Against Mrs. Twitchell," *Springfield (MA) Republican*, 3 December 1887; and "A Belligerant Female Arrested," *Bridgeton (NJ) Evening News*, 24 July 1888.

92. "Where Women Are Not Wanted," *New Haven (CT) Register*, 25 May 1888; and "Arrested for Assault," *New York Times*, 24 July 1888.

93. "Petticoated Sharks," *Harrisburg (PA) Patriot*, 5 July 1888.

94. "A Woman's View of the Federal City," *Evening Star* (Washington, DC), 1 January 1875; "Amusements: Odd Fellow's Hall," *Evening Star*, 9 February 1878; "Fighting for a Fortune," *New York Herald*, 24 October 1878.

95. "Mrs. Pollard's Business," *Chicago Herald*, 15 October 1890; "Lectures," *Evening Star*, 23 May 1892.

96. Fowler, *Twenty Years of Inside Life in Wall Street*, 456.

97. "Lady Cook and Co.," *New York Times*, 21 December 1898.

98. Ritter, *Goldbugs and Greenbacks*, 95–98.

99. Stanton, "Greenbacks or Gold." See also John Magwire, "What Is the True Financial Policy?" *The Revolution*, 19 and 26 November 1868. Victoria Woodhull also supported a convertible currency. See Woodhull, *A Speech on the Principles of Finance*.

100. Underhill, *Woman Who Ran for President*, 209–13.

101. Norgren, *Belva Lockwood*, 151–52.

102. Lebsock, "Radical Reconstruction and the Property Rights of Southern Women," 197.

103. Norgren, *Belva Lockwood*, 111–14.

104. Braukman and Ross, "Married Women's Property Law and Male Coercion," 57, 61.

105. Sawtelle, "How Marriage Affects a Woman's Property," 774.

106. Ibid., 774–75; "Married Women's Property Acts in the United States and Needed Reforms Therein," *Albany Law Journal*, 207–8; Stewart, "English and American Law," *The Central Law Journal*, 219.

107. McMath, *American Populism*, 125.

108. Buhle, *Women and American Socialism*, 68.

109. *New York Herald*, 6 July 1879; "Mind Reading and Stock Speculation," *Wall Street Daily News*, 21 July 1880; *Wall Street Daily News*, 2 February 1881.

110. "The Kings of Wall-Street," *New York Times*, 19 November 1881; "Cowhided by Grace Courtland," *New York Times*, 15 July 1883; "Grace Courtland's Cowhide," *The National Police Gazette*, 4 August 1883. Courtland published a memoir of her career as a psychic: *A Marked Life: Autobiography of a Clairvoyant* (1879).

111. Grace Courtland, *The Kings of Wall Street*, 1, 5, 7; *Toledo Blade*, 19 April 1883. See also "The Wall Street Witch," *Chicago Inter-Ocean*, 5 March 1881; "The Wall Street Witch," *Indianapolis Sentinel*, 15 August 1881; and "Grace Courtland Back Again," *Truth* (New York), 9 September 1883. Courtland's career as a financial authority was short-lived. By 1886 she was appearing at Austin and Stone's Dime Museum in

Boston alongside Balbroma the Fire-King and the Murray Triplets. In 1890 she was featured at Wonderland in Denver, where "she tells all the ladies' fortunes free of charge." Twenty-five years later she was advertising her services as a fortune-teller in Texas. *Boston Herald*, 11 April 1886; *Denver Rocky Mountain News*, 5 January 1890; *Fort Worth Star-Telegram*, 29 November 1914.

112. Walch, *Doctor Sphinx*, 332–33, 337–38.

113. Phelps, "Women and Money." Phelps's sarcastic dismissal of idealized womanhood seems like a rejoinder to John Ruskin's "Of Queens Gardens" from *Sesame and Lillies* (1865).

114. Phelps, "Women and Money."

115. DuBois, *Feminism and Suffrage*, 136.

116. "Female Financiers," *Augusta (GA) Chronicle*, 23 January 1906. For the careers of Green and Reader, see Chapter 5.

117. For Gail Hamilton's defense of Sarah Howe, see Chapter 3.

118. "Letter to the Editor," *Boston Daily Advertiser*, 11 October 1880; *Woman's Journal* quoted in *Boston Daily Advertiser*, 18 October 1880. See also "Woman's Business Ignorance," *Harper's Bazaar* 14 (January 1881): 18.

119. "Women and Money," *Harper's Bazaar* 11 (February 1878): 122.

120. "Business Education for Girls," *Chicago Inter-Ocean*, 14 January 1888, 11.

121. Prescott, "Economic Independence of Women," 528–29.

122. Solomon, *In the Company of Educated Women*, 85–86; Radke-Moss, *Bright Epoch*, 143–51, 166–74.

123. Gilman, *Women and Economics*. For recent studies of Gilman's life and work, see Judith Allen, *The Feminism of Charlotte Perkins Gilman* (Chicago: University of Chicago Press, 2009); and Cynthia J. Davis, *Charlotte Perkins Gilman: A Biography* (Stanford, CA: Stanford University Press, 2010).

124. Gilman, *Women and Economics*, 9, 86, 117, 121, 330.

125. Ibid., 122, 152, 293–94.

126. Evans, "About Men," 15.

127. Green, "The Benefits of a Business Training for Women," 8; Creighton, "Women and Finance," 15–21; Wilbur, *Everyday Business for Women*.

128. Wilbur, *Everyday Business for Women*, vii, 130.

129. U.S. Census Bureau, 1940, *Comparative Occupation Statistics for the United States*, 135.

130. For statistics on women's financial assets, see Chapter 2.

131. Shelby, "A Woman's Approach to Economics," 60–64.

132. Seeger was the father of the folksinger Pete Seeger. The anecdote is related in a book review by Paul Levy, "He Had a Hammer," *Times Literary Supplement* (November 27, 2009): 35.

133. For a discussion of this exchange see Laura Claridge, *Emily Post: Daughter of the Gilded Age, Mistress of American Manners* (New York: Random House, 2008), 305–6.

134. Kelland, "Wives Are Either Tightwads or Spendthrifts," 12, 104–10.

135. Post, "Kelland Doesn't Know What He Is Talking About," 13, 110–13.

Chapter 5. Call Me Madam Ishmael

1. For a good, brief overview of Hetty Green's life, see Ralph W. Hidy, "Hetty Howland Robinson Green," in *Notable American Women, 1607–1950* (Cambridge, MA: Harvard University Press, 1971), edited by Edward T. James, 2:81–83. See also her obituary in the *New York Times*, "Hetty Green Dies, Worth $100,000,000" 4 July 1916.

2. S. E. Kiser, "Dreamers," *Charlotte Observer*, 4 May 1901. In 1909, Carolyn Wells published a similar verse in the *Saturday Evening Post*:

If you were Rockefeller
And I were Hetty Green,
Quite thoughtlessly and gaily
We'd spend our income daily.
We'd be a little sweller
Than anyone we'd seen;
If you were Rockefeller
And I were Hetty Green.

Reprinted in the *Denver Post*, 8 November 1909. See also Virginia G. Drachman, *Enterprising Women: 250 Years of American Business* (Chapel Hill: University of North Carolina Press, 2002), 72.

3. "The Classiest Hats in New Jersey," *Jersey Journal* (Jersey City, NJ), 2 October 1908. For other advertisements that invoke Hetty Green, see *Columbus (Ga.) Ledger*, 1 March 1912; *Elkhart (IN) Truth*, 22 March 1909; *Baltimore American*, 25 March 1908; and *Salt Lake Telegram* (Salt Lake City, UT), 17 October 1914.

4. *Baltimore American*, 10 February 1907; "Arctic Circle Has Its Hetty Green," *Charlotte (NC) Observer*, 31 October 1909; "Richest Colored Woman Visits in City," *Riverside (CA) Independent Enterprise*, 20 September 1915; "A Miniature Hetty Green," *Colorado Springs (CO) Gazette*, 4 October 1907. For other examples of such comparisons, see *Indianapolis Freeman*, 14 May 1904 and *Cleveland Plain Dealer*, 25 March 1912.

5. Sparkes and Moore, *Hetty Green*, 64–65.

6. Ibid., 14.

7. Green, "Why Women Are Not Money Makers," 201; Nicholls, "Hetty Green: A Character Study," 383; "When Hetty Green Was a Young Belle," *Montgomery (AL) Advertiser*, 4 September 1910. Green's supposed financial precocity was even the subject of jokes. See, for example, "The Business Instinct," *Biloxi (MS) Daily Herald*, 15 November 1902; and "Georgie's Paw's Idea of Hetty Green, *Philadelphia Inquirer*, 10 August 1902, Comic Magazine.

8. "Will of Edward Mott Robinson," *Salem (MA) Register*, 6 November 1865; Sparkes and Moore, *Hetty Green*, 91–94.

9. "Will of the Late Edward Mott Robinson," *New Bedford (MA) Mercury*, 29 June 1866; "A Millionaire Spinster in Trouble," *Daily Constitutionalist* (Augusta, Ga.), 26 October 1866.

10. For a discussion of the court battle over Sylvia Howland's will, see Louis Menand, "She Had to Have It," *The New Yorker* (23 and 30 April 2001): 62–70. Over time, Green wore down her trustees, and as they died she managed to have them replaced by persons more amenable to her. Eventually, the three administrators of her father's trust were her husband, her son, and her daughter. Sparkes and Moore, *Hetty Green*, 230–32.

11. *Sandusky (OH) Register*, 20 November 1865; *New London (CT) Democrat*, 12 March 1870.

12. Slack, *Hetty: The Genius and Madness*, 65–66; "Will of Edward Mott Robinson," *Salem (MA) Register*, November 1865.

13. Slack, *Hetty*, 72–73.

14. Wallach, *The Richest Woman in America*, 80–81.

15. *Cleveland Plain Dealer*, 6 June 1870.

16. "About a Bellows Falls Man's Wife," *Argus and Patriot* (Montpelier, VT), 18 February 1880.

17. Sparkes and Moore, *Hetty Green*, 156–60.

18. Ibid., 5–7.

19. Ibid., 8–10.

20. Ibid., 10, and "His Toy Taken Away," *New York Times*, 9 October 1885.

21. "A Woman Multi-Millionaire," *Frank Leslie's Popular Monthly* 51 (April 1901): 623; "Wily Hetty Green," *St. Albans (VT) Daily Messenger*, 13 October 1893; "Stories of Hetty Green," *Salt Lake Telegram* (Salt Lake City, UT), 2 August 1902; and Sparkes and Moore, *Hetty Green*, 139.

22. Sparkes and Moore, *Hetty Green*, 139.

23. "Hetty Green's Advice to Women," *Trenton (NJ) Evening Times*, 28 June 1896.

24. Hidy, "Hetty Green," *Notable American Women*, 82; "Hetty Green's Riches," *New Orleans Times-Picayune*, 15 February 1887.

25. "The Richest Woman in the World," *Harper's Bazaar* (14 October 1899): 881; Hodges, "The Richest Woman in America," 4.

26. "Wall Street Shys at Women," *Watertown (NY) Daily Times*, 18 September 1897.

27. "Mrs. Hetty Green's Millions," *Arkansas Gazette*, 3 March 1889; "Wall Street Shys at Women," *Watertown (NY) Daily Times*, 18 September 1897.

28. "Hetty Green, Great Woman Financier, believes in 'Buy-At-Home' Principle and Practices It in Her Own Business," *Montgomery (AL) Advertiser*, 10 March 1915.

29. Lewis, *The Day They Shook the Plum Tree*, 144.

30. "Mrs. Hetty Green: How the Multi-Millionaire Woman Makes Investment of Her Money," *Daily Journal and Tribune* (Knoxville, TN), 16 June 1895.

31. Hodges, "The Richest Woman in America," 4; Simonson, "Pastels in Sage-Green and Gold," 787; "Hetty Green's Son and Heir Trained by Her," *New York Times*, 9 July 1916.

32. "Hetty Green's Son and Heir Trained by Her," *New York Times*, 9 July 1916; Sparkes and Moore, *Hetty Green*, 274.

33. "Mrs. Hetty Green," *Daily Journal and Tribune* (Knoxville, TN), 16 June 1895.

34. Flynn, "The Witch of Wall Street," 12–15, 54, 56. Flynn expanded his portrait of Green in his biographical collection *Men of Wealth* (New York: Simon and Schuster, 1941).

35. See, for example, Peter Wyckoff, "Queen Midas: Hetty Robinson Green," *New England Quarterly* (June 1950): 147–71; Ishbel Ross, *Charmers and Cranks: Twelve Famous American Women Who Defied the Conventions* (New York: Harper and Row, 1965), 33.

36. Sobel, *The Big Board*, 114; Lewis, *The Day They Shook the Plum Tree*, 8.

37. Norris and Ross McWhirter, eds., *Guinness Book of World Records* (New York: Sterling, 1968), 337.

38. Janet L. Coryell, "Hetty Green," in *Encyclopedia of American Business History and Biography: Banking and Finance, to 1913*, edited by Larry Schweikart (New York: Facts on File, 1990), 233–38; Fraser, *Every Man a Speculator*, 100. Coryell also wrote the entry for Green in John A. Garraty and Mark C. Carnes, eds., *American National Biography* (New York: Oxford University Press, 1999), 9:491–93.

39. Two popular biographies helped revive Green's reputation: Charles Slack, *Hetty Green: The Genius and Madness of America's First Female Tycoon*, and Janet Wallach, *The Richest Woman in America: Hetty Green in the Gilded Age*. Slack's book is more balanced in its assessment of Green and more judicious in its evaluation of source materials. Wallach's biography is more partisan and accepts uncritically Green's perspective and testimony throughout. Neither book is carefully documented, and in many cases it is impossible to identify the historical sources for events described. Recent scholarly work on Green includes Virginia Drachman, *Enterprising Women: 250 Years of American Business* (Chapel Hill: University of North Carolina Press, 2002), 69–73; Yohn, "Crippled Capitalists," 85–109; and Yohn, "'Men Seem to Take Delight in Cheating Women,'" 226–42.

40. Using GenealogyBank.com, a databank of more than 6,500 historical newspapers from across the United States, I found almost 12,000 articles about Hetty Green for the years 1885–1916, the period of her greatest celebrity. This survey does not represent 12,000 distinct articles, as the same wire-service stories could be published in several different papers. It nonetheless includes several thousand different stories about Green over a thirty-year period, representing the most comprehensive analysis of what Green's contemporaries said about her.

41. "Mrs. Hetty Green and Her Adversaries," 848; Hodges, "The Richest Woman in America," 3; "Hetty Green Talks," *Irish World* (NY), 2 March 1895 (reprinted from *New York World*).

42. "Mrs. Hetty Green and Her Adversaries," *Harper's Bazaar*, 848; "Hetty Green's Riches," *New Orleans Times-Picayune*, 15 February 1887 (reprinted from the *Chicago Herald*).

43. "A Woman of Millions," *Wisconsin Labor Advocate*, 10 December 1886; *Cleveland Plain Dealer*, 27 April 1907; *Grand Rapids (MI) Press*, 15 December 1905; Clews, *Twenty-Eight Years in Wall Street*, 441; "Wall Street Shys at Women," *Watertown (NY) Daily Times*, 18 December 1897. Catherine Vernon, the female banker in Margaret

Oliphant's novel *Hester* (1883), was also described as having a "masculine mind." Quoted in Wagner, *Financial Speculation in Victorian Fiction*, 161.

44. "Our Richest Woman," *Daily Inter-Ocean* (Chicago), 27 November 1892 (reprinted from the *New York Herald*).

45. "Avaricious Hetty Green," *Columbus (GA) Daily Enquirer*, 5 November 1886 (reprinted from the *Indianapolis Journal*); "An Uninspiring Example," *Miami Herald*, July 7, 1916; Clark, "The Truth About Hetty Green," *Belleville (IL) News Democrat*, 14 August 1916. See also "Stingiest Woman on Earth," *Kansas City Times*, 30 August 1891, and "Thrift Made Hateful," *San Diego Evening Tribune*, 9 September 1916.

46. Westbrook, *Wall Street in the American Novel*, 9; "Satan and Fire," *Grand Forks (ND) Evening Times*, 21 February 1910.

47. "Our Richest Woman," *Daily Inter-Ocean* (Chicago), 27 November 1892.

48. "Hetty Green May Be Insane," *San Jose (CA) Evening News*, 16 April 1904; "'Hetty Green Is Insane,'" *Boston Journal*, 16 April 1904. Other newspaper stories sometimes implied that Green was mentally imbalanced. See, for example, "Hetty Green Is Queer," *Worcester (MA) Daily Spy*, 10 January 1895, and "Why Psychology Believes Hetty Green Was a Miser," *Richmond (VA) Times Dispatch*, 23 July 1916.

49. "Mrs. Hetty Howland Robinson Green, at 71 Years of Age," *New York World*, 26 November 1905, Metropolitan Section. The *Baltimore Sun* criticized the *World* piece for not having asked Green herself whether she was happy. "Does Mrs. Hetty Green Know What Happiness Is?" *Baltimore Sun*, 30 November 1905.

50. "Woman Pities Hetty Green," *Fort Worth Star-Telegram*, 11 January 1906; "Unhappy Hetty Green," *Baltimore Sun*, 12 February 1908; "Perfect Peace Is Rule in This House: Twenty-Five Years of Happiness Is Claimed by Woman Who Is in Poverty," *Cleveland Plain Dealer*, 17 July 1908.

51. "What Hetty Green Missed," *Fort Worth Star-Telegram*, 1 August 1916; "The World's Richest Woman," *Gulfport (MS) Daily Herald*, July 14, 1916.

52. "Henrietta Howland Robinson Green," *National Cyclopaedia of American Biography* (New York: James T. White, 1916), 15:128. A number of American magazines published positive profiles of Hetty Green, in which they systematically refuted negative stereotypes about her. See, for example, Simonson, "Pastels in Sage-Green and Gold," 483–90; Hodges, "The Richest Woman in America," 3–4; and Nicholls, "Hetty Green: A Character Study," 382–88.

53. Quincy, "Peggy Quincy's Opinion of Mrs. Hetty Green," *Boston Journal*, November 10, 1906.

54. Sparkes and Moore, *Hetty Green*, 270.

55. Lipscomb, "Woman as a Financier," 470; Dodge, *What Women Can Earn*, 334.

56. Among almost 12,000 newspaper articles about Green from 1885 to 1916, she was referred to as "the witch of Wall Street" only twelve times. On the other hand, she was called "the queen of Wall Street" or "the queen of finance" more than 500 times. She was designated "the richest woman in America" or "the richest woman in the world" more than 2,500 times.

57. "A Woman of Millions," *Wisconsin Labor Advocate*, 10 December 1886; "The Feminine Sex the Superior One," *Columbia (SC) State*, 18 September 1904.

58. Conner, "Hetty Green, Multimillionaire, America's Chief Money Lender," *Montgomery (AL) Advertiser*, 7 October 1906.

59. Simonson, "Pastels in Sage-Green and Gold," 483; "Hetty Green's Good Example," *Idaho Statesman* (Boise), March 11, 1909.

60. T. D. MacGregor, "Talks on Thrift," *Trenton (NJ) Evening Times*, 11 June 1914.

61. "About Women," *American Farmer* (January 1896): 6.

62. "Personal," *Harper's Weekly* (December 3, 1892): 1,167.

63. "Sensible Hetty Green," *Wheeling (WV) Register*, 12 December 1897; "Hetty Green's Good Example," *Idaho Statesman* (Boise), 11 March 1909.

64. "Hetty Green's Son and Heir Trained by Her," *New York Times*, 9 July 1916.

65. "Hetty Green's Good Example," *Idaho Statesman*, 11 March 1909.

66. "Dogmatic Moralizing," *Oregonian* (Portland, OR), 19 August 1911; "Stories and Anecdotes of the Late Hetty Green," *Miami Herald*, 15 July 1916.

67. "Hetty Green Talks," *Irish World* (NY), 2 March 1895; "Mrs. Hetty Green Now Patronizing Clipping Bureau," *Salt Lake Telegram* (Salt Lake City, UT), 11 June 1908.

68. "Seventy Years Rest Lightly on Mrs. Hetty Green," *New York Times*, 5 November 1905; Sparkes and Moore, *Hetty Green*, 182.

69. Fraser, *Every Man a Speculator*, 101–2.

70. *The Sayings of Uncle Rufus*.

71. For examples of Green being referred to as "Aunt Hetty," see *Daily Illinois State Journal*, 12 March 1895; *Pawtucket (RI) Times*, 11 May 1899; *Grand Forks (ND) Herald*, 11 January 1901; *Kalamazoo (MI) Gazette*, 3 March 1909; *San Jose (CA) Evening News*, 6 December 1912.

72. "Stories and Anecdotes of the Late Hetty Green," *Miami Herald*, 15 July 1916; "Hetty Green's Philosophy," 320; "Mrs. Green a Wit," *Oregonian* (Portland, OR), 4 July 1916.

73. "Hetty Green Still Young," *Oregonian* (Portland, OR), 20 November 1911.

74. "Personal and Pertinent," *Harper's Weekly* (2 December 1905): 1,733.

75. "Mrs. Hetty's Business Methods," *Philadelphia Inquirer*, 7 August 1899. See also "Hetty Green Gives Good Advice to Girls," *Pawtucket (RI) Times*, 21 November 1912.

76. "Wilks Grilled by Hetty Green," *Baltimore American*, 21 February 1909.

77. "Would Kill Son Like Harry Thaw," *Trenton (NJ) Evening Times*, 14 August 14, 1906; "Stories and Anecdotes of the Late Hetty Green," *Miami Herald*, 15 July 1916.

78. Harwood, "Young Girls of Today Are Too Extravagant," 2.

79. "How I'd Run the World," *Kansas City Star*, 16 February 1911 (reprinted from *New York World*); "Hetty Green's Son and Heir Trained by Her," *New York Times*, 9 July 1916; "Hetty Green's Christmas," *Cleveland Plain Dealer*, 30 December 1896; "Hetty Green's Philosophy," *Literary Digest* (5 August 1916): 319.

80. "Hetty Green Says She Made Her Money by Not Spending It," *Montgomery (AL) Advertiser*, 9 April 1911; Nicholls, "Hetty Green: A Character Study," 384; "Sylvia's Beau Is Given Pointers," *Cleveland Plain Dealer*, 20 February 1909.

81. "Hetty Green Talks," *Albuquerque Journal*, 13 April 1915; "Hetty Green Pessimistic," *Baltimore Sun*, 13 October 1907; "Hetty Green Gets Gossipy," *Biloxi (MS) Daily Herald*, 12 April 1900.

82. "Mrs. Hetty Green's Ramblings," *New York Herald Tribune*, 19 January 1895; "Rich Hetty Green," *Boston Herald*, 3 February 1895.

83. "Her Other Side: Extremely Radical Sentiments Charged to Hetty Green," *Idaho Statesman*, 22 February 1895; "Hetty Green on Trusts," *Baltimore Sun*, 12 November 1906. See also "Hetty Has Her Views," *Daily Inter-Ocean* (Chicago), 8 January 1895.

84. Simonson, "Pastels in Sage-Green and Gold," 485; Harwood, "Young Girls Are Too Extravagant," 2.

85. Wallach, *The Richest Woman in America*, 177.

86. "Hetty Green's Filth House," *Daily People* (NY), 15 October 1906.

87. "Hetty Green, Multimillionaire," *Montgomery (AL) Advertiser*, 7 October 1906; and "Frills Annoy Hetty Green," *Columbia (SC) State*, 9 October 1907.

88. Nicholls, "Hetty Green: A Character Study," 384; "Business Code of Hetty Green," *Aberdeen (SD) Daily News*, 13 July 1916; "Women and Trusts," *Dallas Morning News*, 5 January 1897; "Blames Women for Hard Times," *Trenton (NJ) Evening News*, 2 September 1908.

89. "How Hetty Green Makes Her Money," 39; "And Who Loves His Own Wife," *Oregonian* (Portland, OR), 30 June 1907.

90. "Hetty Green on Simple Life," *Kalamazoo (MI) Gazette*, 23 March 1905; Sparkes and Moore, *Hetty Green*, 305; Hodges, "The Richest Woman in America," 4.

91. "Why Women Don't Get Rich," *New York Times*, 28 April 1901; Green, "Why Women Are Not Money Makers," 201.

92. Green, "Why Women Are Not Money Makers," 201.

93. Hetty Green, "The Benefits of a Business Training for Women," *Woman's Home Companion* (February 1900): 8. Green actually gave a lengthy interview to the journal's editor, C. Montgomery McGovern, who then arranged her words into a seamless article.

94. Ibid., 8. For examples of newspapers reprinting parts of the *Woman's Home Companion* article, see "Hetty Green on the Business Woman," *Philadelphia Inquirer*, 24 February 1900; and "Gives Advice to Her Sex," *Afro-American Advance* (Minneapolis), 3 February 1900.

95. "Mrs. Green a Wit," *Oregonian* (Portland, OR), 4 July 1916; "Why Women Don't Get Rich," *New York Times*, 28 April 1901; Green, "Why Women Are Not Money Makers," 201.

96. Green, "Benefits of a Business Training," 8.

97. Green, "Why Women Are Not Money Makers," 201; "'Hetty' Scores 'Butterflies,'" *Trenton (NJ) Evening News*, 27 April 1903.

98. "The Happiest Women," *Tucson Daily Citizen*, 11 January 1907; "Personal and Pertinent," *Harper's Weekly* (2 December 1905): 1,733.

99. "Mrs. Green a Wit," *Oregonian* (Portland, OR), 4 July 1916; "Why Women Don't Get Rich," *New York Times*, April 28, 1901; "How I'd Run the World," *Kansas City Star*, February 1911; "How Hetty Green Makes Her Money," 39.

100. See, for example, Simonson, "Pastels in Sage-Green and Gold," 483–89; and "Hetty Green: Feminine Counterpart of and Successor to Russell Sage," *Daily People*

(NY), 12 August 1906. Sage's reputation was somewhat salvaged by his widow, who later gave away much of his fortune. Green made no charitable or institutional bequests so that her life story was left for others to interpret.

101. "A Prodigy Because a Woman," *New York Times*, 5 July 1916.

102. "Hetty Green Lays Down Law," *Irish World* (NY), 9 February 1895.

103. "Women as High Financiers," *Daily People* (NY), 31 May 1908; Tompkins, "Ella Rawls Reader, Financier," *Everybody's Magazine* 13 (September 1905): 310, and (October 1905): 458; "Rich Women Work Hard and Long," *Boston Herald*, 17 October 1909.

104. "A Woman Mine Boss," *Biloxi (MS) Daily Herald*, 16 December 1902; "A Woman Cotton Expert," *Washington Bee* (Washington, DC), 24 September 1904; "Women in Wall Street and the Part They Play," *Baltimore Sun*, 24 November 1907; "Women of Wall Street," *Colorado Springs (CO) Gazette*, 26 January 1908. See also "Women as High Financiers," 3.

105. Yohn, "Crippled Capitalists," 95.

106. "Woman 60 Years Old, Worth $50,000,000, Manages Great Chemical Plant," *New York Times*, 4 September 1904; "Anne Weightman Walker, Multimillionaire Business Woman," *Idaho Statesman*, 3 October 1904.

107. "Woman 60 Years Old," *New York Times*; "Anne Weightman Walker," *Idaho Statesman*.

108. "Rich Woman at Work," *Dallas Morning News*; "Two Women Financiers: Hetty Green and Anne Weightman Walker," *Springfield (MA) Republican*, 25 February 1906; "America's Richest Woman Will Live Over Store," *Philadelphia Inquirer*, 20 February 1906.

109. "Two Women Financiers," *Springfield (MA) Republican*.

110. "Woman 60 Years Old," *New York Times*; "Celebrates Wedding by Giving $1,000,000," *New York Times*, 27 February 1908; "Rich Woman at Work," *Dallas Morning News*.

111. "Mrs. Walker to Quit Business," *Colorado Springs (CO) Gazette*, 27 December 1904; "Penfield's Widow Dies in New York," *Hartford (CT) Courant*, 27 February 1932.

112. "Morgan Stirs Up the Senate," *Baltimore American*, 17 March 1905; "Senator Morgan for Investigation," *Baltimore American*, 18 March 1905.

113. "Petticoat Diplomacy in the Dominican Affair," *Salt Lake Telegram* (Salt Lake City, UT), 18 March 1905; "Woman Financier Whom Senate Has Discussed," *San Jose (CA) Mercury News* (Associated Press), 26 March 1905; "A Woman Who Tried to Run a Republic," *Belleville (IL) News Democrat*, 8 April 1905.

114. Tompkins, "Ella Rawls Reader," 311–16.

115. Ibid., 311–16.

116. Ibid., 458–65.

117. Ibid., 691–97, 834–38.

118. Reader is altogether absent from histories of the Dominican Republic and American foreign policy in the Caribbean, such as Frank Moya Pons, *The Dominican Republic: A National History* (New Rochelle, NY: Hispaniola Books, 1995); and

Richard H. Collin, *Theodore Roosevelt's Caribbean* (Baton Rouge: Louisiana State University Press, 1990). Likewise, histories of Malaysia and the Sultan of Johore make no mention of Reader. Nesalamar Nadarajah, *Johore and the Origins of British Control, 1895–1914* (Kuala Lumpur: Arenabuku, 2000), includes a very different narrative concerning the railway contract for Johore.

119. See "A New Zealander's Clever Wife," *Evening Post* (New Zealand), 20 February 1907. For a more skeptical take on the *Everybody's* profile, see "Female Frenzied Finance," *New Orleans Item*, 28 September 1905.

120. "A Woman Who Tried to Run a Republic," *Belleville (IL) News Democrat*; "Strange Case of Athole Reader," *Evening Post* (New Zealand); and "Ella Rawls Reader, the Financial Rival of Hetty Green," *Boston Herald*, 5 May 1907.

121. Tompkins, "Ella Rawls Reader," 310–12, 465.

122. Ibid., 694–95, "Woman Financier Whom Senate Has Discussed," *San Jose (CA) Mercury News*; "Finance and Frills," *Boston Herald*, 7 April 1907, 36; "A New Zealander's Clever Wife," *Evening Post* (New Zealand).

123. "Finance and Frills," *Boston Herald*.

124. "Ella Rawls Reader, the Financial Rival of Hetty Green," *Boston Herald*.

125. Tompkins, "Ella Rawls Reader," 837; Ella Rawls Reader, "Why Most Women Do Not Succeed in Business," *Idaho Falls Times*, 23 May 1905.

126. Reader, "Why Most Women Do Not Succeed in Business"; Tompkins, "Ella Rawls Reader," 459.

127. Tompkins, "Ella Rawls Reader," 312, 461.

128. "Ella Rawls Reader Controls New Mine," *Philadelphia Inquirer*, 22 April 1907; "A New Zealander's Clever Wife," *Evening Post* (New Zealand); "Mrs. Ella Rawls Reader, Promoter, Declares Her Mining Lands Suffered Damages," *Cincinnati Post*, 31 March 1906; "Reader Loses Mine Suit," *Oregonian* (Portland, OR), 15 May 1909.

129. "Arrested for Perjury in Suit for Million and Half," *Denver Post*, 10 January 1907; "Cleverest of Women," *Baltimore Sun*, 11 January 1907.

130. "Women in Wall Street," *New York Times*, 12 December 1909. The *Times* also noted the irony of *Everybody's Magazine* puffing Reader in its 1905 profile, as the magazine usually was "particularly zealous in its pursuit of swindlers of all kinds."

131. "Strange Case of Athole Reader," *Evening Post* (New Zealand), 13 June 1907.

132. Deland, *The Iron Woman*. For an analysis of this novel see Susan Albertine, "Breaking the Silent Partnership: Businesswomen in Popular Fiction," *American Literature* 62 (June 1990): 238–61.

133. Hyne, *Kate Meredith, Financier*, 190–91, 245, 248–49.

Epilogue and Conclusion

1. "Women Traders Going Back to Bridge Games," *New York Times*, 30 October 1929.

2. Hansl, "Leaders Discuss Women in Finance," *New York Times*, 15 March 1936; "American Board Opens Ranks," *New York Times*, 29 October 1958.

3. "The Missing Link," *My Little Margie*, 1952.

4. *The Lady and the Stock Exchange*, New York Stock Exchange, 1962. Screenplay by Robert M. Fresco.

5. Gary B. Charness and Uri Gneezy, "Strong Evidence for Gender Differences in Investment," Departmental Working Papers, Department of Economics, University of California, Santa Barbara, 2007; "Prince Charming Isn't Coming," *Marketplace* (radio program), 25 January 2008.

6. See Chapter 3.

7. Smith Barney advertisement, *New York Times Magazine* (5 October 1997): 33.

8. Citibank advertisement, *Martha Stewart Living* (February 2002): 5.

9. Orman, *Women and Money*, 5–14.

10. Lucht, *Sylvia Porter*, 37.

11. Cooper and Grinder, "Women on Wall Street," 10; Campbell, *Careers for Women in Banking and Finance*, 12.

12. Ellebracht, "Riding the Rails with Madam Railroad," 23.

13. "Banker in High Heels."

14. Fowler, "Broker Preaches Gospel of Mutuals."

15. Fisher, *Wall Street Women*, 48–49; Caplan, *Petticoats and Pinstripes*, 111.

16. Caplan, *Petticoats and Pinstripes*, 128–29.

17. Ibid., 135–43; Cooper and Grinder, "Women on Wall Street," 10–11. See also Muriel Siebert, *Changing the Rules: Adventures of a Wall Street Maverick* (New York: Free Press, 2007).

18. Fisher, *Wall Street Women*, 45–46; Caplan, *Petticoats and Pinstripes*, 151–68.

19. Enid Nemy, "Muriel Siebert, a Determined Trailblazer for Women on Wall Street, Dies at 80," *New York Times*, August 26, 2013.

20. Caplan, *Petticoats and Pinstripes*, 183.

21. Fisher, *Wall Street Women*, 7, 50–52.

22. Antilla, *Tales from the Boom-Boom Room*, 43–44, 64–66, 107, 177–78.

23. Ibid., 93, 95–98, 138–39, 150–51.

24. Ibid., 139, 186–91, 198–99.

25. Susan Antilla, "'Too-Hot' Banker Simply Can't Measure Up," *Star-Ledger*, June 9, 2010.

26. Thomas, "A Fragile Foothold,"; Dominus, "Exile on Park Avenue," 32–39; Solomon, "Questions for Abby Joseph Cohen," 14.

27. Kantor and Silver-Greenberg, "Wall Street Mothers, Stay-Home Fathers."

28. Rukeyser, "Women of Wall Street," 112, 152–53.

29. *Wanda Whips Wall Street*, Platinum Pictures, 1982. Screenplay by Rick Mars.

30. Brady, "In Step with Maria Bartiromo," 18; Halle, "Martha, My Dear," 6.

31. Dominus, "Exile on Park Avenue," 35.

32. Antilla, "'Too-Hot' Banker."

33. See "Business Women's Clothes," *Aberdeen American*, 21 September 1916.

34. Stanley, "With Wall St. Center Stage"; Ryzik, "Where Women Run Wall Street."

35. Sullivan, "The He Hormone," 46–51, 58, 69, 73–79. For an earlier analysis of Sullivan's screed, see Yohn, "Crippled Capitalists," 104.

36. "Wall Street's Secret Weapon for Getting an Edge," CNBC, 11 July 2012.

37. Nicholas D. Kristof, "Mistresses of the Universe," *New York Times*, 7 February 2009.

38. Kolhatkar, "What If Women Ran Wall Street?," 36–41. Adams, "Testosterone and High Finance Do Not Mix"; Zaloom and Schull, "The Shortsighted Brain," 515–38.

Bibliography

Primary Sources

MANUSCRIPT SOURCES

ACE Archives, Philadelphia:
   Insurance Company of North America Records.
Franklin D. Roosevelt Library, Hyde Park, New York:
   Eleanor Roosevelt Papers.
Newark Public Library, Charles F. Cummings New Jersey Information Center:
   Mutual Benefit Life Insurance Company Records.
New Jersey Historical Society:
   Fidelity Trust Company Records.
New York Historical Society:
   G. V. Fox Papers. Series X, volume 4, Property Book.
   Morton, Bliss and Company, Stockbrokers. Ledgers, 6 volumes (1884–1899).
      Letter Books of George Bliss, 12 volumes (1876–1891).
   George P. Butler and Brother, Stockbrokers. Ledgers, 4 volumes (1905–1910).
      Letter Books, 3 volumes (1906–1910).
New York Stock Exchange Archives:
   Admissions Committee. Minute Books.
   James Mitchell. Scrapbooks.
   Special Committee on 'Bucket Shop' Organizations.
   William C. Van Antwerp. Letter Books.
Prudential Insurance Archives, Newark, NJ:
   Company flyers.
Schlesinger Library, Harvard University:
   Bureau of Vocational Information Archives.

BOOKS

A Banker's Daughter. *A Guide to the Unprotected in Everyday Matters Related to Money and Income*. London: Macmillan, 1863.

Bartlett, Frederick Orin. *The Wall Street Girl*. New York: Houghton Mifflin, 1916.

Boyesen, Hjalmar Hjorth. *A Daughter of the Philistines*. Boston: Roberts Brothers, 1883.

Brandeis, Louis. *Other People's Money and How the Bankers Use It*. New York: F. A. Stokes, 1914.

Byrnes, Thomas. *Professional Criminals of America*. New York: Cassell, 1886.

Campbell, Helen. *Mrs. Herndon's Income*. Boston: Roberts Brothers, 1886.

Clews, Henry. *Twenty-Eight Years in Wall Street*. New York: Irving, 1888.

Clews, James Blanchard. *Fortuna: A Story of Wall Street*. New York: J. S. Ogilvie, 1898.

Courtland, Grace. *The Kings of Wall Street, or The People vs. Monopoly*. Np, 1881.

———. *A Marked Life: Autobiography of a Clairvoyant*. London: Low, 1879.

Cromwell, John Howard. *The American Business Woman: A Guide to the Investment, Preservation and Accumulation of Property*. New York: G. P. Putnam's Sons, 1900.

Day, Clarence. *Life with Father*. New York: Modern Library, 1920.

Deland, Margaret. *The Iron Woman*. New York: A. L. Burt, 1911.

Denison, Thomas Stewart. *An Iron Crown: A Tale of the Great Republic*. Chicago: T. S. Denison, 1885.

Dickinson, Anna. *A Paying Investment*. Boston: James R. Osgood, 1876.

Dodge, Grace. *What Women Can Earn*. New York: Frederick A. Stokes, 1899.

Dreiser, Theodore. *The Financier*. New York: Harper and Brothers, 1912.

Flagg, W. J. *Wall Street and the Woods, or Woman the Stronger*. New York: Baker and Taylor, 1885.

Fowler, William Worthington. *Twenty Years of Inside Life in Wall Street*. New York: Orange Judd, 1880.

Frazer, Elizabeth. *A Woman and Her Money*. New York: George H. Doran, 1926.

French, Alice. *The Lion's Share*. Indianapolis: Bobbs-Merrill, 1907.

Gilman, Charlotte Perkins. *Women and Economics*. 1898. Reprint, New York: Harper and Row, 1966.

Hale, Edward Everett. *Sybil Knox, or Home Again: A Story of Today*. New York: Cassell, 1892.

Hannaford, Phebe A. *Women of the Century*. Boston: B. B. Russell, 1877.

The Hardships of English Law in Relation to Wives. London, 1735.

Herrick, Robert. *The Gospel of Freedom*. New York: Macmillan, 1898.

Hill, Joseph A. *Women in Gainful Occupations, 1870 to 1920*. Washington, DC: GPO, 1929.

Hyne, C. J. Cutcliffe. *Kate Meredith, Financier*. New York: The Authors and Newspapers Association, 1906.

Keenan, Henry. *The Money-Makers*. New York: D. Appleton, 1884.

Kirk, Ellen Warner. *Queen Money*. Boston: Ticknor, 1888.

Lefevre, Edwin. *The Making of a Stockbroker*. New York: Doubleday, 1924.

———. *The Reminiscences of a Stock Operator.* New York: George H. Doran, 1923.

Mott, Bessie Q. *An American Woman and Her Bank.* New York: Doubleday, Doran, 1929.

Nichols, J. L. *Safe Methods of Business.* Naperville, IL: J. L. Nichols, 1907.

Norris, Frank. *The Pit: A Story of Chicago.* New York: Curtis, 1902.

Oldham, Mary Kavanaugh, ed. *The Congress of Women: Held in the Woman's Building, World's Columbian Exposition, Chicago, U.S.A., 1893.* Chicago: Monarch, 1894.

Penny, Virginia. *The Employments of Women: A Cyclopedia of Women's Work.* Boston: Walker, Wise, 1863.

Percy, H. C. *Our Cashier's Scrap-Book.* New York: G. W. Carleton, 1879.

Pinto, Erasmus. *Ye Outside Fools! Glimpses Inside the London Stock Exchange.* London: Lovell, Adam, Wesson, 1877.

The Sayings of Uncle Rufus. New York: Jesse Haney, 1881.

Seward, Anne. *The Women's Department.* New York: Bankers' Publishing, 1924.

Sinclair, Upton. *The Moneychangers.* New York: B. W. Dodge, 1908.

Smith, E. V. *Plain Truths about Stock Speculation.* New York: E. V. Smith, 1887.

Smith, Matthew Hale. *Bulls and Bears of New York.* Hartford, CT: J. B. Burr, 1875.

Smith, William Hawley. *The Promoters: A Novel without a Woman.* New York: Rand, McNally, 1904.

Somerset, Sophia Vernon. *A Good Investment, or For Love or Money.* London: Griffith, Farran, Okeden and Welsh, 1891.

Stanton, Elizabeth Cady, and Susan B. Anthony. *The Selected Papers of Elizabeth Cady Stanton and Susan B. Anthony.* Vol. 2, *Against the Aristocracy of Sex, 1866–1873,* Ann D. Gordon, ed. New Brunswick, NJ: Rutgers University Press, 2000.

Stanton, Elizabeth Cady, Susan B. Anthony, and Matilda Joslyn Gage. *History of Woman Suffrage.* 3 vols. Rochester, NY: Susan B. Anthony, 1886.

Tilton, Theodore. *Victoria C. Woodhull: A Biographical Sketch.* New York: McDivitt, Campbell, 1871.

U.S. Bureau of Labor. *Report on Conditions of Woman and Child Wage-Earners in the United States.* 19 vols. Vol 9, *History of Women in Industry in the United States.* Washington, DC: GPO, 1910.

U.S. Census Bureau. Sixteenth Census of the United States, 1940. *Comparative Occupation Statistics for the United States, 1870 to 1940.* Washington, DC: GPO, 1943.

———. *A Social-Economic Grouping of the Gainful Workers of the United States.* Washington, DC: GPO, 1938.

Van Antwerp, W. C. *The Stock Exchange from Within.* New York: Doubleday, 1913.

Walch, Caroline. *Doctor Sphinx.* New York: F. Tennyson Neely, 1898.

Webster, Henry Kitchell. *The Banker and the Bear: The Story of a Corner in Lard.* New York: Macmillan, 1900.

Wendt, Paul Francis. *The Classification of Financial Experience of the Customers of a Typical Wall Street Firm from 1933 to 1938.* Marysville, TN: The Author, 1941.

Wharton, Edith. *The Buccaneers.* 1938. Reprint, London: Fourth Estate, 1993.

———. *The House of Mirth*. 1905. Reprint, New York: Signet Classics, 1964.

Wilbur, Mary Aronetta. *Everyday Business for Women: A Manual for the Uninitiated*. New York: Houghton Mifflin, 1910.

Woodhull, Victoria. *The Great Social Problem of Labor and Capital*. New York: Journeyman Printers' Cooperative Association, 1871.

———. *The Human Body: The Temple of God*. London: np, 1890.

———. *The Impending Revolution*. New York: Woodhull, Claflin, 1872.

———. *The Principles of Social Freedom*. New York: Woodhull, Claflin, 1871.

———. *A Speech on the Principles of Finance*. New York: Woodhull, Claflin, 1871.

ARTICLES

"About Women." *Zion's Herald* 88 (September 1910): 1,233.

"Accuse Woman of Swindle." *New York Times*, 13 June 1917.

"Actress's Estate Valued at $80,193." *New York Times*, 18 July 1916.

"Afraid of Broker Hatch's Ghost." *Trenton Evening News*, 24 May 1888.

"American Woman Is Accused of Forgery." *New York Times*, 3 September 1901.

Anderson, Mrs. Finley. "Women in Wall Street." *Frank Leslie's Popular Monthly* 47 (March 1899): 22–25.

"Anne Weightman Walker, Multimillionaire Business Woman." *Idaho Statesman*, 3 October 1904.

"Another Coil Taken." *Boston Daily Advertiser*, 22 October 1880.

"Another Woman's Bank." *New York Herald*, 14 November 1887.

Anthony, Susan B. "The Working Woman." *The Revolution*, 10 March 1870, 154–55.

"The Arrested Female Broker." *New York Times*, 22 December 1881.

"Arrested for Perjury in Suit for Million and Half." *Denver Post*, 10 January 1907.

"Asking About Mrs. Dow." *New York Times*, 11 January 1882.

"At Her Old Tricks Again." *New York Times*, 4 December 1884.

Atwood, Albert W. "Secret of Riches: Common Stocks." *Saturday Evening Post* 200 (2 June 1928): 31.

"Avaricious Hetty Green." *Columbus (Ga.) Daily Enquirer*, 5 November 1886.

"Baird and Warner Plan." *Magazine of Wall Street* (28 March 1925): 970.

"Banker in High Heels." *Greater Philadelphia Magazine* (July 1952): n.p.

Barnard, Eunice Fuller. "Ladies of the Ticker." *North American Review* 227 (April 1929): 405–10.

———. "Women in Wall Street Wielding a New Power." *New York Times*, 23 June 1929.

Barrett, Walter H. "Investment in Stocks and Bonds." *The Ladies Home Journal* 10 (March 1893): 10.

"The Bewitching Brokers." *New York Evening Telegram*, 18 February 1870.

"The Bewitching Brokers." *New York Herald*, 10 and 13 February 1870.

"Blames Women for Hard Times." *Trenton (NJ) Evening News*, 2 September 1908.

Bok, Edward William. "The Return of the Business Woman." *The Ladies' Home Journal* 17 (March 1900): 16.

"The Boston Woman's Bank." *New York Times*, 23 April 1881.

Brainerd Fuller, Mrs. "Women as Political Economists." In *The Congress of Women,* edited by Mary Kavanaugh Oldham. Chicago: Monarch, 1894.

"The Broad Street Novelty in Brokerage." *The World,* 8 February 1870.

"The Broken Bank." *Boston Daily Advertiser,* 18 October 1880.

"The Broken Bank." *Boston Globe,* 18 October 1880.

"Broker Hatch." *Wheeling (WV) Register,* 9 May 1888.

"A Broker's Commissions." *New York Times,* 7 April 1880.

Burns, Shirley. "Male Vampires." *Forum* 57 (February 1917): 183–85.

"Business Code of Hetty Green." *Aberdeen (S.D.) Daily News,* 13 July 1916.

"Business Education for Girls." *Chicago Inter-Ocean,* 14 January 1888.

"The Business Woman's Investments." *Magazine of Wall Street* (24 October 1925): 1,199 and 1,246.

"A Capitalist Charged with Fraud." *New York Times,* 22 November 1884.

"Cassie Chadwick Dies in Prison." *New York Times,* 11 October 1907.

Cather, Willa. "The Novel Demeublé," in *Not Under Forty.* New York: Knopf, 1936.

"Charge Big Fraud." *Grand Rapids (MI) Press,* 29 October 1906.

"Charged with Running a Bucket Shop." *New York Times,* 5 April 1893.

Clark, Sam. "The Truth About Hetty Green." *Belleville (IL) News Democrat,* 14 August 1916.

"Cleverest of Women." *Baltimore Sun,* 11 January 1907.

"The Coming Woman." *New York Herald,* 2 April 1870.

"A Commonplace Swindler." *New York Times,* 9 December 1887.

"Confessions of a Stockbroker." *The Independent* 61 (20 December 1906): 1,469.

"The Confidence Woman." *New York Times,* 20 January 1888.

Conner, Eliza Archard. "Hetty Green, Multimillionaire, America's Chief Money Lender." *Montgomery (AL) Advertiser,* 7 October 1906.

"Convicting a Female Stock Broker." *New York Times,* 12 June 1884.

Creighton, Louisa. "Women and Finance." *Financial Review of Reviews* 59 (1910): 15–21.

"A Crowd Around the Bank." *Boston Globe,* 17 October 1880.

"Death of Mrs. Howe." *New York Times,* 21 January 1892.

"The Defunct Bank." *Boston Daily Advertiser,* 19 October 1880.

Deland, Margaret. "The House of Rimmon," in *The Wisdom of Fools,* 116–28. New York: Houghton Mifflin, 1897.

Denison, Edward E. "Fleecing the Public of Its Liberty Bonds." *La Follette's Magazine* (June 1922): 91, 93.

"Denounced in Court." *New York Times,* 17 September 1897.

"The Deposit Company." *Boston Daily Advertiser,* 4 October 1880.

"Does Mrs. Hetty Green Know What Happiness Is?" *Baltimore Sun,* 30 November 1905.

Dorman, Marjorie. "A Woman Broker in Wall Street!" *Canton (OH) Sunday Repository,* 13 January 1924.

"Ella Rawls Reader Controls New Mine." *Philadelphia Inquirer,* 22 April 1907.

"Ella Rawls Reader, the Financial Rival of Hetty Green." *Boston Herald*, 5 May 1907.

"Ella Wants $25,000." *Boulder (CO) Daily Camera*, 3 March 1893.

Evans, Frances. "About Men." *Ladies Home Journal* 16 (January 1899): 15.

"The Evolution of Mrs. Hetty Green." *Kansas City Star*, 29 May 1908.

"Excluding Women from Brokers' Offices." *New York Times*, 13 July 1902.

"A Faithless Trustee." *New York Times*, 24 November 1877.

"Faithless Trustees." *New York Times*, 23 April 1877.

"A Female Broker." *Daily Inter-Ocean* (Chicago), 3 December 1887.

"The Female Broker." *Philadelphia Inquirer*, 22 December 1881.

"The Female Broker Again." *New York Times*, 18 July 1883.

"A Female Broker Arrested." *New York Times*, 21 December 1881 and 8 December 1887.

"Female Bucket-Shops." *The New England Farmer* 63 (April 1884): 4.

"A Female Ferdinand Ward." *Columbus (GA) Daily Enquirer*, 25 December 1887.

"Female Financiers." *Augusta (GA) Chronicle*, 23 January 1906.

"Female Frenzied Finance." *New Orleans Item*, 28 September 1905.

"The Female Stock Broker." *New York Times*, 8 April 1884.

"A Female Stock Broker Under Surveillance." *Philadelphia Public Ledger*, 23 December 1881.

Field, Arthur. "A Woman's Romance in Wall Street." *Demorest's Family Magazine* 30 (January 1894): 151–58.

"Finance and Frills: Is It Possible for Women to Understand Business?" *Boston Herald*, 7 April 1907.

"Finance Queen's Chum Held on Fraud Charge." *Columbus (GA) Daily Enquirer*, 29 May 1908.

"A Financial Fraud." *New York Journal*, 26 January 1883.

Fowler, Elizabeth. "Broker Preaches Gospel of Mutuals." *New York Times*, 7 July 1957.

Frazer, Elizabeth. "Did You Lose Your Shirt in the Market?" *Saturday Evening Post*, 8 September 1928.

———. "The Widow's Mite." *Saturday Evening Post*, 6 September 1924, 21, 93–96, 101–2.

"Frills Annoy Hetty Green." *Columbia (SC) State*, 9 October 1907.

"Gail Hamilton's Defense of the Ladies' Deposit." *Boston Daily Advertiser*, 5 October 1880.

"Gail Hamilton's Letter." *Boston Daily Advertiser*, 7 October 1880.

"Grace Courtland's Cow Hide." *National Police Gazette*, 4 August 1883.

Green, Hetty. "The Benefits of a Business Training for Women." *Woman's Home Companion* (February 1900): 8.

———. "Financial Fools and Their Money." *Daily Illinois State Journal*, 11 December 1899.

———. "Why Women Are Not Money Makers." *Harper's Bazaar* (March 1900): 201.

Greig, J., and M. Gibson. "Women and Investment." *Financial Review of Reviews* (June 1917): 174–82.

Guenther, Louis. "In the Land of Pirate Finance." *Forum* 61 (May 1919): 621–25.

———. "Pirates of Promotion." *World's Work* (October 1918): 584–91; (November 1918): 29–33; (March 1919): 509–18.

"Guilty on Four Counts." *The Boston Globe*, 26 April 1881.

Hansl, Eva. "Leaders Discuss Women in Finance." *New York Times*, 15 March 1936.

Harper, Ida Husted. "The Advance of Woman." *Duluth (MN) News Tribune*, 6 September 1903.

Harwood, Henry A. "Young Girls of Today Are Too Extravagant, Declares Hetty Green." *Salt Lake Telegram* (Salt Lake City, UT), 23 August 1907.

"The Hatch Inquest." *New Haven (CT) Register*, 15 May 1888.

Henrotin, Ellen. "The Financial Independence of Women," in *The Congress of Women*, edited by Mary Kavanaugh Oldham, 348–53. Chicago: Monarch, 1894.

"Her Other Side: Extremely Radical Sentiments Charged to Hetty Green." *Idaho Statesman*, 22 February 1895.

"Hetty Green Dies, Worth $100,000,000." *New York Times*, 4 July 1916.

"Hetty Green Gets Gossipy." *Biloxi (MS) Daily Herald*, 12 April 1900.

"Hetty Green Gives Good Advice to Girls." *Pawtucket (RI) Times*, 21 November 1912.

"Hetty Green, Great Woman Financier, Believes in 'Buy-At-Home' Principle and Practices It in Her Own Business." *Montgomery (AL) Advertiser*, 10 March 1915.

"'Hetty Green Is Insane,' Says Noted Alienist." *Boston Journal*, 16 April 1904.

"Hetty Green Is Queer." *Worcester (MA) Daily Spy*, 10 January 1895.

"Hetty Green Lays Down Law." *Irish World* (New York), 9 February 1895.

"Hetty Green, Multimillionaire." *Montgomery (AL) Advertiser*, 7 October 1906.

"Hetty Green on Simple Life." *Kalamazoo (MI) Gazette*, 23 March 1905.

"Hetty Green on Trusts." *Baltimore Sun*, 12 November 1906.

"Hetty Green Opposes Foreign Marriages." *Columbia (SC) State*, 13 October 1907.

"Hetty Green Pessimistic." *Baltimore Sun*, 13 October 1907.

"Hetty Green Says She Made Her Money by Not Spending It." *Montgomery (AL) Advertiser*, 9 April 1911.

"Hetty Green Still Young." *Oregonian* (Portland, OR), 20 November 1911.

"Hetty Green Takes Mrs. Chadwick's Part." *Fort-Worth (TX) Star Telegram*, 15 December 1904.

"Hetty Green Talks." *Albuquerque Journal*, 13 April 1915.

"Hetty Green Talks." *Irish World* (NY), 2 March 1895.

"Hetty Green's Advice to Women." *Trenton (NJ) Evening Times*, 28 June 1896.

"Hetty Green's Christmas." *Cleveland Plain Dealer*, 30 December 1896.

"Hetty Green's Filth House." *Daily People* (NY), 15 October 1906.

"Hetty Green's Good Example." *Idaho Statesman*, 11 March 1909.

"Hetty Green's Philosophy." *Literary Digest* (5 August 1916): 320.

"Hetty Green's Religion." *Boston Sunday Globe*, 8 September 1895.

"Hetty Green's Riches." *New Orleans Times-Picayune*, 15 February 1887.

"Hetty Green's Son and Heir Trained by Her." *New York Times*, 9 July 1916.

"Hetty Has Her Views." *Daily Inter-Ocean* (Chicago), 8 January 1895.

"Hetty Scores 'Butterflies.'" *Trenton (NJ) Evening News*, 27 April 1903.

Hodges, Leigh Mitchell. "The Richest Woman in America." *Ladies' Home Journal* 17 (June 1900): 4.

"Hold 'Yogi' Garnett for Duping Women." *New York Times*, 19 October 1909.

"How Hetty Green Makes Her Money." *Baltimore American*, 4 December 1904.

"How I'd Run the World." *Kansas City Star*, 16 February 1911.

"How May a Woman Invest a Small Sum?" *The World's Work* 11 (February 1906): 149–50.

"How the Trick Is Done." *New York Times*, 10 December 1887.

"Imbecile Finance." *New York Times*, 2 December 1904.

"Irrepressible Hetty." *Oregonian* (Portland, OR), 28 January 1895.

"Just a Few Thousand Dollars." *The Independent* (2 June 1881): 22.

"Katherine M. Giles, Great Statistician, Tells How She Won Her Success." *New Orleans Times-Picayune*, 17 October 1915.

Kelland, Clarence Budington. "Wives Are Either Tightwads or Spendthrifts." *American Magazine* (December 1928): 12, 104–10.

"The Kings of Wall Street: Grace Courtland Tells What She Thinks of Them." *New York Times*, 19 November 1881.

"Ladies as Stock Speculators." *New York Times*, 3 February 1880.

"The Ladies' Deposit." *Boston Daily Advertiser*, 29 October 1880 and 5 November 1880.

"The Ladies' Deposit." *Boston Herald*, 17 October 1880.

"Ladies' Deposit Banking—How It Is Supposed to Work." *Boston Daily Advertiser*, 4 October 1880.

"The Lady Brokers of Wall Street." *New York Herald*, 18 May 1870.

"Lady Cook and Co." *New York Times*, 21 December 1898.

"'Lady Lansmere' Played Possum." *New York Herald*, 4 March 1893.

Laurence, William Beach. "The Marriage Laws of Various Countries, as Affecting the Property of Married Women." *Albany Law Journal* (15 October 1870): 281–88.

Lawson, Thomas. "Frenzied Finance." *Everybody's Magazine* 12 (January 1905): 40–53; (February 1905): 173–86.

Lefevre, Edwin. "A Woman and Her Bonds," in *Wall Street Stories*. New York: S. S. McClure, 1901.

"Lillian Scofield Again." *New York Herald*, 26 April 1895.

"Lillian Scofield Held for Theft." *New York Herald*, 15 October 1890.

"Lillian Scofield Smiles." *New York Herald*, 1 March 1890.

Lipscomb, Mary A. "Woman as a Financier," in *The Congress of Women*, edited by Mary Kavanaugh Oldham, 469–70. Chicago: Monarch, 1894.

"Local Business Troubles." *New York Times*, 13 November 1880.

"Losing Her Money in the Street." *New York Times*, 1 April 1884.

"Many Women Defrauded." *Hartford (CT) Daily Courant*, 15 April 1887.

"Marie Latouche Goes Free." *New York Herald*, 15 February 1888.

"Married Women's Property Acts in the United States and Needed Reforms Therein." *Albany Law Journal* 48 (9 September 1893): 207–8.

Merz, Charles. "The Bull Market." *Harper's* 158 (April 1929): 640–46.

"Mind Reading and Stock Speculation." *Wall Street Daily News*, 21 July 1880.

"Miss Eastwick Committed." *New York Times*, 2 October 1901.

"Miss Eastwick Sentenced." *New York Times*, 19 November 1901.

"Miss Eastwick Subject to Hallucinations." *New York Times*, 4 September 1901.

"Miss Eastwick to Be Released Today." *New York Times*, 18 April 1902.

"Miss Mattern's Suit." *New York Times*, 6 May 1887.

"Miss Mattern's Ventures." *New York Times*, 20 March 1887.

"Money Poured into Fraud Stock Office." *New York Times*, 23 November 1910.

"'Mother Jones' Puts Blame for Economic Conditions on Shoulders of Women," *Macon (GA) Telegraph*, 16 July 1916.

"Mrs. Anne M. Weightman Walker." *Morning Olympian* (Olympia, WA), 31 May 1905.

"Mrs. Carrie Morse's Victims." *New York Times*, 6 April 1884.

"Mrs. Chadwick Got Millions on Securities." *New York Times*, 30 November 1904.

"Mrs. Chadwick Guilty." *New York Times*, 12 March 1905.

"Mrs. Ella Rawls Reader Has Gone to Law with Husband." *Augusta (GA) Chronicle*, 7 April 1912.

"Mrs. Ella Rawls Reader, Promoter, Declares Her Mining Lands Suffered Damages." *Cincinnati Post*, 31 March 1906.

"Mrs. Giles Is Famous Expert." *Winston-Salem (NC) Journal*, 1 April 1928.

"Mrs. Green a Wit." *Oregonian* (Portland, OR), 4 July 1916.

"Mrs. Hetty Green and Her Adversaries." *Harper's Bazaar* 28 (19 October 1895): 848.

"Mrs. Hetty Green: How the Multi-Millionaire Woman Makes Investment of Her Money." *Daily Journal and Tribune* (Knoxville, TN), 16 June 1895.

"Mrs. Hetty Green's Millions." *Arkansas Gazette*, 3 March 1889.

"Mrs. Hetty Green's Ramblings." *New York Herald Tribune*, 19 January 1895.

"Mrs. Hetty Howland Robinson Green, at 71 Years of Age." *New York World*, 26 November 1905, Metropolitan Section.

"Mrs. Hetty's Business Methods." *Philadelphia Inquirer*, 7 August 1899.

"Mrs. Howe a Fugitive." *New York Times*, 15 April 1887.

"Mrs. Howe and Her Bank." *New York Times*, 7 December 1884.

"Mrs. Howe of Woman's Bank Fame Again." *Boston Daily Advertiser*, 15 April 1887.

"Mrs. Howe's 'Bank' Again." *New York Times*, 16 April 1887.

"Mrs. Howe's Statement." *Boston Daily Advertiser*, 2 October 1880.

"Mrs. Howe's Unsavory Record." *Boston Herald*, 15 October 1880.

"Mrs. Lillian Scofield Again." *New Haven (CT) Register*, 1 February 1889.

"Mrs. Pollard's Business." *Chicago Herald*, 15 October 1890.

"Mrs. Sarah E. Howe at Liberty." *Boston Journal*, 28 March 1889.

"Mrs. Sophronia Twitchell Dead: She Was a Well Known Figure on Wall Street and a Female Suffragist." *New York Herald*, 4 August 1893.

"Mrs. Walker to Quit Business." *Colorado Springs (CO) Gazette*, 27 December 1904.

"A Mysterious Bank." *Boston Daily Advertiser*, 25 September 1880.

"New and Old South Sea Bubbles." *World's Work* 41 (November 1920): 31–33.

Nicholls, C. W. de Lyon. "Hetty Green: A Character Study." *Business America* (May 1913): 382–88.

Norman, Henry. "The Feminine Failure in Business." *Forum* (April–May 1920): 455–61.

Norris, Frank. "A Deal in Wheat," in *A Deal in Wheat and Other Stories of the New and Old West*, 1–26. London: Grant Richards, 1903.

"A Noted Female Swindler." *New York Times*, 9 December 1888.

"A Notorious Woman's Suit." *New York Times*, 31 January 1883.

"Off with Millions: Sweet-Faced Sophia Beck Managed a Fake Concern." *Oregonian* (Portland, OR), 27 March 1905.

"Old Eight Percent." *Boston Herald*, 15 October 1880.

"Old Miser Gleefully Tells How She Swindled a Presbyterian Church." *Olympia (WA) Daily Recorder*, 25 April 1903.

"100,000 Women Play the Market Here." *New York Sun*, 7 November 1929.

"Oscar in Wall Street." *New York Times*, 20 September 1882.

"A Peculiarly Heartless Swindle." *New York Times*, 11 October 1879.

"A Pen Picture of the Remarkable Head of the Establishment." *Boston Herald*, 15 October 1880.

"The Petticoat Financiers in Another Flutter." *New York Sun*, 26 March 1870.

Phelps, Elizabeth Stuart. "Women and Money." *The Independent*, 24 August 1871.

"Playing the Stock Market." *Christian Century* 46 (21 February 1929): 255.

Post, Emily. "Kelland Doesn't Know What He Is Talking About." *American Magazine* (December 1928): 13, 110–13.

Powell, Richard Stillman. "The Views of Viola: On Stocks and Things." *Puck* 46 (24 January 1900): 4.

Prescott, Lydia A. "The Economic Independence of Women." In *The Congress of Women*, edited by Mary Kavanaugh Oldham, 526–30. Chicago: Monarch, 1894.

"Present Day Sampson Discovers His Delilah." *Grand Forks (ND) Herald*, 22 May 1908.

"A Prodigy Because a Woman." *New York Times*, 5 July 1916.

"Pulpit Attack on Mrs. Green." *New York Times*, 24 February 1903.

"The Queens of Finance." *New York Herald*, 22 January 1870; 5 and 6 February 1870.

"In Quest of Great Fortune." *Omaha World Herald*, 8 January 1895.

Quincy, Peggy. "Peggy Quincy's Opinion of Mrs. Hetty Green." *Boston Journal*, 10 November 1906.

"Radcliffe Girl Is Bond Salesman." *Boston Herald*, 11 July 1915.

Raskob, John. "Everybody Ought to Be Rich." *The Ladies' Home Journal* 46 (August 1929): 9.

Reader, Ella Rawls. "Why Most Women Do Not Succeed in Business." *Idaho Falls (ID) Times*, 23 May 1905.

"Reader Loses Mine Suit." *Oregonian* (Portland, OR), 15 May 1909.

Reede, Mrs. B. C. "A Business Woman." *The Revolution*, 14 February 1870, 100–101.

"Reynolds Tells Story of How He Was Duped." *New York Times*, 12 December 1904.

"Rich Hetty Green." *Boston Herald,* 3 February 1895.

"Rich Woman at Work." *Dallas Morning News*, 12 September 1904.

"Rich Women Work Hard and Long." *Boston Herald*, 17 October 1909.

Richardson, Eudora Ramsey. "The Queen Sits in the Counting House." *Bankers' Magazine* (August 1920): 212–14.

"The Richest Woman in the World." *Denver Post*, 5 March 1899.

"The Richest Woman in the World." *Harper's Bazaar* (14 October 1899): 881.

"Our Richest Woman." *Daily Inter-Ocean* (Chicago), 27 November 1892.

Riggs, Oscar Willoughby. "Petticoated Sharks." *Harrisburg (PA) Patriot*, 5 July 1888.

"The Right View of It." *Boston Daily Advertiser*, 8 October 1880.

Robison, H. G. "Women Learn How to Invest on Big Scale." *New York Times*, 25 July 1926.

"Russell Sage's Victory." *New York Times*, 5 June 1887.

Sawtelle, Lelia Robinson. "How Marriage Affects a Woman's Property." *The Chautauquan* 12 (March 1891): 774–75.

"Says Woman Aided Swindle." *New York Times*, 19 December 1914.

"Second Mrs. Chadwick Works Several Rich Pittsburg Men." *Aberdeen (SD) Daily News*, 17 February 1908.

"Sensible Hetty Green." *Wheeling (WV) Register*, 12 December 1897.

"Seventy Years Rest Lightly on Mrs. Henry Green." *New York Times*, 5 November 1905.

"She 'Squealed' Says Vahey of Mrs. Biggs." *Boston Herald*, 3 April 1907.

Shelby, Gertrude Mathews. "A Woman's Approach to Economics." *The Bookman* (1926): 60–64.

Simonson, George Montfort. "Pastels in Sage-Green and Gold." *Godey's Magazine* (November 1895): 483–89.

Smith, Edgar Lawrence. "Speculation and Investment." *Atlantic Monthly* 136 (October 1925): 524–47.

"The Social Evil." *Woodhull and Claflin's Weekly*, 23 July 1870.

"Social Leader 'Gets Back' at Hetty Green." *Indianapolis Freeman*, 12 September 1908.

"Sophia Beck Fined $500." *New York Times*, 10 July 1910.

"Speculating Women." *New York Times*, 17 January 1875.

Stanton, Elizabeth Cady. "Finance for the People." *The Revolution*, 26 November 1868, 330.

———. "Greenbacks or Gold." In *Papers of Elizabeth Cady Stanton and Susan B. Anthony*, edited by Patricia G. Holland and Ann D. Gordon. Microfilm edition, reel 18, 451. Wilmington, DE: Scholarly Resources, 1991.

———. "Wall Street." *The Revolution* 16 April 1868, 225–26.

Starkweather, Louise A. "Woman as an Investor," in *The Congress of Women*, edited by Mary Kavanaugh Oldham, 62–66. Chicago: Monarch, 1894.

Stewart, David. "Married Women Traders." *American Law Register* 24 (June 1885): 355–62.

Stewart, William Downie. "English and American Law." *The Central Law Journal* 5 (7 September 1877): 219.

"Still Working the Women." *Boston Herald*, 9 December 1888.

"Stingiest Woman on Earth." *Kansas City Times*, 30 August 1891.

"Stories and Anecdotes of the Late Hetty Green." *Miami Herald*, 15 July 1916.

"Stories of Hetty Green." *Salt Lake Telegram* (Salt Lake City, UT), 2 August 1902.

"The Story of Adele Spitzeder, Mrs. Howe's Model." *Boston Daily Advertiser*, 18 October 1880.

"Sue Broker for $30,000." *New York Times*, 10 March 1905.

"Swindled Society Ladies." *Elkhart Daily Review* (IN), 8 December 1887.

"Think Confidence Queen Is Caught." *Cleveland Plain Dealer*, 26 September 1909.

"30 Billions in Bonds Handled by Woman." *New York Times*, 6 April 1927.

Tompkins, Juliet Wilbor. "Ella Rawls Reader, Financier: The Story of the Greatest Business Woman in the World." *Everybody's Magazine* 13 (September 1905): 310–16; (October 1905): 458–65; (November 1905): 691–97; (December 1905): 832–38.

"A Trustee Charged with Fraud." *New York Times*, 16 January 1879.

"Two Adventuresses." *The Nation* (15 December 1904): 475.

"Two Women Financiers: Hetty Green and Anne Weightman Walker." *Springfield (MA) Republican*, 25 February 1906.

"Using Her Eyes on the Jury." *New York Times*, 17 May 1884.

"Victim of Blackmailers." *Daily Inter-Ocean* (Chicago), 16 May 1883.

Walker, Alfred. "Hints to Women on the Care of Property." *Harper's Bazaar* 11 (20 April 1876): 250.

"Wall Street Aroused." *The New York Times*, 6 February 1870.

"Wall Street Aroused." *The Revolution*, 24 February 1870.

"Wall Street Bids for the Woman Speculator." *Literary Digest* 99 (17 November 1928): 86.

"Wall Street Connected to Many Camps and Cottages." *New York Times*, 12 August 1903.

"Wall Street Offers Good Chances to College Women." *New York Times*, 1 March 1914.

"Wall Street Shys at Women." *Watertown (NY) Daily Times*, 18 September 1897.

"Wall Street Splurge May Lead Ex-Stenog to Prison." *Charlotte (NC) Sunday Observer*, 9 December 1928.

"The Wall Street Witch." *Chicago Inter-Ocean*, 5 March 1881.

"Wanted to Be a Second Hetty Green." *St. Louis Republic*, 24 June 1900.

Ward, John T. "The Forgotten Woman." *Springfield (MA) Republican*, 25 June 1933.

Warwick, Walter. "Wall Street Wrecks." *Christian Union* 17 (13 March 1878): 221–22.

Welch, Margaret Hamilton. "Woman's Use of Money." *Congregationalist* 86 (March 1901): 348.

"When Hetty Green Was a Young Belle." *Montgomery (AL) Advertiser*, 4 September 1910.

"Where Women Are Not Wanted." *New Haven (CT) Register*, 25 May 1888.

White, Goodell. "Women's Savings Club Earns $80 per Share." *Magazine of Wall Street* (28 March 1925): 942–43.

"Why Psychology Believes Hetty Green Was a Miser." *Richmond (VA) Times-Dispatch*, 23 July 1916.

"Why Women Don't Get Rich." *New York Times*, 28 April 1901.

"Widows Duped by Land Sharks." *Duluth (MN) News-Tribune*, 24 March 1906.

"Wily Hetty Green." *St. Albans (VT) Daily Messenger*, 13 October 1893.

"Wily Women." *Cleveland Plain Dealer*, 20 May 1888.

Witten, George. "Pretty Girls and Handsome Men." *Outlook* 5 (1 October 1924): 173–74.

"Woman a Leader as a Promoter." *Grand Rapids (MI) Press*, 19 May 1908.

"Woman as a Financier." *The Phrenological Journal of Science and Heath* (June 1877): 416.

"Woman Brains of Syndicate." *New York Times*, 27 March 1905.

"Woman Broker Still Sought." *Wilkes-Barre (PA) Times-Leader*, 1 June 1908.

"A Woman Cotton Expert." *Washington Bee* (Washington, DC), 24 September 1904.

"Woman Financier Whom Senate Has Discussed." *San Jose (CA) Mercury News*, 26 March 1905.

"Woman Has Million of Storey Cash." *Philadelphia Inquirer*, 26 March 1905.

"The Woman in the Case." *Canton (OH) Repository*, 11 May 1888.

"Woman Manages Bond Department for Women." *Boston Herald*, 23 April 1916.

"A Woman Multi-Millionaire." *Frank Leslie's Popular Monthly* 51 (April 1901): 623.

"A Woman of Millions." *Wisconsin Labor Advocate* (La Crosse), 10 December 1886.

"Woman Saves Girls Who Made Bad Investments." *Colorado Springs (CO) Gazette*, 27 December 1911.

"Woman Seeks a Seat on the Stock Exchange." *New York Times*, 14 January 1927.

"Woman 60 Years Old, Worth $50,000,000, Manages Great Chemical Plant." *New York Times*, 4 September 1904.

"Woman's Ability to Earn Money." *Woodhull and Claflin's Weekly*, 17 September 1870.

"A Woman's Adventure in Investments." *The World's Work* (December 1913): 144.

"The Woman's 'Bank.'" *Boston Daily Advertiser*, 5 October 1880.

"A Woman's Bank Account." *Current Literature* 4 (June 1890): 460.

"The Woman's Bank of Boston." *The Bankers' Magazine* 35 (November 1880): 351–52.

"Woman's Business Ignorance." *Harper's Bazaar* 14 (January 1881): 18.

"The Woman's Deposit at Munich." *Boston Daily Advertiser*, 12 October 1880.

"Woman's Investment Invasion." *Wall Street Journal*, 11 August 1927.

"A Woman's Poor Speculation." *New York Times*, 18 October 1882.

"Woman's Progress—The Female Operators of Wall Street." *New York Sunday News*, 30 January 1870.

"Woman's Right to Speculate." *New York Times*, 22 February 1871.

"Women and Money." *Harper's Bazaar* 11 (February 1878): 122.

"Women and Their Bank Accounts." *The American Farmer* (15 September 1893): 6.

"Women and Trusts." *Dallas Morning News*, 5 January 1897.

"Women and Wall Street." *North American Review* 229 (January 1930): 121.

"Women and Wealth." *Grand Forks (ND) Evening Times*, 24 December 1909.

"Women Are Honest." *Michigan Farmer*, 15 April 1884.

"Women as Bank Depositors." *New York Times*, 5 December 1897.

"Women as Bankers." *New York Times*, 25 January 1906.

"Women as High Financiers." *Daily People* (NY), 31 May 1908.

"The Women Brokers of Broad Street." *New York Courier*, 14 February 1870.

"Women Gamblers in Wall Street: By One of Them." *Forum* (January 1918): 101–8.

"Women in Wall Street." *New York Times*, 31 March 1872.

"Women in Wall Street." *New York Times*, 12 December 1909.

"Women in Wall Street and the Part They Play." *Baltimore Sun*, 24 November 1907.

"Women Make Best Assistants in Get-Rich-Quick Games." *Boston Herald*, 17 December 1911.

"Women Now Investing Millions: Housewives Big Stock Buyers." *New York Times*, 16 February 1927.

"Women of Wall Street." *Colorado Springs (CO) Gazette*, 26 January 1908.

"Women Seeking 'Points': Unwelcome Visits to Wall Street Magnates." *New York Times*, 24 September 1882.

"Women Squeal." *Cleveland Plain Dealer*, 13 May 1894.

"Women Stockholders Rapidly Increase." *Nation's Business* 18 (May 1930): 116.

"Women Traders Going Back to Bridge Games." *New York Times*, 30 October 1929.

"Women Who Earn $10,000 a Year." *Evening Star* (Washington, DC), 27 June 1915.

"Women Who Speculate." *New York Herald*, 11 November 1894.

"Women's Investment Invasion." *Barron's* 7 (15 August 1927): 4, 18.

"Women's Ownership of Corporations." *Current Opinion* 56 (April 1914): 304.

"Woodhull and Claflin in Court." *New York Daily Tribune*, 22 February 1871.

"Woodhull, Claflin and Co." *The (NY) Sun*, 7 February 1870.

"Working Girls Buying Wall Street Securities." *New York Times*, 5 January 1928.

"Would Kill Son Like Harry Thaw." *Trenton (NJ) Evening News*, 14 August 1906.

Secondary Sources

BOOKS

Ackerman, Kenneth D. *The Gold Ring: Jim Fisk, Jay Gould, and Black Friday, 1869*. Falls Church, VA: Viral History Press, 2011.

Antilla, Susan. *Tales from the Boom-Boom Room: Women vs. Wall Street*. Princeton, NJ: Bloomberg Press, 2002.

Balfour, Robert, ed. *Culture, Capital and Representation*. New York: Palgrave, 2010.

Basch, Norma. *In the Eyes of the Law: Women, Marriage, and Property in Nineteenth-Century New York*. Ithaca, NY: Cornell University Press, 1982.

Brody, Miriam. *Victoria Woodhull: Free Spirit for Women's Rights*. New York: Oxford University Press, 2003.

Campbell, Dorcas. *Careers for Women in Banking and Finance*. New York: E. P. Dutton, 1944.

Caplan, Sheri J. *Petticoats and Pinstripes: Portraits of Women in Wall Street's History*. Santa Barbara, CA: Praeger, 2013.

Cleary, Patricia. *Elizabeth Murray: A Woman's Pursuit of Independence in Eighteenth-Century America*. Amherst: University of Massachusetts Press, 2000.

Conger, Vivian Bruce. *The Widow's Might: Widowhood and Gender in Early British America*. New York: New York University Press, 2009.

Cowing, Cedric B. *Populists, Plungers, and Progressives: A Social History of Stock and Commodity Speculation, 1890–1936*. Princeton, NJ: Princeton University Press, 1965.

Davidoff, Leonore, and Catherine Hall. *Family Fortunes: Men and Women of the English Middle Class, 1780–1850*. Chicago: University of Chicago Press, 1987.

Dubois, Ellen Carol. *Feminism and Suffrage: The Emergence of an Independent Women's Movement in America, 1848–1869*. Ithaca, NY: Cornell University Press, 1978.

Fabian, Ann. *Card Sharps, Dream Books and Bucket Shops: Gambling in 19th-Century America*. Ithaca, NY: Cornell University Press, 1990.

Fisher, Melissa S. *Wall Street Women*. Durham, NC: Duke University Press, 2012.

Fraser, Steve. *Every Man a Speculator: A History of Wall Street in American Life*. New York: HarperCollins, 2005.

Freeman, Mark, Robin Pearson, and James Taylor. "Between Madam Bubble and Kitty Lorimer: Women Investors in British and Irish Stock Companies." In Laurence, Maltby, and Rutterford, *Women and Their Money*, 95–114.

Frisken, Amanda. *Victoria Woodhull's Sexual Revolution: Political Theater and the Popular Press in Nineteenth-Century America*. Philadelphia: University of Pennsylvania Press, 2004.

Froide, Amy. *Never Married: Singlewomen in Early Modern England*. Oxford: Oxford University Press, 2005.

Gabriel, Mary. *Notorious Victoria: The Life of Victoria Woodhull, Uncensored*. Chapel Hill, NC: Algonquin Books, 1998.

Galbraith, John Kenneth. *The Great Crash: 1929*. Boston: Houghton Mifflin, 1988.

Geisst, Charles R. *Wall Street: A History*. New York: Oxford University Press, 1997.

Gildersleeve, Genieve N. *Women in Banking*. Washington, DC: Public Affairs Press, 1959.

Goldsmith, Barbara. *Other Powers: The Age of Suffrage, Spiritualism, and the Scandalous Victoria Woodhull*. New York: Knopf, 1998.

Hawkins, David. *Corporate Financial Disclosure, 1900–1933*. New York: Garland, 1986.

Henry, Nancy. "'Ladies Do It?': Victorian Women Investors in Fact and Fiction." In O'Gorman, *Victorian Literature and Finance*, 111–32.

Henry, Nancy, and Cannon Schmitt, eds. *Victorian Investments: New Perspectives on Finance and Culture*. Bloomington: Indiana University Press, 2009.

Hofer, Margaret K. *The Games We Played: The Golden Age of Board and Table Games*. New York: Princeton Architectural Press, 2003.

Holton, Woody. *Abigail Adams*. New York: Free Press, 2009.

Hudson, Lynn M. *The Making of "Mammy Pleasant": A Black Entrepreneur in Nineteenth-Century San Francisco*. Urbana: University of Illinois Press, 2003.

Hunt, Margaret. *The Middling Sort: Commerce, Gender, and the Family in England*. Berkeley: University of California Press, 1996.

Ingrassia, Catherine. *Authorship, Commerce, and Gender in Early Eighteenth-Century England: A Culture of Paper Credit*. Cambridge: Cambridge University Press, 1998.

Itzkowitz, David C. "Fair Enterprise or Extravagant Speculation: Investment, Speculation, and Gambling in Victorian England." In Henry and Schmitt, *Victorian Investments*, 98–119.

Klein, Maury. *Rainbow's End: The Crash of 1929*. Oxford: Oxford University Press, 2003.

Kreisel, Deanna K. *Economic Woman: Demand, Gender, and Narrative Closure in Eliot and Hardy*. Toronto: University of Toronto Press, 2012.

Kwolek-Folland, Angel. *Incorporating Women: A History of Women and Business in the United States*. New York: Twayne, 1998.

Laird, Pamela Walker. *Pull: Networking and Success Since Benjamin Franklin*. Cambridge, MA: Harvard University Press, 2006.

Laurence, Anne. "Women, Banks and the Securities Market in Early Eighteenth-Century England." In Laurence, Maltby, and Rutterford, *Women and Their Money*, 46–58.

Laurence, Anne, Josephine Maltby, and Janette Rutterford, eds. *Women and Their Money, 1700- 1950: Essays on Women and Finance*. London: Routledge, 2009.

Lewis, Arthur H. *The Day They Shook the Plum Tree*. New York: Harcourt, Brace, 1963.

Lucht, Tracy. *Sylvia Porter: America's Original Personal Finance Columnist*. Syracuse, NY: Syracuse University Press, 2013.

Marchand, Roland. *Creating the Corporate Soul: The Rise of Public Relations and Corporate Imagery in American Business*. Berkeley: University of California Press, 1998.

McMath, Robert C., Jr. *American Populism: A Social History*. New York: Hill and Wang, 1993.

Michie, Ranald. *The London and New York Stock Exchanges, 1850–1914*. London: Allen and Unwin, 1987.

Nelson, Elizabeth White. *Market Sentiments: Middle-Class Market Culture in Nineteenth-Century America*. Washington, DC: Smithsonian Books, 2004.

Norgren, Jill. *Belva Lockwood: The Woman Who Would Be President*. New York: New York University Press, 2007.

O'Day, Rosemary. *Women's Agency in Early Modern Britain and the American Colonies, 1450–1700*. London: Routledge, 2007.

O'Gorman, Francis, ed. *Victorian Literature and Finance*. Oxford: Oxford University Press, 2007.

Orman, Suze. *Women and Money: Owning the Power to Control Your Destiny*. New York: Spiegel and Grau, 2010.

Ott, Julia C. *When Wall Street Met Main Street: The Quest for Investors' Democracy*. Cambridge, MA: Harvard University Press, 2011.

Parsons, Wayne. *The Power of the Financial Press: Journalism and Economic Opinion in Britain and America*. New Brunswick, NJ: Rutgers University Press, 1989.

Perkin, Harold. *Origins of Modern English Society*. London: Routledge, 1969.

Phillips, Nicola. *Women in Business, 1700–1850*. Woodbridge, UK: Boydell, 2006.

Poovey, Mary. *Genres of the Credit Economy: Mediating Value in Eighteenth- and Nineteenth-Century Britain*. Chicago: University of Chicago Press, 2008.

————. "Writing about Finance in Victorian England: Disclosure and Secrecy in the Culture of Investment." In Henry and Schmitt, *Victorian Investments*, 39–57.

Radke-Moss, Andrea G. *Bright Epoch: Women and Coeducation in the American West*. Lincoln: University of Nebraska Press, 2008.

Ritter, Gretchen. *Goldbugs and Greenbacks: The Antimonopoly Tradition and the Politics of Finance in America, 1865–1896.* Cambridge: Cambridge University Press, 1997.

Robb, George. "Ladies of the Ticker: Women, Investment and Fraud in England and America, 1850–1930." In Henry and Schmitt, *Victorian Investments*, 120–40.

———. *White-Collar Crime in Modern England: Financial Fraud and Business Morality, 1845–1929.* Cambridge: Cambridge University Press, 1992.

Robertson, Nancy Marie, and Susan M. Yohn. "Women and Money: The United States." In Laurence, Maltby, and Rutterford, *Women and Their Money*, 218–25.

Rotundo, Anthony E. *American Manhood: Transformations in Masculinity from the Revolution to the Modern Era.* New York: Basic Books, 1993.

Russell, Norman. *The Novelist and Mammon: Literary Responses to the World of Commerce in the Nineteenth Century.* Oxford: Oxford University Press, 1986.

Sachs, Emanie. *The Terrible Siren: Victoria Woodhull.* New York: Harper and Brothers, 1928.

Salmon, Marylynn. "Equality or Submission? Feme Covert Status in Early Pennsylvania." In *Women of America: A History*, edited by Carol Ruth Berkin and Mary Beth Norton, 92–111. Boston: Houghton Mifflin, 1979.

———. "Republican Sentiment, Economic Change, and the Property Rights of Women in American Law." In *Women in the Age of the American Revolution*, edited by Ronald Hoffman and Peter J. Albert, 447–75. Charlottesville: University of Virginia Press, 1989.

Slack, Charles. *Hetty: The Genius and Madness of America's First Female Tycoon.* New York: Ecco, 2004.

Sobel, Robert. *The Big Board: A History of the New York Stock Market.* New York: Free Press, 1965.

———. *The Curbstone Brokers.* New York: Macmillan, 1970.

Solomon, Barbara Miller. *In the Company of Educated Women: A History of Women and Higher Education in America.* New Haven, CT: Yale University Press, 1985.

Sparkes, Boyden and Samuel Taylor Moore. *Hetty Green: A Woman Who Loved Money.* Garden City, NY: Doubleday, Doran, 1930.

Staves, Susan. "Investments, Votes and 'Bribes': Women as Shareholders in the Chartered Companies." In *Women Writers in the Early Modern Political Tradition*, edited by H.L. Smith, 259–78. Cambridge: Cambridge University Press, 1998.

———. *Married Women's Separate Property in England, 1660–1883.* Cambridge, MA: Harvard University Press, 1990.

Stern, Madeleine B. *The Victoria Woodhull Reader.* Weston, MA: M and S Press, 1974.

Stern, Rebecca. *Home Economics: Domestic Fraud in Victorian England.* Columbus: Ohio State University Press, 2008.

Stiles, T. J. *The First Tycoon: The Epic Life of Cornelius Vanderbilt.* New York: Vintage Books, 2009.

Strom, Sharon Hartman. *Beyond the Typewriter: Gender, Class, and Origins of Modern American Office Work, 1900–1930.* Urbana: University of Illinois Press, 1992.

Taylor, Walter Fuller. *The Economic Novel in America*. New York: Octagon, 1964.

Underhill, Lois Beachy. *The Woman Who Ran for President: The Many Lives of Victoria Woodhull*. Bridgehampton, NY: Bridge Works, 1995.

Wagner, Tamara. *Financial Speculation in Victorian Fiction: Plotting Money and the Novel Genre, 1815–1901*. Columbus: Ohio State University Press, 2010.

Wallach, Janet. *The Richest Woman in America: Hetty Green in the Gilded Age*. New York: Doubleday, 2012.

Warren, Joyce W. *Women, Money, and the Law: Nineteenth-Century Fiction, Gender, and the Courts*. Iowa City: University of Iowa Press, 2005.

Westbrook, Wayne. *Wall Street in the American Novel*. New York: New York University Press, 1980.

Whitfield, Eileen. *Pickford: The Woman Who Made Hollywood*. Lexington: University Press of Kentucky, 2007.

Wright, Robert. *Hamilton Unbound: Finance and the Creation of the American Republic*. Westport, CT: Greenwood Press, 2002.

———. *The Wealth of Nations Rediscovered: Integration and Expansion in American Financial Markets, 1780–1850*. Cambridge, MA: Cambridge University Press, 2003.

Yohn, Susan M. "'Men Seem to Take a Delight in Cheating Women': Legal Challenges Faced by Businesswomen in the United States, 1880–1920." In Laurence, Maltby, and Rutterford, *Women and Their Money*, 226–42.

Zimmerman, David A. *Panic! Markets, Crises, and Crowds in American Fiction*. Chapel Hill: University of North Carolina Press, 2006.

ARTICLES

Adams, Tim. "Testosterone and High Finance Do Not Mix: So Bring on the Women." *Observer*, 18 June 2013.

Alborn, Timothy. "A License to Bet: Life Insurance and the Gambling Acts in the British Courts." *Connecticut Insurance Law Journal* 14 (2008): 1–20.

Bailey, Joanne. "Favoured or Oppressed? Married Women, Property, and 'Coverture' in England, 1660–1880." *Continuity and Change* 17 (2002): 351–72.

Bajtelsmit, Vickie L., and Alexandra Bernasek. "Why Do Women Invest Differently Than Men?" *Financial Counseling and Planning* 7 (1996): 1–10.

Barber, Brad M., and Terrance Odean. "Boys Will Be Boys: Gender, Overconfidence, and Common Stock Investment." *Quarterly Journal of Economics* (February 2001): 261–92.

Berg, Maxine. "Women's Property and the Industrial Revolution." *Journal of Interdisciplinary History* 24 (Autumn 1993): 233–50.

Brady, James. "In Step with Maria Bartiromo." *Parade* (17 April 2005): 18.

Braukman, Stacey Lorraine, and Michael A. Ross. "Married Women's Property Law and Male Coercion: United States Courts and the Privy Examination, 1864–1887." *Journal of Women's History* 12 (Summer 2000): 57–80.

Carlos, Ann, Karen Maguire, and Larry Neal. "Women in the City: Financial Acumen, Women Speculators, and the Royal Africa Company during the South Sea Bubble." *Accounting, Business and Financial History* 16 (July 2006): 219–43.

Carlos, Ann M., and Larry Neal. "Women Investors in Early Capital Markets, 1720–1725." *Financial History Review* 11 (2004): 197–224.

Chused, Richard H. "Late Nineteenth-Century Married Women's Property Law: Reception of the Early Married Women's Property Acts by the Courts and Legislatures." *American Journal of Legal History* 29 (January 1985): 3–35.

Cleary, Patricia. "'She Will Be in the Shop': Women's Sphere of Trade in Eighteenth-Century New York and Philadelphia." *Pennsylvania Magazine of History and Biography* 119 (July 1995): 181–202.

Cooper, Dan, and Brian Grinder. "Women on Wall Street: An Historical Perspective." *Financial History* (2003): 10–11, 30.

Dominus, Susan. "Exile on Park Avenue." *New York Times Magazine* (7 October 2012): 32–39.

Ellebracht, Pat. "Riding the Rails with Madam Railroad." *Financial History* (1999): 21–25, 34.

Flynn, John T. "The Witch of Wall Street." *Mentor* (December 1929): 12–15, 54, 56.

Freeman, Mark, Robin Pearson, and James Taylor. "'A Doe in the City': Women Shareholders in Eighteenth- and Early Nineteenth-Century Britain." *Accounting, Business and Financial History* 16 (2006): 265–91.

Froide, Amy. "The Business of Investing: The Public Stock Portfolios of Female Investors in Eighteenth-Century Britain." Paper presented at the Berkshire Conference on Women's History. Amherst, MA, 2011.

Ginzburg, Benjamin. "Wall Street under the New Deal." *North American Review* 245 (Spring 1938): 58–81.

Goldin, Claudia. "The Economic Status of Women in the Early Republic: Quantitative Evidence." *Journal of Interdisciplinary History* 16 (Winter 1986): 375–404.

Halle, Howard. "Martha, My Dear." *Time Out New York* (February 5–12, 2004): 6.

Hawkins, David F. "The Development of Modern Financial Reporting Practices among American Manufacturing Corporations." *Business History Review* 37 (Autumn 1963): 135–68.

Hochfelder, David. "'Where the Common People Could Speculate': The Ticker, Bucket Shops, and the Origins of Popular Participation in Financial Markets, 1880–1920." *Journal of American History* (September 2006): 335–58.

Horowitz, Helen Lefkowitz. "Victoria Woodhull, Anthony Comstock, and the Conflict over Sex in the United States in the 1870s." *Journal of American History* 87 (September 2000): 403–34.

Hughes, Kathryn. "Respectable Punch." *Times Literary Supplement* (January 25, 2013): 4–5.

Ingrassia, Catherine. "The Pleasure of Business and the Business of Pleasure: Gender, Credit and the South Sea Bubble." *Studies in Eighteenth-Century Culture* 24 (1995): 191–210.

Kantor, Jodi, and Jessica Silver-Greenberg. "Wall Street Mothers, Stay-Home Fathers." *New York Times*, 8 December 2013.

Kerber, Linda K. "Separate Spheres, Female Worlds, Woman's Place: The Rhetoric of Women's History." *Journal of American History* 75 (June 1988): 9–39.

Kolhatkar, Sheelah. "What If Women Ran Wall Street? Testosterone and Risk." *New York* (29 March 2010): 36–41.

Laurence, Anne. "Women Investors, 'That Nasty South Sea Affair,' and the Rage to Speculate in Early Eighteenth-Century England." *Accounting, Business and Financial History* 16 (July 2006): 254–64.

Lebsock, Suzanne D. "Radical Reconstruction and the Property Rights of Southern Women." *Journal of Southern History* 43 (May 1977): 195–216.

Maltby, Josephine, and Janette Rutterford. "'She Possessed Her Own Fortune': Women Investors from the Late Nineteenth Century to the Early Twentieth Century." *Business History* 48 (April 2006): 220–53.

Means, Gardiner. "The Diffusion of Stock Ownership in the United States." *Quarterly Journal of Economics* 44 (August 1930): 561–600.

O'Day, Rosemary. "Matchmaking and Moneymaking in a Patronage Society: The First Duke and Duchess of Chandos, c. 1712–35." *Economic History Review* 66 (2013): 273–96.

O'Sullivan, Mary. "The Expansion of the U.S. Stock Market, 1885–1930: Historical Facts and Theoretical Fashions." *Enterprise and Society* 8 (September 2007): 489–542.

Prince, Melvin. "Women, Men and Money Styles." *Journal of Economic Psychology* 14 (1993): 175–82.

Reed, J. R. "A Friend to Mammon: Speculation in Victorian Literature." *Victorian Studies* 27 (Winter 1984): 179–202.

Robb, George. "Women and White-Collar Crime: Debates on Gender, Fraud and the Corporate Economy in England and America." *British Journal of Criminology* 46 (November 2006): 1,058–72.

Rukeyser, Louis. "Women of Wall Street." *Playboy* (August 1989): 112, 152–53.

Rutterford, Janette, and Josephine Maltby. "'The Widow, the Clergyman and the Reckless': Women Investors in England, 1830–1914." *Feminist Economics* 12 (January–April 2006): 111–38.

Ryzik, Melana. "Where Women Run Wall Street." *New York Times*, 24 July 2016.

Shammas, Carole. "Re-Assessing the Married Women's Property Acts." *Journal of Women's History* 6 (Spring 1994): 9–30.

Solomon, Deborah. "Questions for Abby Joseph Cohen." *New York Times Magazine* (28 January 2011): 14.

Stanley, Alessandra. "With Wall St. Center Stage, Novel about Female Trader." *New York Times*, 1 February 2016.

Sullivan, Andrew. "The He Hormone: The Defining Power of Testosterone." *New York Times Magazine* (2 April 2000): 46–51, 58, 69, 73–79.

Tetrault, Lisa. "The Incorporation of American Feminism: Suffragists and the Postbellum Lyceum." *Journal of American History* (March 2010): 1,027–56.

Thomas, Landon, Jr. "A Fragile Foothold: The Ranks of Top-Tier Women on Wall St. Are Shrinking." *New York Times*, 1 December 2007.

Thompson, Joel E. "Early Books on Investing at the Dawn of Modern Business in America." *Accounting Historians Journal* 35 (June 2008): 83–110.

Traflet, Janice. "'Everybody Ought to Be Rich': The Expanding Ranks of Women Investors and Speculators in the Roaring Twenties." *Financial History* (2009): 20–23, 39.

Vickery, Amanda. "Golden Age to Separate Spheres? A Review of the Categories and Chronology of English Women's History." *Historical Journal* 36 (June 1993): 383–414.

Wright, Robert. "Women and Finance in the Early National U.S." *Essays in History* 42 (2000). Accessed November 28, 2016, at http://www.essaysinhistory.com/articles/2012/100.

Yohn, Susan M. "Crippled Capitalists: The Inscription of Economic Dependence and the Challenge of Female Entrepreneurship in Nineteenth-Century America." *Feminist Economics* 12 (January–April 2006): 85–109.

Zaloom, Caitlin, and Natasha Dow Schull. "The Shortsighted Brain: Neuroeconomics and the Governance of Choice in Time." *Social Studies of Science* 41 (2011): 515–38.

Index

GEORGE ROBB is a professor of history at William Paterson University. He is the author of *White-Collar Crime in Modern England* and *British Culture and the First World War*.

The University of Illinois Press
is a founding member of the
Association of American University Presses.

University of Illinois Press
1325 South Oak Street
Champaign, IL 61820-6903
www.press.uillinois.edu